3/97

To Dr. Lucy —

May all you
be filled with love
& laughter!

xoxo
R. Sfrisso

IN MY WORLD

Designing Living & Learning Environments for the Young

RO LOGRIPPO

John Wiley & Sons, Inc.
New York Chichester Brisbane Toronto Singapore

Library of Congress Cataloging in Publication Data:

Logrippo, Ro, 1946–
     In my world: designing living & learning environments for the
     young / by Ro Logrippo
          p.   cm.
     Includes bibliographical references and index.
     ISBN 0-471-11162-7
     1. Children's rooms. 2. Interior decoration.   I. Title.
II. Title. III. Series.
     NK2117.C4l64   1995
     747—dc20   94-41907

Printed in the United States of America

1 0 9 8 7 6 5 4 3 2 1

A Dedication

To Tony
—whose magical spirit set the dream in motion,

To Mike
—whose loving support kept it alive and in focus,

And to Linda, Mary Ellen, Carolyn and Teddi
—whose "true blue" friendship and belief
guided this meaningful journey.

"You Can Be Whatever You Want to Be"

"There is inside you all of the potential to be whatever you want to be—
All the energy to do whatever you want to do.
Imagine yourself as you would like to be, doing what you want to do,
And each day, take one step towards your dream.
And though at times it may be difficult to continue, hold on to your dream.
One morning you will awake to find that you are the person you dreamed of -
Doing what you wanted to do—
Simply because you had the courage
To believe in your potential
And to hold on to your dream. "

Donna Levine
Copyright © 1987 by Blue Mountain Arts, Inc.

"Keep that motto a daily prayer, each day awakening to more of the magic.
Connect your dreams to the great realities that we see around us.
Seeds planted over years, finally poke their heads above the surface.
Rest assured that all of the work is preparation for harvesting
A bouquet of rainbows."

Tony Torrice
May 12, 1988

CONTENTS

Preface   ix
The Author Acknowledges   xi

_____ CHAPTER 1 _____

A WORLD OF WONDERS   1

The Beginning Stretch   2
A Nest That Nurtures   7
A Theme Come True? Not in My Room   16
Strike up the Bands of Color   19
Home Safety is No Accident   31

_____ CHAPTER 2 _____

UP, DOWN, ALL AROUND   39

What's Up—Paint or Paper?   40
Border Patrol to the Rescue   50
Bridging the Generations with the Write Stuff   52
High Hopes for High Places   56
Don't Overlook What's Underfoot   59
Through These Portals Pass the Playful   66

_____ CHAPTER 3 _____

FURNISHINGS FIT FOR A CHILD   71

Getting a Handle on Hardware   74
Two-for-One Designs with Kids in Mind   77

Overnight Success   81
Desks That Make the Grade   83
The S.O.S. of Good Storage   93
Plain Pieces + Paint + Pizazz = Splashy Furniture   96
Hand-Me-Downs with Pick-Me Up   101
Converting Common Items into Unconventional Decor   104

CHAPTER 4

DETAILS, DETAILS   **111**

Window Wonderland   112
An Illuminating Experience   116
A Permanent Place for Show and Tell   120
Turning Sheet Dreams into Suite Reality   124
Creating Rooms That Click with Kids   130
Giving Child Space a Holiday Face   135

CHAPTER 5

SOMETHING SPECIAL   **141**

Making Room for the Young at Art   147
Setting the Stage for Fantasy Play   150
Widening a Child's Window on the World   153
Turning Nature Outside In   156
Making Your Home One for the Books   160
Decor That Scores Big in a Small World   165
A New Slant on Physical Fitness   168

_____ CHAPTER 6 _____

SPECIAL CHALLENGES   173

Eliminating the Squeeze in Tight Quarters   174
When the Room I Call "Mine" Is Really "Ours"   180
How Design Can Bridge the Divide in Shared Custody   184
A Room for a Child Facing Physical Challenges   189
Creating a Teen Scene Without the Growing Pains   197
Cushioning the Jolt of a Moving Experience   203
Parental Guidance That Camouflages the Blahs   209
Allergy-Free Kids' Rooms: Nothing to Sneeze At   213

_____ CHAPTER 7 _____

IN MY OTHER WORLDS   221

Where the Living Is Easy   222
Recipe for a Child-Friendly Kitchen   226
Making a Splash in a Child's Bath   234
Turning the Closet into the "Other" Room   241
The Inside Story on Play Spaces   247

A Final Note from the Author   254
Bibliography   256
Credits   262
Sources   264
About the Author   271
Index   272

PREFACE

Just as the second building block relies on the first for its support, this book stands on the shoulders of its predecessor: *In My Room: Designing For and With Children.*

With due respect to the cornerstone, before christening its follower, let's flashback to the earlier guide. It laid the foundation for *In My World* and rightfully deserves explanation along with information about the late, great dreamer who envisioned it.

Back in 1981, after 24 months "co-designing" environments with children, Antonio Torrice was brought to my attention as a home furnishings editor by the savvy promoter of an event featuring the former child psychologist and early childhood educator.

From the onset, what was impressive about Tony Torrice was his overwhelming compassion for kids. He believed in giving them a voice in personal space by undertaking a team approach with them. Consultations—conducted eye-to-eye at child level—tapped youthful interests, abilities, and preference for color. "Pick a card," the team's senior member would ask those junior to him, while fanning a rainbow assortment for them.

Inventive Master Plans for clever, yet uncomplicated, spaces resulted from these sessions. They were playful without playing a theme and educational without being didactic. And because kids picked the palettes, they were deliciously colorful—from marmelade and mint to candy-apple red and bubble gum-blue.

While many grown-ups have trouble taking kids seriously, this Pied Piper of kids design thrived on their phantasmagorical ideas and strived to execute them—not as elaborate make-believe rooms, but as wise environments rich in purposeful whimsy.

When a 6-year-old wanted a "marshmellow soft" bed protected by "washable bunnies," her adult collaborator created four enormous canvas rabbits to work double time—performing moveable lounge furniture duty by day and guard duty by night...

When a 3-year-old demonstrated he was too shy to talk within viewer sight, his older colleague provided a closet puppet theater. Its curtain openings for cloth characters enabled the boy to mask his fright while playing puppeteer, a pastime promoting language...

Encouraging strengths and strengthening weaknesses—that's what Tony Torrice's *"living & learning environments"* were all about. From training and experience, their conceptualizer knew that children with some control over their immediate surroundings perceive the possibility of conquering a larger universe.

Before many years elapsed, *In My Room* was in Tony's life plan. Above all, he wanted parents to learn how to draw out children through collaboration with them on engaging personal spaces. What mattered was not how big the budget, but how big the opportunity for a child to express ideas, even if some couldn't materialize. As in selecting food from a menu, freedom to choose never equated to a license for everything desirable.

Amazingly, Tony Torrice's designs never looked formula but always followed one. Described as "the 3 Cs," it equated to Choice, Color, and Convertibility. *Choice* and *color* meant allowing a child to describe and define his or her ideal world. *Convertibility* meant providing flexibility for someone on the grow.

It was easy to catch enthusiasm for publishing and writing about these ideas, especially after seeing remarkable projects and talking to the kids behind them. Undoubtedly, the value in allowing the young to influence surroundings went deeper than instilling a decorating sense, or color and texture appreciation. What was at issue involved fostering self-image, building self-confidence, and strengthening the parent/child bond.

As a journalist, it was a momentous experience for me to interview children who masterminded their own rooms. They were so frank about their entree into furnishings under adult guidance.

"It was the first time a grown-up made me feel my ideas counted," Allison, at 14, told me about her 6-year-old setting eventually showcased in *Better Homes & Gardens.*

"Doing that room was a turning point in my life that made me feel I could cope with my disability," said 17-year-old Scott. He was remembering the room he helped devise at the age of 12 to meet the needs of his deafness and to reflect his special interests.

All the young people I met on the *In My Room* journey did more than impress me with personal stories. They validated the theory that children whose surroundings reflect them grow up believing their thoughts and feelings matter.

After pumping nearly three years of effort and information into that first book, we couldn't conceive what might be missing. But many readers sought personal advice about situations very typical of the times.

"What can be done so a room comforts and connects a child to it and the rest of the family when she only lives in a home part time?" challenged a remarried Dad whose daughter's transitory life translated to shared custody and blended families.

"Can one room work for three kids?," implored the mother of 3-year-old triplets.

"How can I encourage artistry?" wrote a grandmother caring for her son's child.

Fortunately, within months after publication, an ideal vehicle for answering questions presented itself—the *In My Room* column for Universal Press Syndicate. With each monthly installment, more information surfaced than the first book contained. But as clippings faded, they sparked the dream of a new guide dealing not only with decorating ideas but twenty-first-century issues kids face daily and the role of good design in resolving them:

- Moving across the hall, moving away, or making room for a brother or sister
- Bridging the divide in shared custody
- Fighting dust that triggers allergies without surrendering a youthful room look
- Dealing with dilemmas such as recycling standbys and making do with stand-ins

In My World also was conceived as a springboard for ideas for rooms supporting typical interests such as art, sports, and nature. Its pages would cover the rest of the house, too, suggesting how its many areas could be made safe and inviting for kids living there.

Clearly, as the column tackled these and other matters, the new book came more into focus. But the dual drive behind it came to a sad and abrupt halt in the fall of 1992, when Tony Torrice, 41, passed away.

It would have been reasonable, I suppose, as his sole business partner, to close the company doors and simply walk away. But I was too connected to the work by then. Too many columns about children's issues were swirling in my head. A book incorporating them surely loomed on the horizon, not to mention a poll of kids' rooms that I longed to pursue.

And so the company is continuing in the realm of communicating and consulting…

And the column is maturing and reflecting myriad professional thought on children's concerns…

And the poll is taking shape, thanks to an industry education foundation grant…

It all adds up to the book before you. In the six years since it took root, many new shoots of information have been added—from the significance of displaying family photos, to the importance of configuring a computer station so it works ergonomically for a child, to the delight of decorating a child's room to reflect the holidays.

First and foremost, this book zeroes in on *"living & learning environments."* It spotlights not only Tony Torrice's final and favorite projects, but also clever and creative designs by many other gifted professionals nationwide. What unites them is a commitment to themeless settings that inspire and instruct the young people living there.

Those whose work is reflected on the following pages are making bold brushstrokes today on the canvas of children's design. *In My World* proudly presents their imaginative work as the next foundation to build upon.

THE AUTHOR ACKNOWLEDGES

If I were writing a *Who's Who of Incredibly Knowledgeable and Unbelieveably Kind People,* I couldn't find better candidates to highlight than those whose names appear here.

Through my years of gathering information about children's design that seeded this book and numerous articles, these individuals gave substance and meaning to my mission. May this published recognition convince them of my deep and enduring appreciation.

First and foremost, I credit the role played in this publishing scenario by my husband, photographer Mike Spinelli. To me, his creative images are each worth much more than 10,000 words—as the *accurate,* but oft misquoted, saying goes. I treasure every photograph he provided, as well as his love and understanding throughout this endeavor.

In large measure, this manuscript reflects the guidance of children's designer Linda Runion, *ASID.* Her editing, input, and assistance are among this book's chief assets, and I am forever grateful to her for years of listening to—and reading—my design writing.

Many other professionals provided significant insight as well as moral support. For always being there to hear and critique passages, Marian Wheeler, *ASID,* Paula McChesney, *ASID,* and Mary Ellen O'Reilly de Andrea, receive my heartfelt thanks. Your unswerving belief in my abilities buoys me more than you will ever know and I can ever show.

For being the best cheerleader a wordperson could hope for, my editor Amanda Miller deserves unending author praise. Always encouraging, she kept me energized and entertained with sage and saucy responses to my "secret sealed letters." Editorial assistant Mary Alice Yates earns kudos, too, for being helpful, hopeful, and joyful.

The rest of the "dream team" at Wiley who nurtured this project, especially in its final stages, earn my deep gratitude and admiration, too. They include Diana Cisek, Sheila Aronson, Meg Hudak-Day, and Amanda Gerien Clarke. Marsha Cohen, this book's interior designer, also

deserves special praise for masterfully, colorfully, and magically presenting this information.

Because the research that shaped this book began a half dozen years ago when I started writing columns for national syndication by Universal Press Syndicate, I extend sincere appreciation to colleagues there who oversee my efforts. Thanks first to vice president Harriet Choice for seeing the value in an illustrated column about children's environments, and to past and present editors Clare LaPlante, Elizabeth Andersen, Lisa Tarry, Maureen McMeel, Don Frost, and Joyce Mott for tweaking my text and not tampering too much with my headlines. Seeing the material come to life in varied layouts in 200 newspapers endears many home and lifestyle editors to me. Their care and flair in *packaging* my ideas has motivated me often to *decorate* blank pages with the right words.

The professionalism and friendship of my former *San Mateo Times* editor Mary Jane Clinton and my former *Designers West* editor, Julie Goodman, also garner special gratitude.

Unquestionably, this book's content benefits from the research of many others in the education, design, psychology and science fields. On early developmental issues, I appreciate the insight gained in conjunction with cochairmanship of the National Task Force on Day Care Interior Design. Those triggering my early journalistic investigation of design for children include fellow Task Force members: Jacky De Jonge, dean of the College of Human Ecology at the University of Tennessee, Knoxville; Faith Wohl, formerly of Du Pont Co., and currently director of the Government Services Administration Office of Work Place Initiatives; and Robert john Dean, *FASID,* past national president of the American Society of Interior Designers.

Others influencing my writing are the following children's authorities, who thoughtfully responded to my letters asking for their insights about quality children's environments. They include leading child psychologists and authors Penelope Leach of London and Benjamin Spock, M.D., of Maine; former San Francisco Unified School District program director Madelon Halpern; the late clinical child psychologist and author Lee Salk, Ph.D.; former U.S. Secretary of Education Lauro F. Cavazos; former Wellesley Child Study Center Director Marian Blum; UCLA Child Care Services Director June Solnit Sale; Minnesota child care authority Ruth Matson; LEGO Creative Child Care Center architect Nancy Carroll, AIA, and award-winning day-care designers Denise Tom-Sera and Janet Robb.

For shedding light on early childhood issues through interviews, I extend appreciation to Denver child develop- ment specialist Ruth Wimmer; former Children's Museum of Houston executive director Jane Jerry; Children's Museum of Rhode Island museum educator Karen Lambe; Discovery Toys child development specialist Margo Lillig and art therapist Basia Lubicz; New York psychologist Michael Schwartzman, Ph.D.; Cleveland clinical psycholo- gist and photo therapist Jerry Fryrear, Ph.D.; pre-school and elementary teacher Kathleen Allan-Meyer; Environments, Inc. director of research and development Mary Hampton; and Iowa State University College of Design professor Cigdem Akkurt, Ph.D.

I bless the day Pennsylvania middle school teacher Dick Cook and his Abington Heights School Global Studies Class entered my life, and, through ongoing correspon- dence, improved my understanding of teens and their per- sonal space concerns. Others in the academic arena whom I appreciate for their thoughts and guidance include University of Tennessee family life educator Anna Mae Kobbe; Massachusetts reading consultant Jim Trelease; City University of New York Children's Environments Research Group personnel; and former elementary school teachers Mary Ellen de Andrea, Marian Brooks, and Sister Bernice Dudek, BVM.

I appreciate color research supplied by Lea Eiseman of Eiseman Center for Color Information and Training; Victoria Doolittle of Pantone Color Institute; Brad Drexler of Binney & Smith; Maryann McKenna of LEGO; and

artist Betsy Hoffman. And I am grateful to Dianne Koch of Massachusetts who counted 450 variegated handprints in Plympton School Gym to determine student color preferences: Red (140), Blue (100), Green (90), and Orange (70).

For generously imparting some of their vast knowledge about children with special needs, I am indebted to Susan Behar, ASID, Paula McChesney, ASID, and Rhonda Luongo, ASID; children's author Sandra Lee Peckinpah; and Lowell Masters of Academic Achievement Center, a Las Vegas remedial center for students with learning problems.

For enlightening me about allergy-free environments, I thank Stanford University professor and allergist Steven Machfinger, M.D.; University of California, Irvine, and University of California, San Diego, clinical professor and allergist Gerald Klein, M.D.; Allergy-Free/Non-Toxic Design architect Robert Kobet, AIA, Garth Benson of Vesta Labs; Mary Anne Buckley of Allergy Clean Environments; Allergy and Asthma Network/ Mothers of Asthmatics; Mary Ellen Monteleone of the American Lung Association; and friends Kathleen Quale and Rhonda Luongo.

In the area of divorce and its effects on children, I am very thankful for precious interview time granted by reknowned psychologists and authors Judith Wallerstein, Ph.D., of the Center for the Family in Transition, and Joyce Brothers, Ph.D. Also appreciated is the information gleaned from discussions with San Francisco's Kids' Turn director Rosemarie Bolen, and Colorado social worker Linda Sartori, editor of the remarkable "Kids Express" newsletter for children in divorce and separation.

Many relocation specialists contributed information about making a move with kids. My thanks to Cheryl Griffin of North American Relocation Services, Wendy Flanagan of Atlas Van Lines, Beth Copeland of Mayflower Transit, and Fran Denato of Bekins Van Lines Co.

For updating me on computers and kids, I applaud Home PC magazine education editor Carol Ellison; mar- keting specialist Kevin diLorenzo of Ergodyne; Marci Dockery of Copithorne & Bellows, and Ken Tameling of the Steelcase company Turnstone.

For assistance with text and images, I extend immeasureable thanks to Eileen McComb of Benjamin Moore; Debbie Kane of Dutch Boy Paints; Deborah Bahr of Martin-Senour Paints; Nancy Deptola of Kohler Co., Kate Ely of Techline; Nancy Lidner of Gerber Co., Rela Gleason of Summer Hill; Dan Heller of LARS Design; Janet Pearson of Quiltcraft Kids; Vicki Enteen of Laura Ashley Inc.; Susan Van Voorhees of American Olean; Alan Ferguson of Wimmer-Ferguson Child Products; Bob Kleinhans of Tile Council of America; Jeanne Ann Russell of Fabulous Fotoforms; Brendon Nunes of Trintec Industries; Monica Whitaker of Foreign Accents; Sheri Sharpe of Mothers Love and Nancy Snyderman, MD, of ABC-TV.

In the quest for data, many agencies, organizations, and libraries offered learning materials and detailed explanations. My sincere thanks to Burlingame Public Library reference and children's librarians, and to those consulted at National Geographic Society, Juvenile Product Manufacturers Association, National Safety Council, National Safe Kids Campaign, President's Council on Physical Fitness, Reading Is Fundamental, International Reading Association, National Kitchen & Bath Association, Unfinished Furniture Association, International Furnishings and Design Association, and the American Society of Interior Designers.

While many child specialists and designers influenced the content of this book, in many ways it was also shaped by friends who gave opinions and provided a safe harbor for frenzied stops during this monumental venture. For unflagging encouragement and good humor, I thank Teddi Grant, Mary Ellen O'Reilly, Carolyn Mady, Helen Fuson, Terry Nagel, Lily Sarmiento, Jane Grogan, Ann Kezeor, Stephanie Gale, Nancy Adams Cooke, Stephen Pouliot, Charles McCarthy, Carol Parkinson, Linda Harris, Sisi Luopajarvi, Yolanda Torrice, Barbara Bladen, Michelle Carter, Diana Viglianese, Mory Gerstemeier, Polin Cohanne, Marianna Nunes, Jane Boillotat, Allison and Tim Wojciechowski, Marshia and Ed Beck, and Allison Herlick.

For helping me rekindle childhood memories, I thank cousins Carmelia Marks, Lisa Clements, Pat Jensen, and Bob Milito and "big brudda" Jim Logrippo. Special gratitude is also extended to Sam, Sue, Dan and Charlie Spinelli; Bud, Jenny, and Brian Runion, and Lauren Logrippo, as well as my dear deceased Mom and Dad, for always fueling my aspirations.

The cooperation of many parents and children whose homes are featured is tremendously appreciated. Their kindness never ceases to impress me. So, too, do the remarkable talents of dozens of designers coast-to-coast, many of whom undertook or speeded up projects to participate in this book. Beyond those mentioned, special thanks to Lynette Reid, Merrily Ludlow, DeAnna Brandt, Carol Jacobson-Ziecik, Sandy Schiffman, *ASID*, Gary White, *CBD*, Diane Pizzoli, *Allied Member ASID*; and Anita Goldblatt, *Allied Member ASID*.

I also acknowledge the cooperation of magazine editors who lent images for this book. They include Kit Selzer, editor, *Better Homes and Gardens Special Interest Publications Bedroom & Bath*; Bette Boote, managing editor, *House Beautiful*; Mary Beth Jordan, deputy editor, *Child*; and Allison Blumenthal, art director, *Parents*.

Unquestionably, the skilled photographers who participated in this book earn my eternal kudos. I'm proud to feature their work.

Last, but far from least in importance on this list, is the late designer, lecturer, and humanitarian Tony Torrice, *ASID*, whose memory guided the creation of this manuscript. His zeal and innovative ideas about quality children's environments ripple through these pages. Like his enduring friendship, may they inspire others "10 times 10 times 10."

If others who aided this material aren't mentioned, the omission is unintentional. Named or not, you all hug my heart and stir my soul to meet the continual challenge of growing up, while never forgetting the wonderful world of childhood.

—Ro Logrippo, Allied Member ASID, IFDA

A WORLD OF WONDERS

Imagine your first day on a different planet.

The surroundings seem so strange and mysterious, cast in a brightness as yet unknown.

The other beings all loom so large and are incomprehensible, uttering many unfamiliar sounds.

Even the smells, tastes, and things you feel are totally new experiences, dazzling one moment, frightening the next.

There you are, the latest arrival, anxious to explore everything around. But forget any expeditions for now. You're flat on your back, very confined, and completely dependent on everyone else for sustenance, stimulus, care, and company.

Welcome to planet Earth and every baby's introduction to its vast world of wonders.

Cultivating that wonderment for the new addition to your family is what feathering a first environment is all about. But with so many decorative "plumes" to choose from in the marketplace, picking what's right for baby is often as perplexing as picking his or her name.

Some possible scenarios:

- Baby "A" begins life in a burst of brightness. Riotous room colors rival her toys.
- Baby "B" arrives in a fairytale setting. Plot and characters develop in detail at his every turn.
- Baby "C" lives a "hush hush" storyline. Soft pastels cushion her surroundings, taking their cue from pale walls and delicate furniture.

◄ *As playful as the rest of the artistry in this New York loft for a sculptor and his family, the doorway decoration that leads to Cleo's and Kimberly's personal world amuses them daily.*

As parents of A, B, C, and other newborns soon discover, determining how quiet or colorful their son's or daughter's home setting should be is not a one-time decision. If the room stays in step with the budding personality living there, it changes often—from the mobile that eventually loses its appeal to the crib sheets that soon fade from washing.

Change is an inevitable part of growing up. Make way for it as you plan the perfect place for a new life to unfold.

Moving in.
Moving around.
Moving safely.

That's what a baby's never-ending world of wonders, and these first pages, are all about.

THE BEGINNING STRETCH

Jostled by a gentle summer breeze, the tiny multicolored ribbons dance back and forth across the corner of the maple changing table where they're secured.

As Aaron reaches over to touch them with baby soft 4-month-old hands, his mother momentarily stops powdering him to marvel once more at her son's wonderment with everything in his new world. The narrow grosgrain ties, simple details meant to amuse, gently introduce the baby to a new texture and a handful of colors.

But besides delighting Aaron's senses, the simple decor and the stimulation it evokes in a small way demonstrates dramatic findings about brain development and its strong environmental link. Released by the Carnegie Corporation of New York, the 1994 report *Starting Points* recognizes that newborns usually have a well-organized capacity for adapting to environment.

"But the unfolding of the developing brain is not inevitable," the research states. "It depends on a fostering environment that is reasonably stable while at the same time stimulating, responsive, protective and loving." The quality of this environment, plus social experience, have "decisive long-lasting impact on a child's well-being and ability to learn."

CULTIVATING THE EARLY BRAIN

What scientists discovered, reports the Carnegie Task Force on Meeting the Needs of Young Children, is that a child's surroundings influence how many brain cells the body keeps and connects. Just as a statue is shaped by a sculptor chiseling marble, the adult brain is shaped after the very dense immature brain eliminates what's not used. By using outside information, consequently, the brain designs its own architecture, particularly in the early years.

"Even at birth infants show startling intellectual abilities," the Carnegie findings stress. "Newborns touch, see, hear, smell, taste and make sounds to gather information about their world. Parents and other caregivers exercise enormous influence on intellectual development" by providing food, warmth, and touching while protecting children from being overwhelmed by information and experiences.

"Both nature and nurture play a role in human development," the report concludes, thereby echoing other research emphasizing the importance of development in life's first 18 months. According to studies, by this age children raised in poor environments worldwide, already display substantial cognitive deficits that may be irreversible.

FROM THE EYES OF BABES

A thin round of wood painted to look like a wheel is the only hint a child with a vivid imagination needs to be transported on imaginary journeys.

How can parents of new babies take advantage of this research to make their son's or daughter's home environment just right?

Certainly the answer hinges greatly on what that setting contains to soothe and stimulate baby by enhancing baby's environment. But before tackling how to outfit the room with cuddly, challenging, or cute decor, it's important to understand some developmental facts about baby, starting with what he or she can actually see.

In terms of environment for those up to 2 months old, child development specialist Ruth Wimmer points out, something across the room makes little difference to them. That's because at birth babies see only about as far away as 8 inches. By 6 weeks, their range increases to about 12 inches. Even so, they do differentiate shape, size, and pattern.

However, black and white patterns are more appealing because the retina's rods and cones—the structures that perceive color—are still developing. Essentially, what they prefer are simple-to-moderate high-contrast "closeup" designs, although they view the outside edges more often than internal patterns. This discovery by child psychologist Phillip Salapatek, Ph.D., was made at the University of Minnesota during experiments in tracking an infant's gaze.

In the first 60 days of life, a baby's environmental stimulus, beyond a mobile placed nearby, is usually limited to the bedding. But don't assume that it, too, should be of a high contrast design.

"Parents often ask me if they should decorate the nursery in black-and-white checkerboard fabric and wallpaper," says human development researcher Dr. Susan Ludington-Hoe, whose infant stimulation studies and programs are widely recognized. Her emphatic "no" to the question draws this explanation: "Infant preferences change so quickly during the first six months that what's stimulating the first week would be a bore by the second or certainly third month. You don't want to redecorate every two weeks! Instead, consider making liberal use of posters and cardboard flash cards," she advises.

Decorating with a black-and-white scheme elicits strong negative response from Wimmer, too. "That would be like an adult sleeping in an amusement park," says the former director of therapeutic recreation at Denver Children's Hospital.

By about 2 months, vision changes when baby scans and remembers the entire visual field as well as interior patterns and outside edges. Patterns of increasing complexity, such as curved lines and shapes, faces, and targets, are now preferred to straight lines or angular shapes. It's a good idea, therefore, to provide high-contrast toys with mixed patterns of graduated complexity. Until a child is at the toddler stage, however, Ludington-Hoe recommends bypassing the perennial favorite teddy bear in favor of something like a black-and-white panda bear. "A panda puppet is even better," she says, but not only because it's a high contrast design. "When you animate the puppet and add your own voice, it comes alive with sound and movement for your infant."

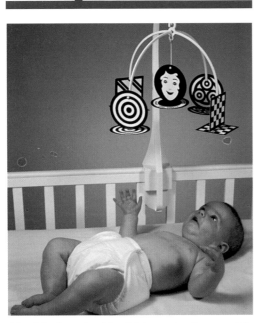

The black and white high contrast geometric patterns in this Stim-Mobile are designed with baby's visual preferences in mind.

At about 4 months, visual environment complexity and novelty are sought. Baby's focus adjusts to objects near or far, and depth perception begins to develop. Full color can be seen now, and curved patterns and shapes continue to be preferred. Only two months later, says Ludington-Hoe, baby will love looking at a color photo of the pattern most interesting to him or her—your face.

But don't equate baby's vision development with the need for a blast of room color.

"Just as a crib is a space that a baby needs to relax in or have alert time in, the whole room needs to be something a child can either relax in or play actively in," Wimmer says. "If it bombards all the time visually, it's a hard place to ever calm down because there are too many distractions."

Sensory overload is what happens to a baby in an environment that continually stimulates, Wimmer maintains. "Such an infant will cry and fuss in protest or quietly withdraw to avoid further sensory bombardment."

Recognizing the need for a nursery item taking sight preferences into consideration, a dozen years ago Wimmer designed a mobile for daughter Katherine. Incorporating three decades of laboratory study by others about how babies see, it featured stripes, faces, bull's eyes and checkerboards, all similar to those that researchers used in tests, taking object size, density, and contour into consideration. The prototype for a revolutionary baby industry product that followed, the mobile had high contrast black-and-white graphics that heed infant visual likes and dislikes. In deference to the fact that monotony tires babies, today's version has 20 viewing surfaces. All toy with the infantile notion of a good time: engaging the eyes back and forth between dark and light.

The mobile designer is quick to point out, however, that sensory stimulation is useful only when baby is alert and playful. For that reason, she suggests that all toys—including her Infant Stim-Mobile designs—be the kind that can be removed easily when unwanted.

"There's a time and place for everything," she explains. "The time for high contrast toys is play time; the time for soothing colors and combinations is quiet time. The nursery should not resemble a Coca-Cola sign or the generic aisle of a grocery store!"

It is interesting to note that Wimmer designed her hanging product line so that they are activated only by gentle air currents or a touch. They are intentionally designed not to make music or move on their own. "Mobiles that use a wind-up music box 'hypnotize' babies with constant motion and repetitive music," the child care specialist says. Instead, she advises parents to entertain baby with a variety of radio or audiotape sounds.

NOW HEAR THIS

In fact, what a baby hears at birth is low sound frequency under 1,000 Hz, because acoustic capacity is still underdeveloped. Speculating that low frequency sounds a baby hears in utero might be calming outside the womb, medical researchers overseas first explored the effects of reproducing these sounds in clinical studies.

Using a specially built microphone, a team of three doctors in Kawasaki, Japan, performed the scientific tests on 700 newborns by exposing them to prerecorded intrauterine sounds. Amazingly, in 85 percent of cases, the acoustic stimulation calmed babies and stopped their crying. Through EEG tracing it was further discovered that 30 percent were actually put to sleep. Similar results occurred in 1985 throughout Australia following testing in major hospitals with the help of Foundation 41, a Sydney research organization. There, too, 85 percent of newborns monitored were calmed after listening to a cassette tape of womb sounds played in maternity wards.

Besides indicating certain sounds can have therapeutic and psychological interest to infants, the research spawned a new kind of pacifier. An audio device, it recreates the "za-za-za" intrauterine sounds of a mother's heartbeat and internal fluids. Soothing Sounds, a product endorsed by the Lamaze Institute for Family Education, has actually modified its cushion-encased recording so its vibrations conform with the adjustments an infant's ears undergo at birth. The benefit of the sound pad versus the audiotape is that babies have to lie down to hear it and, consequently, are calmed off to sleep.

As with other developing senses, a baby's hearing eventually matures. At that point, the need for gentle, rhythmic sound diminishes. In some infants up to 2 years, however, audio pacifiers are reportedly still effective when baby is restless or colicky.

In the vast arena of children's issues, hearing is a salient but often neglected point, contends leading child psychologist and author Penelope Leach, Ph.D., of England.

"Many children intensely dislike high noise levels," Leach writes about early environments including day care settings. "Sound-absorbent ceilings, flooring, drapes, etc., can do a great deal to deaden the sound of small feet, voices and plastic equipment."

TAKING A HINT FROM BABY

As critical as this and other developmental information is for those parenting and creating nurturing settings, it doesn't equate to the need for expensive or expansive tools that enhance baby's environment. Like Aaron's ribbons, objects that offer stimulation can be quite simple.

"A child's imagination is so strong," says San Francisco Bay Area children's designer Bonnie Jaffey. "All it takes is a suggestion to trigger it. If decoration is very defined, a child's imagination has no place to go."

A professional who practices what she preaches, Jaffey initially put her theories to the test in son Aaron's room. By the time he was toddling, his small fingers could twirl wheel-like rounds of thin wood his dad had attached to the changing table's front legs. Painted white with rainbow stripes that looked like spokes, the wheels some days are the driving force behind imaginary train journeys; other days, they are the momentum of a make-believe car.

Besides sparking fantasy play, the ribbons, wheels and other "hints" of decor Jaffey provides all her young clients also serve another purpose. They enable a room's look and a furnishing's function to change with little effort, since they're easy to remove.

In a world with so many wonders, it only makes sense to keep changing some so baby can keep enjoying new experiences as he or she grows. Your keen awareness and attentiveness for the right time to add or subtract these environmental features provides the most invaluable nurturing elements of all—care and love.

A NEST THAT NURTURES

Finding the right formula for baby's room calls for action long before delivery day.

Well in advance of the new arrival, expectant parents should be searching for the right ingredients to fix up baby's first environment. In the ideal scenario, it should be ready for immediate occupancy once homecoming day dawns.

Deciding on the decor to welcome the one taking up residency in your home, starts with a study session on the area to be transformed. Its dimensions, architecture, and other elements impose some constraints that ultimately influence what design plan will work. Doorways, for example, hinder any furniture use. Windows, likewise, restrict the height of items placed in front of them.

On the architectural plus side, there may be a big open wall crying to be accented. If so, make it the focal point. Do something major, such as position the crib there.

Take design cues, too, from carpet and other existing features that aren't going to change. You'll have to work around them if a coordinated look means much to you.

When there's an odd room feature with which to contend, try to find a way to use it to advantage. That's what Sandy Schiffman, *ASID, FIFDA*, did. When faced with an off-center floor-to-ceiling vent in a nursery conversion from a storeroom, the Key West, Florida,

Even grown-ups can join in the fun in this kiddie corral designed like a playpen so a toddler can safely play. Once outgrown, the area can easily be re-worked to house a desk and activity area.

designer turned the unsightly feature into a fanciful maypole for the client's daughter. All it took was encircling the pipe with ribbons and a menagerie of plush toys at play. In this case, the camouflage not only worked, it created the room's dominant attraction—besides baby, of course. Come crawling stage, the ribbons can be removed and the pipe wrapped with reflective material so the toddler can see her ever changing self-image.

A protruding ceiling header was one of California designer Denise Tom-Sera's challenges in son Nikko's room. Her inventive budget-minded solution—make its location look intentional by appearing at both ends to top built-in floor-to-ceiling wall systems. Actually, what transforms the wall areas into corner "units" is pegboard painted a deeper color than the walls. Stuffed toys, hanging there on hooks, seem to float midair and their ever-moving arrangement continually captivates Nikko. He looks at them from his crib placed between the displays, which are trimmed in wavy wood painted turquoise. While the upper display area, designed for visual stimulation, is beyond baby's reach, the entire lower shelf area for playthings is meant to be touched by the toddler and accessible to him.

Besides amusing Nikko Sera at the baby stage, the wall system, as he grows, will suit his needs for seeing personal art and other kinds of treasures surface, thereby keeping in step with his rapid growth and development.

"Everything in the room is a potential toy and teacher," says Tom-Sera, who points out that includes the dresser. Its round, tactile door pulls are painted different shades of the rainbow and further accented on top with metallic marker in a spiral pattern. Explains his mother: "Nikko loves to pull himself up by them, and touch each color as I name each one."

ON YOUR MARK, GET SET. . .

When there isn't a design element or an architectural feature that triggers a plan of action in your situation, you'll need an alternate starting point. One idea is a family heirloom, suggests Janet Anderson Robb, a Colorado designer of children's environments.

A likely candidate is a rocker or a youth chair from your own childhood. Either is ideal for baby's room, even if it requires a little TLC to become presentable or sturdy again. The meaning such pieces hold is worth the effort—not to mention the savings that comes from recycling. Exceptions, of course, include an old crib that does not meet Consumer Product Safety Commission standards *(see "Baby Room Basics", page 12)* or any other furniture that is unsuited for a baby and consequently could be unsafe in this environment.

For Robb personally, the hand-me-down idea translated to using her own babyhood basinette for daughter Anna Sophia. When the baby outgrew the confines of her first sleep space and subsequently moved into a crib, the bassinette stayed. Its new role: a one-of-a-kind display piece for Anna's tiny "Lambie" and other stuffed toys.

Because it's virtually impossible to know your baby's tastes before it's born, Robb sanctions the idea of gingerly decorating your child's first environment with something that stirs an interest in you. Maybe it's a sense of nature and the environment that can be reflected in the window fabric. Maybe it's something more ethereal such as angels or mythical creatures that can be reflected in a framed picture. Whatever personally touches you to act upon it, don't go overboard on the look or your investment. Otherwise, you may be reluctant to alter the setting once it loses appeal for the very person it was meant to amuse.

The hooks and hangings on this pegboard display in the background continually change position to entertain and stimulate baby Nikko from his nearby crib. So do soft toys hung above his sleep area.

For other inspiration about baby decor, try to recall enjoyable images from your own childhood. If nothing comes to mind, let a wallcovering border design spark room detail. Easily "strippable," its replacement will be a snap once a child's own tastes come into play.

As for a particular theme or color in a child's room, both are covered in depth later in this chapter. For now, keep in mind that whatever you do in a nursery doesn't have to be dictated by Madison Avenue marketing trendsetters. What's in fashion may be fun, but it's not a prerequisite for baby's pleasure. Certainly, if you want this kind of flair, it's fine to invest in it. But your motivation is misplaced if it relies solely on what's in vogue.

MOVING FORWARD

Once you think through your baby's space, list the items that need to function in it. Besides a crib, basics to consider are a changing table or station, auxiliary storage such

When there's no place to go but up, a wall grid serves as efficient storage for bearing essentials such as diapers, supplies, and toys to amuse baby with at a changing station.

as a low dresser, and a comfortable adult chair, such as a rocker. Lighting and window coverings are extremely important, too, in a setting where naps and feedings are 'round the clock.

For the best setup, draw a rudimentary layout on paper. Let each furnishing's eventual use be your guide, as well as the relationship of one to the other. If you'll be nursing baby, for instance, position a rocker or comfortable adult chair near the crib. Using similar logic, put the changing area near the storage for baby's diapers, clothing, and other supplies so you won't have far to reach when you need them.

If room is tight, go vertical. Use a wall grid's shelves for necessities. When there's insufficient floor or wall space to meet nursery needs, think about other alternatives, starting with closet reconfiguration. Take Northern California designer Lynnette Reid's situation as an example. Straddled with cramped quarters for little Colby's nursery, the resourceful new mother removed the room's double closet doors to turn the entire alcove into a clever changing station. By lowering, reinforcing, and padding the shelf, Reid transformed it into a useful area of interest. She raised the clothes rod on high for Colby's limited wardrobe and tucked the baby's diapers and other necessities out of sight behind the cotton print she hung in dressing-table fashion under the low shelf.

A standard closet also came to the rescue of Minnesota mother and graphic designer DeAnna Brandt. Determined to keep baby Daniel's floor space open, she stacked wire baskets for laundry, toys, and baby clothes behind bifold closet doors, where each was labeled in front with a picture of the contents to teach early on where everything belonged. As for diapers and baby blankets, they were lined up in vertical rows in hanging plastic storage caddies intended by the manufactuer for sweaters, shoes, and other adult items. Swung open, the storage is easy for Daniel and his parents to access.

Whatever your overall plan, keep baby's growth in mind. Once he or she is mobile, you may need to rearrange furnishings or supplies that otherwise could pose a potential hazard.

READYING FOR THE HUNT

When you've established a detailed plan of action for your own baby's room, you're just about ready to put on your shopping shoes and hunt for furnishings.

To make shopping easier, however, do a bit more homework first. Get current parenting magazines and clip pictures of appealing products. Put them in a special file along with dimensions, overall room snapshots, and swatches of carpet and other materials you'll need to work around. All these practical tools will help take the guesswork out of buying. Samples also assist the in-store designers or salespersons helping you.

Last but not least, before heading out the door, take stock of your budget. If you know what's affordable before you go, you're likely to be more careful about expenditures.

Naturally, with oodles of designs from which to choose, purchases depend on available cash as much as available space. But what you like should influence decisions, too. After all, in a market predominated by wood and white furnishings, choosing one over the other depends mostly on taste. Some people view wood as a warm touch that brings in the outdoors. Some prefer the clean look of white, whether painted wood or laminate. Still others opt for brass cribs—not as commonplace as other options yet widely available.

As you debate the pros and cons of furniture finishes, keep in mind that bedding, curtains, and other fabrics will be what catches both yours and baby's eyes. With regard to material, be practical when it comes to window treatments. Even though they're usually far from baby's range, they should be easy to clean since they absorb room odors.

Blinds, roller shades, and shutters are all easy to keep up. Curtains, on the other hand, involve more maintainence but their designs afford a more juvenile touch. Whatever graces baby's window on the outside world, be sure it has black-out features for naptime.

Baby's ability to sleep comfortably should also influence the decision on what lighting goes in the room. A dimmer allows the best control over artificial light and softens the setting when need be. If there's space on a dresser, you might also want to consider a small lamp. For late night feedings, a dim light works well and can even be provided by a colored bulb.

A simple night light that plugs into the wall is a good idea, too. Not only does it allow you to check baby periodically without altering the illumination, it helps to prevent a tired parent from tripping in the dark.

FIT TO BE RE-TRIED

Even the best plans and purchases don't always add up to what you imagined. Once everything is arranged according to layout, step back with a critical eye and judge what's before you.

If the look doesn't tie together well, don't be afraid to do some rearranging. Considering how many changes this setting will undergo, you may as well get used to trying a different formula early on.

Baby Room Basics

If you brush up on the latest information about safe, sound and sensible furnishings, outfitting baby's room with the basics is as easy as A, B, C.

One security measure for buyers is the safety certification given by the Juvenile Product Manufacturers Association. The "JPMA Certified" seal, found on cribs and certain other baby equipment, ensures that a model has passed rigorous standards for structural integrity. But once an item is purchased, the seal and other tags should be removed; they pose a choking hazard. Before filing them away, read any instructions.

Points to ponder about major buys for baby's room include the following, not all of which come under JPMA certification yet.

CRADLES AND BASSINETS

Although only safe for a few months until babies can raise up on their own, cradles and bassinets are popular for newborns because they are cozier at this stage than a crib. The benefit of these sleeping units is portability. They can be easily transported to wherever you want baby to be.

Cradles that suspend from a base should have a wide and sturdy support with secure pivoting hardware that locks in a stationary position. The higher the sides, the less likelihood of baby taking a tumble, although a rocking mechanism should only provide slight motion.

If the bassinet is wicker, check to see no broken or loose ends protrude inside where they could hurt baby or outside where they could hurt a caregiver. Whether buying one new or using an heirloom, make certain the lining is securely in place, with no ribbons, buttons, or other trims posing a danger.

CRIBS

As with other large pieces, know where this one will go before you bring it home. For starters, rule out a place near draperies, blinds, or decorative accessories with long wall-mounted cords. All of these pose a threat if baby becomes entangled in them.

If space is limited and a crib won't be reused for later children, a crib that converts to other uses may be desirable. Convertible options range from built-in storage components that detach as single units, to fully removeable rails that allow the mattress to become the foundation for a youth bed conversion. A mattress extension and spring, either optional or provided, can add years of usefulness.

"Convertibles," while pricier than others, may save money in the long run, since their growth potential means less replacement furniture. From a child's perspective, however, the downside to longevity is living longer with a look reminiscent of baby days.

All cribs have adjustable side rails that drop to help baby in or out. Two side drops allow greater flexibility for repositioning a crib in the event of a move or room reconfiguration. Be sure rail slats or spindles meet current standards, with spacing no more than $2\frac{3}{8}$ inches apart and drop side catches that don't release accidentally.

Shy away from cribs that may signal poor construction. Warning signs include the following:

- Unsturdiness or shakiness
- Surface cracks
- Missing slats or hardware

As for secondhand merchandise, be cautious even if it belongs to a good friend. The dangerous features just mentioned also come from wear and tear, and older models also may have design details no longer considered safe. Absolute "no-nos" today include:

- Paint that isn't lead free
- Decorative cut-outs where a child could get stuck
- Corner posts or knobs that could catch baby's clothing. Neither should project more than $\frac{1}{16}$ inches above the crib end. Corner canopies or posts over 16 inches high are both OK.

If you're hesitant in the least about a used item, pass it up. A potential risk isn't a bargain. Even new models should be checked often for loose parts that are produced by squirming or moving around.

Once baby can mastermind a crib escape, or reaches a height of 35 inches, bid the equipment a final "night night." It's time to introduce more grown-up slumber options.

CRIB MATTRESS

A separate purchase, a mattress should fit snugly in the frame with no more than two fingers width between it and the side of the crib. If it's possible to put more fingers in this space, a larger mattress is needed to prevent possible suffocation.

Typically, baby mattresses measure $28\frac{5}{8}$ by $5\frac{3}{8}$ inches, with a standard thickness ranging from 5 to 6 inches.

CRIB BEDDING

In regard to bedding, JPMA suggests bumper pads that fit around the entire crib and tie or snap securely into place. Once it is tied, trim away excess strap or ribbon so it can't get tangled and cause strangulation. When baby can sit, ban the bumper. It could aid in a crib escape.

While sheet and bumper patterns differ greatly, a delicate design may be more restful than a wild one. Even so, try to vary bedding for baby's visual pleasure. Besides alternating sets, if your skills include sewing, make a pad with two-sided designs, or with vinyl pockets where high contrast patterns can be inserted on a rotating basis.

About pillows: don't put one under baby's head or leave one in the crib.

A delicate design may be more restful than a wild one. Even so, for the baby's visual pleasure try to vary the bedding once in a while.

CHANGING TABLES

Besides sturdy construction, look for a change station with straps that help prevent baby from falling. If a unit lacks these, purchase a strap for separate installation. Whenever baby is on the table, be sure straps are in use as a restraining measure. But never leave baby unattended on it.

Convertible changing tables are also part of the bedtime story. Those designed for flexibility feature a detachable changing station that secures to the top of the storage unit.

Since styles vary in height by as much as 10 inches, get one that feels right for your height or changing baby will be uncomfortable. Also scrutinize how a unit looks without its change station. Some design elements, such as visible top hardware, may not appeal in the metamorphosis.

If you opt for a convertible unit with a built-in dresser—or if you put a change station on top of a conventional dresser—locate the piece near shelving or a wall grid that provides easy and open access to needed baby products stored there.

14

BOOKSHELVES

Whether high or low, rounded edges, stable construction, and safe positioning are what you need to concern yourself with regarding the purchase of freestanding shelving, especially for a baby's room.

If it's at all unsteady, anchor the piece to the wall with appropriate screws.

What you plan to display should guide your purchase, too. If you want to keep a toddler from inspecting every book in his or her personal library, for instance, choose a shelf unit with closed storage doors on the bottom and open shelving on top. This style has the advantage of being harder for kids to climb.

If you want a toddler to have ready access to lightweight toys and a few other playthings, consider a low, open-shelf unit.

DRESSERS

A dresser, which averages about 30 inches tall, has the advantage of being low enough to use as a change table when a waterproof pad is placed on it.

Although your immediate need may be for baby item storage, look beyond the early years so that whatever you buy will function at least through preschool.

Because of its height, a three- or four-drawer dresser functions better for a young child than a high chest. The latter may hold more, but its 42- to 48-inch average height will frustrate a child needing items from upper drawers.

Besides sturdy construction, consider a piece that's easy for a child to grasp and open when the stage for encouraging independence arrives. Hardware too far apart frustrates a child who can't possibly spread arms wide enough to maneuver both sides at once.

ROCKERS

While the old rock-a-bye baby rhyme called for a treetop and wind so baby's cradle could sway, nowadays the nurturing routine relies on a rocker conveniently placed in baby's room.

Current versions come with footstools and/or gliding mechanisms, but the old wooden standby still works well, too. Besides comfort, look for a rocker that provides plenty of room for cradling baby in your arms and no awkward cushion or upper chair features that restrict you from holding baby's head on your shoulder.

As for the fabric on the seat and backrests, something washable is always preferable. If you don't like any patterns available, consider slipcovers for the cushions.

Whatever you choose, be sure it can't tilt back too far when you rock-a-bye baby.

Watch out, too, for side or back spindle designs that could entrap baby's arms or legs.

15

A THEME COME TRUE?
NOT IN MY ROOM!

Close your eyes and picture 1-year-old Lily's bedroom scene.

As in a prehistoric kingdom, dinosaurs reign supreme, roaming her room by way of clever designs.

- Multicolored stegosaurs detail the lampshades and light switches.
- Animated tyrannosaurs accent the window coverings and wallpaper.
- Bold brontosaurs emblazon Lily's sheets and the rest of her bedding.

Now imagine her older brother Charlie's quarters right next door: An out-of-this-world setting, it's been transformed from an earthly scene with oodles of items guaranteed to make it look like a mock-up of Mission Control.

- Walls and ceiling are plastered with posters of planets and glow-in-the dark stars.
- Floor space is predominated with a NASA-inspired spaceship bed.
- Futuristic furnishings by the dozens send a nonstop signal to this would-be astronaut to blast off.

What do you think of Lily's and Charlie's bedrooms? Are they storybook settings or good intentions gone awry? Consider the longevity factor of both scenes before responding to that question. Therein the answer lies.

As whimsical as these fictitious children's settings sound, they probably would be shortlived dreamlands to any children who would live there. The reason is simple. Decorating in an overall theme locks the room into a specific time frame. What kids consider delightful today will be deemed uncool tomorrow when they're likely to view their magical settings as traces of babyhood.

With children's tastes and current fads ever changing, it's almost certain that a look will be outgrown long before the items portraying it wear out. Once that interest is lost, a theme room will annoy the very one it used to amuse.

LOCALIZING A LOOK

There are several ways without bombarding an environment to satisfy childhood cravings for decorations inspired by their favorite real and imagined characters.

If your children have their hearts set on a particular look, suggest limiting it to one wall. Transform that area into a large bulletin board that constantly changes with pinned-up pictures, stickers, or other trinkets, including those of personalities they particularly admire.

To save the wall from push pins and tacks that could damage it, pad the area to be covered with either adhesive-backed corkboard squares or sheets of sound deadening material covered with fabric your child selects.

BORDER PAPERS

Wallpaper borders printed in a child's favorite design are another imaginative way to give a young fan's room some punch that pleases. After narrowing selections to a manageable number, encourage your son or daughter to look at samples with you. But be careful not to choose something that caters to your taste instead of your child's.

Besides costing less than overall wallcovering because of the amount used, borders are an attractive alternative and easy to apply. Position the pattern midway around the room just a few inches above your child's head, unless this placement fights with the architecture of the space. In that case, raise or lower the ornamental strip to avoid the problem. What a midwall border achieves is the effect of visually lowering the ceiling to child height. In so doing, you also allow the child to enjoy the border since it will then be within his or her close range of vision.

Wall decorations and characters that can be removed easily and repositioned are other possibilities for a border. What makes these changeable sticker-like designs so desireable in a child's room is their ability to foster the creation of a different storyline at any time. In other words, they nurture imagination.

Stencils play up a theme with minimal expense, too. An enjoyable do-it-yourself project, stenciling enables you to repeat a pattern around a room. For flexibility and practicality, use washable latex enamel paint and thick ready-to-use paper or plastic stencils like the kind you find in activity books in a craft store. Be original and mix a few designs for some real pizazz. Take those dinosaurs, for instance. With many species to select from, you can create a caravan of the extinct creatures so they playfully march in unison from one wall to the next. Let your child pick the colors of each.

Magazines provide many wall border opportunities. If your preteen likes fancy cars, for instance, specialty publications geared for collectors will supply plenty of full page photos that can be used to line the walls with many makes and models. Whole publications are devoted monthly to dolls, teddy bears, and a score of other topics appealing to young people. To add durability to the clippings, laminate them before hanging.

Also browse through calendars illustrated with professional quality photos. Because they're printed on sturdier paper than magazines, their pages make more durable wall borders. Keep the cost down by purchasing calendars beyond the half-yearly mark when stores discount them considerably.

KEEPING COMPANY WITH FICTITIOUS CHARACTERS

Peanuts. Garfield. These are just a couple of cartoon characters your child may like and long for as bedroom company. As with any other character or personality that appeals to someone young, exercise restraint in decorating a setting with them. In other words, a little detail goes a long way.

The funnies provide some interesting possibilities especially if you're on a tight budget. Save the Sunday papers, for instance, and cut out the color comic strips of the character your son or daughter likes best. Glue them to cardboard and, when dry, cover with clear contact paper to make them impervious to water or sticky fingers. Suspend them with thread from wire clothes hangers and presto! You've made an amusing mobile that can be changed inexpensively from week to week.

A child's small collectibles also afford the opportunity of carrying out a special theme in moderation.

For example, a collection of baseball cards, small stuffed animals, or other light-weight "hangables" could be ideal components for a one-of-a-kind mobile with special significance. Hung from the ceiling over the bed, this decoration could be a soothing diversion at bedtime.

The bed itself is an ideal place for theme characters to prevail. To satisfy the young person who will regularly be kept company by them, let him or her decide what the bedding pattern will be.

In a shared space, allow each child to make an individual selection. After all, there's no need for the sheets on both beds to match. If you like a uniform look, coordinate the covers.

OLDER CHILDREN

Fashions and fads have as much place in a young adult's room as toys do in a nursery. Just as a preschooler thrills in seeing his or her primitive artistry displayed, older children like to show off objects that reflect individual style or personal interest in real-life heroes and heroines.

While it's important to recognize the need for expression, it's also wise not to encourage older children to go overboard with themed decor either. A few posters, and so forth, strategically placed, allow opportunity for something new to surface.

As you watch team pennants, rock star paraphernalia, and other expressions of teenage tastes appear, keep in mind that you're helping someone on the brink of maturity establish an identity and create a "signature" look.

BROADENING A CHILD'S FOCUS

No matter what age your child is, it's only natural for his or her interests to change periodically. All the more reason to focus special interests in a special area.

Think about it. If the whole room is teddy bears or hot rods, they're always there, impossible to ignore. By encouraging kids to change or adapt their environments, you allow them to explore new interests and discover new tastes.

S T R I K E   U P   T H E   B A N D S
O F   C O L O R !

It was a "true blue" day at the children's museum, and the young visitors, like partygoers bearing gifts, raced to the blank white wall clutching unwrapped treasures. As they placed items on the clear shelves hung there, a collection of azure to indigo articles grew.

A plastic cup the color of blueberries... shoelaces and scarves the shade of peacock feathers... pop-beads that matched the sky... a rubber ball as bright as cobalt... a big brimmed hat "blooming" with bachelor buttons and forget-me-nots.

Together, these and other finds turned the blank wall behind them into the color of many oceans.

"The Color Wall made kids more sensitive to colors and observant of life," says American Youth Museum past president Jane Jerry about a prior New England color

Crayon-colored cushions and banners turn this playroom corner into a magical setting that promotes motor skills as well as visual perception.

exhibit. She could tell parents appreciated the display's ability to instill color awareness in their children. But the former executive director of the Children's Museum of Houston wonders how many ever realized its potential for being copied on a small scale at home. Part of a shelf in a child's room, she says, could be a changing display area for toys and other objects that reinforce how multicolored a world this is, both by nature and design.

Because parents can provide one-on-one guidance that a museum or school often can't, they can capitalize at home on lessons triggered elsewhere. To enhance the experience of color, for instance, think in terms of an interdisciplinary approach. Play music or read a book about whatever hue is being explored. As Jane Jerry vouches, "A parent can become just as involved as a child and get just as much out of it."

EXPLORING THE WORLD OF COLOR

By allowing a child's colorful expressions to surface like the Color Wall at a level within their reach, California art therapist Basia Lubicz believes you contribute to a child's "personal resonance" with color. "The whole idea," she says, "is being supportive of a child's exploration and feelings about color."

However, the very concept of trying to influence a child's color choices draws serious criticism from outspoken members of the art, design, and education communities.

Says Nashville furniture artist Betsy Hoffman, who teaches children's art to kindergarten through fifth graders: "If you're discouraged when you're young to experiment with different colors and told 'that isn't going to work,' you become inhibited." To counter such attitudes, she urges her classes to unleash their artistry on all kinds of surfaces, from wood to maps to kites. "So many kids think they can only paint on paper," she says. "Letting them paint on other materials opens up a whole world of possibilities."

With that in mind, Hoffman suggests children 4 years old and up be alloted part of a wall at home as a free expression area where it's OK to be creative. By that age, she says, kids will understand they can't take over every wall in the house, just the one specified. Lubicz, who concurs with the idea, also recommends door space for artistry since it's easy to hang a roll of paper there that encourages ever-changing murals. It doesn't matter how simple or complex they are, she says. What's important is knowing "this is my special place."

Using children's art for room accents is one of the best ways to color their private world so it's meaningful to them. But let them be the judge about what belongs on exhibit.

As tempting as it may be to single out particular efforts so they coordinate with the rest of your child's room, resist the urge.

"If you impose your sense of color, you dictate an emotional relationship that your child might not have," says San Francisco designer Victoria Stone. When that happens, she says, the child's room becomes less a statement about the one living there and what makes him or her feel good and more a statement about the parent. "Let children pick their own colors," she says, "and they're more apt to feel comfortable in their own environment."

Tapping in to colors your kids like is as easy as paying attention to the crayons they choose most for drawing. Whether they pick one color or an explosion of colors is inconsequential, says child development specialist Margo Lillig of Discovery Toys. "Both are healthy," she says. After all, kids, like grown-ups, vary.

In light of how vibrant most children's playthings are, it's interesting to note the views of a leading supplier of colorful early learning materials.

"Color can greatly enhance the aesthetic appeal and sensory stimulation of the spaces in which children live, learn, discover and dream," remarks Irene Hoogenboom of Environments, Inc., when asked about the importance of colorful products for children. "It can be a powerful way to seduce spirits, encourage creative response and suggest possibilities to active imaginations.

"In a world that can be so bright and beautiful, color is an integral part of a magic environmental mirror that reflects to each child the wonder and value of his individual existence," the merchandiser continues. "Its effective use is a joyous and everyday rein-forcement of our message to children: 'You are worthy of beauty. Your spaces are special places where important things happen!' "

SCHOOL GAZE, SCHOOL GAZE

Because a child's room should be a learning as well as a living environment, the use of color in it should have more than decorative significance.

To realize the teaching potential of color, visit children's public spaces, including a variety of schools. Often their rudimentary displays foster color sensitivity, and with little effort and expense these can be duplicated at home.

An instructional tool easy to imitate is a color mobile of the kind Lillig once made to teach 4-year-olds about the spectrum. The day "red" was the topic of discussion, her kindergarten class was welcomed by real apples, plastic strawberries, and other crimson objects suspended from on high. By mixing things naturally red with things intentionally made rosy, an interesting lesson was conveyed about color properties and varieties.

Home mobiles like Lillig's can make an even greater impact on young viewers by involving them in the process of selecting hangables. This not only draws interest in the project and intensifies color awareness, she contends, but also builds a sense of self esteem.

Other classroom "color tools" that could easily take up residence where you live include:

- **Seasonal Displays:** Because holidays and seasons are all associated with a specific palette, encourage room decor that reflects what's happening on the calendar. A vase of wildflowers can tell the story of spring. A basket of leaves turning color can signify fall. A display of miniature flags can mark Independence Day.

- **Carpet Squares:** Just the right size for kids to sit on or play with, these small islands of color are good for a reading post or whatever else stirs the imagination. Discontinued samples, sold inexpensively through large dealers, come in three sizes:13 by 18 inch-es; 18 by 27 inches and 27 by 54 inches. The larger two are bound on all sides. Try to mix colors and weaves so a child can experience a variety.

- **Ceiling Banners**: Depending on design, this colorful touch can teach or simply delight the viewer. Nylon taffeta is the ideal banner material because of its sheen and ability to sway when touched by the slightest breeze. For personal detail, applique a name or initials on a banner. Variations on this look that also appeal to a child range from flags and windsocks to fabric canopies suspended by clear fishing line.

- **Color "Calendar":** Squares or circles of variegated construction paper hung like a calendar have a dual purpose. Besides familiarizing children with the spectrum, it gives them a vehicle for describing their emotions in relation to color. As California art therapist Basia Lubicz explains about materials such as this: "Children have their own idiosyncratic feelings about color. It's important to help them express themselves."

TAKING A CUE FROM COLOR

Obviously, introducing kids to the wonders of color starts long before their first day of school or their first visit to a children's museum. It begins at home—first while focusing on bedding and clothing, and later while zeroing in on toys and furnishings.

Once a child reaches the toddler stage, spectral cues in the environment can be enabling as well as enhancing. A good example of this is color-coded storage, since it visually signals what goes where.

The value of color coding kids' stuff repeatedly influences the work of children's designer Anita Goldblatt, *Allied ASID*, who years ago switched from designing institutional learning settings to doing residential settings for kids. In making the transition, the New Yorker clung to what she learned in the classroom: Children innately like to sort things.

Consequently, Goldblatt makes it easy for clients' very young children to organize small toys like LEGOs by providing clear containers for every toy brick color. The contents of each are identified on the outside with either a colored picture cut from the box it came in, or with a colored toy part taped on the inside corner of the storage container. Labeled in such a way, the designer points out, a child's belongings can be put away even by visiting playmates.

To color code alternate storage containers already in use, get peel-off colored lettering available at most stationery stores. As interests change and new toys replace the old, relabeling is a simple matter.

Putting color to work in a kid's room can also be done by detailing drawers with multicolored hardware, or by differentiating closet shelves with paint, self-adhesive paper, or fabric. Naturally, to maximize the benefits of color coding, let your child determine what goes where. This contributes to a sense of pride as well as ownership.

Judging by the description on the outside of each drawer, everything under the sun seems suitable for this storage unit. Once a plain changing table, hands-on artistry transformed it to a family heirloom.

"When children feel they possess the room, the room speaks to them," designer Goldblatt says. "Then it's not just a room within the house, but their room that they've helped design." One way to evoke this reaction, she finds, is getting kids' input on colors by asking which ones make them feel happy.

A perfect example of that philosophy successfully carried out is evidenced in the Manhattan loft where artist/sculptor Rodney A. Greenblat and his wife, hat designer Deena Lebow, make their home with twin daughters Cleo and Kimberly. In the girls' room particularly, color, language, and art "communicate" to them on a single piece of furniture updated from changing station to dresser when they turned a few years old. To help them recall where belongings go, their father, owner of the Center for Advanced Whimsy, painted all five drawers differently in the twins' favorite colors. Then, he decorated them with comic and storybook symbols and words describing everything inside.

The bubble gum pink drawer, for instance, has the top of a little girl's blue outfit painted on one side; its matching bottoms are painted on the other. In red paint between them, a hand-written message proclaims: "Cute Outfits." Two drawers down, the purple drawer says "Frilly Nighties," and just below that, the bottom yellow drawer advertises "Things We Don't Use" with doodles dancing around it.

With rainbow splashes here and there, the twins' domain preaches what their dad's artistry teaches: If you want something unique for your child's room, make it yourself with their input, including colors they enjoy.

LET THERE BE COLORED LIGHT

Equally as important as color pigment in a child's world is color illumination. That's why a personal environment should provide possibilities for experiencing both.

Besides enjoying a rainbow, one magical way to illuminate a young mind about the wonders of light is to hang a prism in the window. When it catches the sun at different intervals during the day, the light refracted from it breaks into six component colors.

"Prisms are a terrific way to turn a child's mental wheels thinking about color," says Connecticut architect Nancy Carroll, *AIA*, who has several prisms hanging within young son Brett's line of vision. The award-winning designer of the LEGO Creative Child Care Center, Carroll also recommends occasionally hanging different colors of cellophane in a child's windows so the outdoor environment appears to be tinted. To really entertain and educate a young observer further, just layer the colored gels.

In the same way that a color calendar can elicit thought about emotional feelings, colored light can evoke or indicate a certain mood. For a younger child, using a colored bulb in a lamp is an inexpensive way to mark special occasions while teaching a lesson in creating atmosphere. To add a mysterious indoor element to Halloween, for instance, a child may enjoy placing an orange bulb in a bedside lamp. When all other lights are out, the glow that's cast may make the entire room appear like a jack-o'lantern.

A more pervasive way to alter a room with colored lights is to turn on overhead track fixtures outfitted with different colored filters or gels. Bathed in a color the young person chooses, a room changes its look on the spur of the moment and thereby allows for youthful reflection or special enjoyment.

COLOR MY WORLD

Whether *in the pink, feeling blue, seeing red,* or *green with envy,* all children deserve a personal experience of color. As their grown-up guides, parents have the privilege of fanning their curiosity about it.

Catching Inner Rainbows

Like metal to magnet, visual childhood perceptions latch onto the spectrum. Once absorbed and recorded, the colorful images are strung together as private history recalled throughout life again and again. Consider these colorful impressions of early life:

- The soft, inviting tones that identify a mother's flesh
- The comforting patchwork that distinguishes personal belongings
- The warm or cool light that streaks across a room

"With as much care and concern given to feeding, nurturing and loving children, we should be attentive to the quality of color and light imposed on them during formative years." These words of the late Tony Torrice, *ASID*, reflect more than 20 years of researching color and its effect on young people, with whom he "co-designed" environments from 1979 to 1992, drawing from a background in child psychology and early childhood education.

By letting a child choose part of the spectrum surfacing in personal quarters, the one-time teacher believed, you open a doorway of expression, not only fostering positive self image but also satisfying a survival need. Comprehending the importance of this hinged greatly, he realized, on understanding color's effect on human anatomy at any age.

"As any sunbather soaking up rays knows," Torrice explained, "the body absorbs color through skin when light bounces off it, interacting with the energy inherent in its makeup. Absorb too much sunlight, and sunburn results on parts of the body exposed."

But the color researcher was quick to point out that whether a person is sun-

26

Joining forces with children on what their personal space will look like fosters pride in the space as well as self-confidence and self-image.

bathing or not, when light hits the skin, it absorbs color in the same way a prism does when struck by light. It breaks it into rainbow components in spectral order from red to purple.

Russian scientists were the first to isolate colors relating to specific body functions. In the 1940s, Semyon and Valentina Kirlian captured on photographic plates color images of life forms, including Semyon's hand, subjected to electrical charges. Described as corona discharges, the colors that emanated from humans, animals, and plants were examined in the research institute where they worked. To accurately measure information, the couple devoted 10 years to developing instruments. Their conclusion: the skin absorbs light in much the same way as Sir Isaac Newton's prism bent light.

Taking the Kirlian theory into consideration, along with color studies of children in clinical, hospital and residential settings, Torrice ascertained an association between the organs of the body and the wavelengths of light normally absorbed by them. What he deduced follows:

- Red is absorbed at the base of the spine and consequently concerns itself with motor skill activities.
- Orange relates to the circulatory and nervous systems.
- Yellow corresponds to the chest, heart, and lungs, concerning itself with respiration and cardiopulmonary activities.
- Green relates to the throat and vocal cords.
- Blue deals with eyes, ears, and nose, which involve sight, sound, and smell.
- Violet is absorbed on top of the head, corresponding to brain activity. In a child, it may signify a mind concerned, deep in thought, or afraid of something confusing.

To clarify his position, Torrice described how he envisioned the human color absorption process.

"Like a prism suddenly illuminated, the body bends natural and artificial light while receiving it, channeling it through a system of reactions en route to the brain. Along the way, the body is affected from the spine to the pituitary gland which depends on light for human growth and development. During this light bombardment, those organs molecularly sympathetic with the wavelength vibrating towards it, will absorb it simply and easily."

The damaged body is the exception to this rule, as the Kirlians discovered and Torrice concurred. "If a child is deaf, for instance, wave lengths of light commonly absorbed by the body's audio apparatus may find great difficulty in their normal pathway," Torrice contended. To compensate for lack of light to a certain area, he believed, persons reached out for the deficient color to include it in their immediate surroundings. Amazingly, he found that the young people he studied shared an affinity for the same colors if they shared a physical deficiency. In the playroom he designed at San Francisco Children's Hospital with areas zoned in color for specific play, children with specific ailments sought out the color area correlating with their ailment. Those with mending muscles, opted most for the red area. Those with throat problems gravitated most toward the green area. Interestingly, Torrice also discovered that the restorative effect of colors, in this renovated health environment, was emphasized by the decrease in patient hospital stays.

The color theorist stressed, however, that choosing a specific color didn't necessarily indicate physical affliction. It could also signal a body area undergoing development. Take, for example, a child with a propensity for green, the color associated with the throat. Rather than experiencing speech problems, he speculated, that child may be learning a second language and therefore concentrating on vocal skills.

As simplistic as the concept of physiological response to color may be, it never was intended to be a formula for acquiring certain skills.

"These theories cannot be reversed to achieve a desired result," Torrice wrote. "Filling an environment with green may not encourage language aptitude. Flooding a room with blue may not improve sight or hearing.

"Color cannot be prescribed as if it were a bottle of blue or a gram of green. Each individual receives and responds to color as light in their own unique way. All the more reason to ask a child to choose color preference. Each individual child, as each individual adult, selects the best situation to survive when given the opportunity to choose what they really need and not just like."

Lending weight to Torrice's highly publicized theories are scientific studies brought to light in 1988 during an international science conference in New York. The findings indicate that keratinocytes (cells of the epidermis) are highly sensitive to colored light and aid in the conversion of spectral colors to chemical reactions within the body.

In his own lectures and writings, Torrice emphasized that every human being responds to color differently. A 10-year-old Los Angeles boy inclined toward blue might have a totally different preference were he in New York City. What's important is being able to select what color actually fulfills personal need at a particular time and place.

To enable a boy or girl to zero in on the intensity of a preferred color, the children's designer suggested color games of choice in conjunction with paint chips ranging from light to dark in the color or colors most desired. *(See "Cushioning the Jolt of a Moving Experience" in Chapter 6 for details.)*

"Like a radio station turned up or down," Torrice explained, "the child will perceive how 'loud' or 'soft' his choice should be." What is actually chosen represents how bright or muted the palette in personal space should be, although even slight use of it will impact a child. "There is no need to saturate a setting in one color," Torrice stressed. "A can of paint or a piece of fabric can profoundly change a child's outlook." But the more preferences that do materialize in fabrics, carpet, and decorative elements, he added, the more they become the child's "signature," serving as imprints of innermost feelings.

Just as we outgrow clothes and tastes, at any age we can outgrow color. A child who picks blue at 5, may or may not at 15. And once grown, people tend to select color based on fashion trends and advertising.

But as Tony Torrice's work, highlighted in this book, shows, a child not yet biased by outside influences spontaneously selects color true to the inner self. Like food or shelter, the need for a personal experience of color is no less for a child than for an adult.

Staking Neutral Territory

Because children's toys and clothing are primarily of bold colors, some specialists take a firm stand that children's environments be just the opposite.

"If the background is neutral," contends Denver child development specialist Ruth Wimmer, "it can accept a changing array of colorful objects from a kite over the bed to a poster on the ceiling."

Echoing these sentiments is Connecticut architect Nancy Carroll, *AIA*, who believes, "If you keep things neutral, a child's colorful art work and toys pop out and become important, rather than the walls in their room." An attitude that prevails in children's public spaces, it could apply in home settings, too, she says.

In looking at the issue of color in a child's environment, London psychologist and child development author Penelope Leach considers a child's perspective above all.

"The adult view of child-friendly decor—primary colors and cartoon pictures—has no basis in children's own preferences," she says. "Such schemes can be visually 'noisy' and stressful. More emphasis should be put on subtle colors, textures and lighting." While Leach's observations to the National Task Force on Day Care Interior Design were about day care settings, they certainly carry over to residential space. As she herself states: "The day care environment should not be completely different from the 'real world' outside it."

Believing that "interior space should not bombard children visually," Wellesley Child Study Center former director Marian Blum takes a dim view of children's spaces that use bright, primary colors to excess. "Children discover and learn best in an environment that is tranquil, welcoming, consistent and orderly," she responded when polled a few years ago about her feelings on children's environmental design.

In establishing color schemes of children's settings, vast differences between adult and child color perceptions cannot be overlooked, says former longtime San Francisco Unified School District child development program director Madelon Halpern, also a respondent in the environmental poll.

Because adults are the audience of advertisers, she points out, they have learned "a syllabus of valuation based on color" which is unknown to children who are "innocent of these expectations and respond to color in their own growing ways. If a child loves a teddy bear," she explains, "he may grow up feeling brown is a warm, comforting color."

With so many children's materials fabricated in the brightest primary colors, Halpern worries that "a child's toys, his working tools, can teach one monotonous lesson: everything is red, yellow and blue. Good teaching," she says, "brings the multicoloredness of life into the classroom. Young children, if allowed to, will play happily with sand, mud, water and items that adults would consider too worn or faded to be of any interest. This behavior leads many adults to believe children do not actually perceive color, that true color perception arises at a later age. In truth," she adds, "the mind of a very young child is not that easy to fathom. Much of the failure to respond to color as adults expect, is sheer inexperience with the social significance—the code as it were, of color."

Obviously, not all educators realize this when dealing with institutional settings.

"Schools frequently use bright colors to encourage 'bright' behavior," says Halpern. "Young children, on the other hand, do not perceive color as adults do and may remain oblivious to the stimulus. Yet color in the environment is important. Bland and insipid surfaces—what we think of as the institutional look—depress teacher performance and narrow the child's visual growth."

With so much at play when it comes to color and surroundings, Halpern favors a diverse approach.

"To enrich that process of discovery," she says, "good teachers incorporate a variety of textures, shapes, densities and tastes, as well as color, in the objects with which children play and learn."

HOME SAFETY IS NO ACCIDENT

Imagine a day when "Home Safe Home" is as accurate a motto as Home Sweet Home.

There would be no accidents where we live.

Hospital emergency rooms would no longer need to treat the tens of thousands of children they see annually for injuries related to nursery equipment alone.

And no one would die or suffer the consequences of residential fires, falls, drownings, or other mishaps that yearly claim the lives of kids or leave them with brutal aftereffects such as scars.

Working toward the goal of no home-related tragedies, especially for defenseless children, means more than installing childproof latches and safety gates all over the world. It calls for vigilance all over the house, starting in a child's bedroom.

A BURNING ISSUE

With fire a universal danger causing more children's home fatalities than anything else, kids who know how to act quickly if one starts, can literally save their own lives. Points to make to a child about this life-threatening situation include these:

1. If the door to a room is closed, feel the knob. If it's warm or hot, keep the door closed and line the bottom of it with clothes or towels to keep the smoke out. Escape through a window, if possible.

2. If the knob is cool, open the door slowly to check for smoke. If the exit path is not too smoky, leave the room but close the door behind you. Stay low and crawl below smoke to reduce inhaling toxic fumes. If clothes ignite, don't run; this fans the flames. Stop right away, cover your face with your hands, and drop to the floor, rolling back and forth to snuff flames. "Stop, drop, and roll" is what children are taught to remember.

3. If there's no smoke outside the door, exit quickly. Don't stop to get anything.

4. If you're trapped, call 911 if you can. Yell out the window, but close it if smoke comes in. Never hide in a closet or under a bed; both hinder fire fighters searching for you.

5. Under no circumstances should you re-enter a burning building.

To hinder fatality, install smoke detectors outside sleep areas on all levels. Involve kids in monthly testings using real smoke so they can recognize an alarm. Give them the semi-annual task of being sure batteries are replaced. Never remove them, even temporarily.

If you live in a multiple-story building, get a portable rope or chain escape ladder for each upper bedroom. Store it near a window, so it can be hooked to the sill and thrown out. Test the equipment regularly with your children so they aren't afraid, if necessary, to use it by themselves. If home is a high rise, warn kids about not using elevators in a fire.

Practice home fire drills twice a year with the entire family. But be sure to do some in the dark of night when deadly fires often occur. If it's difficult to find your way around during "lights out", get phosphorescent markers to place near all exits.

Because electricity poses a fire hazard, cover outlets with childproof devices. Look for something as unobtrusive as possible so it won't draw a curious child's attention.

Post emergency numbers by all phones. Fire, police, and ambulance should top the list. Also include doctors, hospitals, electric and water companies, neighbors and nearby realatives. Note parent work numbers, too. Teach younger kids how and when to call 911.

If you live in a remote area, let kids memorize your home's description and the closest cross street. In a crisis, these could be vital to those trying to reach your address.

HANDLE WITH CARE

Besides constant surveillance, childproofing a child's world starts with outfitting the nursery with items designed with care and caution. There are a couple of devices guaranteed to promote safety. They are:

Monitors: Like an intercom that allows you to listen to what's going on, an electronic room monitor provides added assurance that baby is OK when you're not in the room. Simply leave the monitor near the crib and keep the receiver with you to detect anything out of the ordinary. But turn off the transmitter when it's not in use, to protect your privacy from neighbors who can overhear what's being said if their CB radios, cordless telephones, or own monitors are on the same frequency.

Safety Gates: Once crawling begins, block doorways and stairways with gates anchored securely. Look for pressure-mounted or hinged attachments with straight top edges or rigid mesh screens, and choose a gate easy for adults to manipulate so it will be used consistently. If pressure bars expand, install them with the bar side away from baby.

Only newer accordion-style gates are certified by the Juvenile Product Manufactures Association; older models do not pass the current standards. Close any gate when you leave the room, and never leave baby unattended.

Once out of a crib and on his or her own two feet, a child requires other safety strategies. Security measures include:

Safe Curves: Think "round" when it comes to furnishings, from rounded edges on dressers to rounded tables and chairs. To round off corners that could be hazardous, use corner guards designed to provide extra cushioning and protection.

Sturdy Construction: All furniture should be tough enough to withstand an active child. Durable wood, rugged plastic, and sturdy metal are good options. Make sure screws are tight and unexposed not only at the time of purchase but upon periodic safety checks. Fasten heavy furniture, such as bookcases to the wall.

Removable guardrails provide extra safety for young children at sleeptime.

Regulation Details: Hand-me-downs may be one-of-a-kind treasures, but beware. The price for that charm may be fancy hardware that's dangerous in a child's hands, or it may be construction unstable from years of use. Store heirloom pieces for later use and pick quality new furnishings that meet current regulations.

Guardrails: Whether you are using bunk beds or an individual bed, guardrails on the upper sides deter falls. Be sure the space between the frame and the rail is not wide enough for a child to wriggle into.

Safety Hinges: Traditional toy chests should have spring-loaded supports that prevent the lid from slamming shut, and ventilation holes and an interior lock release in case a child gets trapped inside. For peace of mind, disarm locks altogether. It's a good idea to remove locking devices from wardrobes and closets, too.

A cord corral keeps an emergency from happening in a setting where children might be tempted to play with cords and ties that pose the risk of strangulation.

FOUR ON THE FLOOR

To determine what dangers lurk from your child's vantage point, get on your hands and knees to survey for these:

Climb Ups: Rearrange storage cubes and other furniture that might enable young climbers to investigate new heights. Make sure nothing climbable is under a window.

Cover Ups: If electrical outlets are within a child's reach, block them with safety devices such as plugs or outlet plates.

Trip Ups: To prevent tripping on toys, books, or other belongings, encourage neatness early on through good example. To make sure electrical cords don't cause tripping or other dangers, tack them under pieces of furniture, tape them to walls or wrap them securely around table legs. Window cords should be corralled, too, on specific hardware designed for that purpose.

Slip Ups: Keep floor coverings slip-resistant. Use nonskid pads on area rugs, and tack down carpet edges. Don't overdo the waxing on wood floors, or a serious slip may occur.

SHEDDING A LITTLE LIGHT

To a very young child, a floor lamp may look just like another piece of play equipment. Since it can tip over easily, rely instead on illumination from an overhead fixture such as a pull-down light with a retractable cord.

Provide a night light so you and your child can find your way through the room when it's dark. Keep a flashlight handy, too.

KNOCK, KNOCK

Regardless of size or location, doors pose threats to inquisitive kids. A few aids that prevent injury include:

✔ **STOPS:**
Designed to fit over most doors, stops adjust the extent to which an interior door closes so small hands can't get scrunched.

✔ **LOCKS:**
Safety locks enable doors and drawers to open a crack so kids can't get at the contents or hurt fingers trying.

✔ **COVERS AND SLEEVES:**
Door sleeves and knob covers deter children from locking themselves in a room.

OUT OF HARM'S WAY

Those product stickers that warn "Never Leave Child Unattended" are there for a reason. Remember, no protection in the world compares with a parent's watchful eye. Nor is there any better way to instill safety rules in a child than through the good example set by a parent who makes safety a family priority every day.

Cleaning solutions and other items that can be dangerous in a child's hands should be stored in locked cabinets. Plastic links too difficult for kids to manipulate keep them from what's behind these doors.

Before butying furniture check to be sure if the hardware is safe and easy for a child to manipulate.

On Your Mark?
Get Set for Emergency Preparedness

In a fire or other disaster, would your family panic?

Formulating emergency plans is part of safety preparedness. Teach kids what to do and where to go in a crisis, and chances are they'll act quickly and correctly if one occurs.

Since different regions of the world experience different calamities, from earthquakes to hurricanes to tornados, check with community resources such as the Red Cross to learn about local disaster plans.

Because fires are a universal danger and there's no time for planning when one occurs, the National Fire Prevention Association underscores the importance of sitting down as a family to make a step-by-step plan for escape in the event of an emergency. If home is in a high-rise building, show children the shortest route to a safe exit and warn them NOT to use elevators.

Wherever you live, fire preparation should include:

- Drawing a floor plan noting two ways (i.e., a door and a window) out of every room, especially bedrooms. Inspect each site to be sure kids comprehend emergency exits and procedures. If they'll need to break a window or remove a screen, show them how.

- Agreeing on a meeting place outside where all gather to wait for the fire department. This designated spot allows for counting heads and informing the fire fighters if anyone is trapped inside the burning building. Stress that under no circumstance should you ever go back into a building on fire.

- Practicing your escape plan at least twice a year by having home drills. Everyone, including children, should participate and someone should be appointed as a monitor. Impress upon children that this is not a race or a game, although it's important for all to get out quickly as well as carefully.

To engage kids more in the process of preparing for an emergency, let them plan when home fire drills will occur. Even if they learn disaster preparedness in school, it's important to tailor their knowledge to fit your living situation.

An Open and Shut Case

Whether open or closed, windows pose several potential perils in children's rooms in an emergency. Consider the following:

The Glass: Windows within 18 inches of the floor should be glazed with tempered safety glass. If it breaks, it will be in rounded pieces less dangerous than the shards created when nontempered glass breaks. To keep kids from slamming into sliding glass doors, stick on colored decals at child eye level.

The Hardware: Since window screens offer little resistance as a barrier to curious children, keep kids safely inside with locks that allow the window to open only a few inches. As extra security on double-hung windows, choose a keyed sash lock, but hang the key on a screw high enough to be out of child reach yet easy enough for a family member or sitter to find in an emergency. Keyed locks also work on sliding windows and doors; so do "Charley bars" that wedge a slider shut.

The Covering: A quick tug on a dangling curtain cord can trigger a serious accident if the fabric falls down over a child. Prevent this either by wrapping cords around a tie-down fixture secured near the top of the window or by putting them in cord corrals. Safer window coverings might be shades or blinds.

CHAPTER 2

UP, DOWN, ALL AROUND

Tiny Teddi, confined to her crib, awakens and sees a rainbow of light dancing on high. Its soft rays are deflected to the ceiling from a prism hanging high inside the 9-month-old's far corner window.

Peppy Linda gets the urge to hop and runs straight to her room. In time-honored fashion, the 4-year-old skips joyfully from one spot to another, landing each time on a different colored carpet square.

Shy yet spirited Courtney loves chasing butterflies, so the 8-year-old reaches up from her bed to touch a row of them. Pink, yellow, lavender, and green squishy creatures, they're really sponge cutouts shaped like the real thing and hung as a border that rims the walls.

Adventurous Kevin, astronaut-in-waiting, yearns for exploration beyond books and movies. Between daydreams of future missions, the 12-year-old stares at model spacecraft suspended by invisible filiment from the far reaches of his personal "sky."

Up.
Down.
All Around.

As Teddi, Linda, Courtney, and Kevin already know, there's no limit, where kids are concerned, to an inner sanctum's area of decorative delights. The trick to detailing any of them is tuning in to what your child likes without overdoing it.

While stores, magazines, catalogs, and children's public spaces are always good starting points for ideas, don't neglect what's already under your roof. That includes your child's imagination—and yours, too, for that matter.

Look through the art box for suspendible ideas.

Examine treasured greeting or collectible cards for wall border opportunities.

◀ *A ladder that's custom made with easy-to-grasp cutout openings lends an assist to a boy intent on reaching a hideaway loft situated above the closet.*

Study trinkets with a new perspective. Strung on clear fishing line to hang in a window, they can offer a daydreamer many hours of enjoyment.

With paint or with other products, if the statement is fairly simple on walls, doors, ceilings, and floors, you enable a young person's private domain to change as easily as the child's own whims of fancy.

In time, all youthful scenes should undergo some metamorphosis.

Teddi's prism may come down.

Linda's rug squares may be covered.

Courtney's butterflies may take flight.

And Kevin's spacecraft may land in another universe.

Enjoy a youthful look while it lingers. Then help a growing child raise the curtain on a new stage.

Childhood settings, like museum displays, deserve periodic change to keep the viewers continually stimulated. Who knows? The replacements may be just as magical and just as meaningful as what preceded them.

WHAT'S UP—
PAINT OR PAPER?

Like the rest of the house, what's up in your child's room can be as simple as plain paint or as elaborate as detailed wall covering.

But unlike other areas in your home, the decision about what covers the walls in a kid's quarters hinges on adolescent whims. After all, growing up means growing into new looks and out of old ones. That's why it's wiser to choose a wall treatment that changes face readily.

THE POWER OF PAINT

Without question, paint is not only the easiest wall finish to apply but also the easiest to redo when it's time to update the scenery. It's the least expensive means of decorating a surface, too, if you opt for a single color overall. The more colors and techniques you use, the more it costs. On the other hand, paint applied creatively is more distinctive than a solid-covered surface.

When it comes to color, paint can change the character of a room quicker than anything else. But let your child pick the palette that predominates, or at least surfaces, to some degree since he or she will be living with what's chosen. After all, it's important that these surroundings be personally pleasing.

Involve your child in color selection by showing him or her all six colors of the rainbow: red, yellow, orange, green, blue, and violet. Once the child spontaneously chooses a preferred color, let them define its exact hue. To do this, supply paint chips that range from light to dark. If the choice is narrowed to two or three, buy the smallest quantity of paint available so sample patches of color can be applied next to each other on the surface to be covered. This exercise takes into consideration that a color viewed on a paint chip will change dramatically when applied to a large area. If the final selection is a bold choice, balance the intensity with a companion color such as white or beige.

When two or more children share a room, paint is a terrific way to define territory. One vivid way to do this is by designating a wall for each roommate that he or she can enliven in whatever part of the spectrum the child likes. The end result, to your adult eye, may resemble a kaleidescope of color, but if a little fabric that picks up every shade is added to the room, you'll be surprised at how it pulls the look together. Those added elements could include anything from colorful throw pillows to original art a child produces.

In a setting shared by two bunkmates, you might even try another interesting decorative approach. Visually divide the room in half horizontally by allowing each one's favored color to surface in either the upper or lower section, depending on where his or her sleep area is located. Come naptime, sleeptime or other times when relaxing in bed, the color closest to each one's space seems to predominate that child's private corner.

A SIGNATURE LOOK

More playful looks are possible with paint when special techniques enter the picture. A few that fit into a child's world include spattering, sponging, stencilling and foam stamping, all of which give pizzazz to plain walls, or even furniture, as the next chapter will explore. Entire books have been written on special finishes; these should be consulted along with how-to videos if a unique look intrigues you. As for some basics:

What better way to offset a sponged wall treatment than with sponges! These butterfly-shaped designs serve as decoration and dado, visually lowering the ceiling to child height.

- Sponging involves dabbing paint on a surface with a sea sponge. The mottled effect is magical if several colors, or several shades of the same color, are randomly applied in imaginative fashion. An enjoyable do-it-yourself weekend project that can involve parent and child or the whole family, sponging has a free-form finished look as appealing as fingerpainting.

- Spattering is just as splashy. All it takes is a flick of the wrist with a brush wet with paint. What lands on the wall in front of it creates a flecked pattern as fanciful as confetti.

- Foam stamping, which also adds whimsical flair, is as easy as using rubber stamps and ink pads. For a good assortment of high-density foam designs with kid appeal, visit toy and bath stores that sell sponge tub toys, lightweight blocks, or precut letters and shapes.

- Stenciling, a centuries-old craft, is a look that calls for repetitive shapes and patterns. An inexpensive way to detail walls, ceilings, and other architectural elements, it has a childlike quality if the stencils used are simple designs such as flowers or animals. Paint them on long strips of poster board, however, if you want a wall border that changes easily.

As with any special finish, consult a paint store for product information and application guidelines. Add an undercoat or two as well as a clear protective overcoat if the store recommends it. No matter what course of action is taken, however, before any artistry is applied to the walls, remove dirt and grease that have built up.

MURAL, MURAL ON THE WALL

Artistic murals give another decorative one-of-a-kind look that adds atmosphere, and often depth, to a setting. If this appeals to your child, however, keep it simple with generic designs such as stars, clouds, and rainbows that invite rather than stifle imagination.

An overall scene, like the same meal served over and over, can quickly lose its attraction and begin to bother the very one it was meant to amuse. That's why a little bit of fantasy in a child's bedroom goes a long way. A mural confined to part of a wall or even a singular piece of furniture is a big statement all by itself.

The ceiling is a good candidate for this decorative treatment. Paint it azure blue, let it dry and then add some large splotches of white paint. You'll wind up with a summer sky and clouds that beckon daydreamers even when it's dreary outside. Or if the ceiling peaks, consider a fingerpaint look that resembles thatching—a technique designer Carolyn Carnell, *Allied ASID*, used effectively in a third-story setting to lend a cottage feeling to it. For other interesting, uncomplicated ceiling ideas, look in the section titled "High Hopes for High Places" later in this chapter.

One further note about scenic designs. When a mural decorates a child's bathroom, playroom, or other area occupied for shorter periods than a bedroom, it's less likely to fatigue the viewer day in and day out. Even so, try to keep the theme fairly simple so it doesn't overwhelm the viewer or "time lock" the surroundings.

An old, narrow two-tier medicine cabinet turns into a Victorian facade once a false roof is added along with skillful artistry. A wall mural completes the scene in this child's bath.

GETTING THE HANG OF IT

What do circus stripes, storybook scenes, teddy bears, and Mickey Mouse have in common? They're part of an endless parade of youthful patterns that fill wallcovering books by the thousands.

With all the themes that entice kids today, it's not difficult to march through these pages and find a design to match any interest. But before you turn Junior's or Missy's room into a mini Big Top or Magic Kingdom, think twice. As delightful as a wallpaper pattern can be, it can also be limiting in a child's bedroom setting where tastes change more frequently than the wind. When that happens, the indoor scenery may be seen as a vestige

Like background music that doesn't interfere with other activity, subtle wallcovering creates a framework that can stay while other room elements change.

of the past that constantly reminds the viewer of a childhood phase now outgrown.

Without doubt, however, there are advantages to a wallcovering—particularly if it's designed to be washable or scrubbable. Fingerprints and other childish smudges on these coverings can be wiped away. If you use the same cleaning method on a wall covered with latex paint, however, expect a noticeable change in finish.

Whereas vinyl is "scrubbable," many other wallcoverings are not and can start to deteriorate when you attempt to remove stains from them with water or chemicals. To be on the safe side, ask a wallcovering dealer to explain the properties of the paper you pick or to point out only the books that feature scrubbable or washable patterns.

With so many variables to hanging paper, you want to be well advised and well prepared before you undertake this venture. Inexperience can cause irreparable mistakes that botch the job and burst the budget.

Whether using a professional paperhanger or not, get expert advice on how many rolls your project will take. If that means heading for the nearest wallcovering store that offers experienced help, arm yourself first with the square footage of all the walls, being sure to add or subtract the square footage of any doors or windows. In the event that you underestimate your needs, be sure to write down the "run number" on the back of the rolls already purchased so that you can reorder from the same dye lot.

If you decide on wallpaper after measuring the pros and cons, keep this in mind. Patterns, including stripes, dots, or subtle geometrics on a neutral ground, create an overall background. As long as they are not overwhelming designs, they can stay for a longer period while other elements change.

Like wandering through a supermarket and studying all the merchandise, however, the task of looking through wallcovering books is too tedious for a very young person to tackle. It makes more sense for an adult to narrow the field to three or four patterns in a child's favorite colors and designs. Even given these few choices from which to pick, a young person still gets the message that his or her ideas are being incorporated in a personal environment.

DETAILS THAT PACK A PUNCH

As you explore wallcovering possibilities, check out borders. A fraction of the width of a whole roll, borders generally range from 2 to 27 inches wide, with 6 to 8-inch widths the norm.

Although giving only a hint of design as compared to a whole roll, borders still pack decorative punch, especially when they complement the room's walls, fabric, flooring, or other decorative features. Unlike large rolls, which may be unwieldy for neophytes to put up, small prepasted borders are easy to get the hang of without professional help.

Far less expensive than their full-size cousins, borders play a definite role in a child's domain when they encircle a room midway and visually bring the ceiling down to a child's proportions. Place the trim one foot above your son's or daughter's current height, unless this placement would interrupt light switches or fight with the room's architecture. If that's the case, raise or lower the ornamental strip a few inches.

To give the border added impact, consider painting the wall area below it in one of the colors that are featured in it.

As a child stretches toward adulthood, remove the old border and hang its replacement higher. If you choose a strippable pattern to begin with, taking it down is simply a matter of loosening a corner and pulling upward. Within minutes, the entire task can be finished. When in doubt, get an opinion and an estimate from a wallpaper hanger.

Whether a large roll of wallpaper or a small border roll, those labeled "prepasted" are ideal choices. All it takes to activate the paste is placing each strip in water. Detailed instructions are usually packaged with each roll. If not, refer to the product book where you found the pattern.

A few other wallcovering tidbits worth noting:

- Keep the remnants of a wallcovering project. Besides offering insurance against the day when you might need to replace a torn or battered wall section, they're perfect finishing touches for a child's treasure box, pencil holder, scrapbook, lampshade, and so forth.

- Give yourself a dose of reassurance about what the pattern will look like in your home by purchasing page, strip, or roll samples, which are usually nominally priced. Tack them up and live with them for awhile before you and your child make up your minds. By the way, not every manufacturer offers the option of samples. It's wise to take advantage of the service from those who do offer it.

- Resist the temptation to "childproof" wallcovering in a child's room by hanging it only way beyond his or her reach. Like any other decoration placed on high, wallpaper beyond a child's vantage point will also be beyond his or her realm of enjoyment.

In a room with delicate patterns, even a small element such as a lamp in a playful design becomes a focal point. The border paper it matches can also be used to create other decor.

- Resist, too, the urge to be clever by restricting wallpaper to a single wall, whether an overall treatment or just a border. While this cuts the cost of covering every wall, it also cuts the look of a room. Like woodwork, what decorates the walls looks better if it continuously follows the flow of architectural features. If it abruptly stops short, it jars the eye and is ineffective. The exception to this is a room with a defined recess or alcove. In that situation, you may want the architectural element to be the room's focal point. Isolating wallpaper to such an area would not only lead the eye there, but also make an effective statement.

As you'll soon read on the upcoming pages, heading for the border in decorating circles means more than resorting to wallpaper trim. It has many decorative translations including some with global implications.

Wallpaper:
Some Pluses and Minuses

Besides the ability to create instant decor in a child's room, wallcovering also has the following advantages:

- It's available in extensive patterns.

- It's available in extensive textures, both real and look-alike, that range from burlap and grass cloth to linen and vinyl.

- It hides disfigured walls.

- It can minimize architectural flaws by camouflaging them or giving the illusion of doing so.

- It has a longer life and a cleaner life span than latex paint if the material from which it's made is durable.

With regard to the cleanability aspect, scrubbable products are designed to hold up against common soil marks that mild soap and water remove. For the best results, of course, take action promptly.

Unquestionably, wallcoverings have disadvantages in a child's room, too, besides time-locking a setting, as previously discussed. Let me count the "nays":

- The expense is substantial if the room is large and requires many rolls, if the pattern is pricey, or if the design repeats every so many inches and therefore calls for extra rolls in order to match them up properly.

- The application is time consuming and adds cost to the purchase price if lack of homeowner skill demands the services of a professional paper hanger. The project is even more labor intensive if preparation means stripping existing paper, cleaning the surface of old residue, and "sizing" the walls with special paste.

- The process can be complicated if the wall is already covered with non-strippable paper that comes off only with special chemical strippers, steaming devices, and/or concerted elbow grease.

Brushing Up on Paint

For a child's room, the ideal paint treatment is a combination of eggshell and glossy finishes.

Eggshell, a water- or oil-based paint that literally gives a slight sheen, works well on most surfaces, however, a water-based "latex" paint dries more quickly.

Glossy paint, on the other hand, is preferable on doors, window frames, and shelves, which get more hand use and therefore require a tougher treatment with protective qualities. Dirty fingerprints and stains can be wiped clean from higher-sheen surfaces, whereas they either cannot be removed easily from a flat finish, or if they can, may result in a noticeable change in finish.

For years, the only glossy paint made was oil-based. Today there's also water-based paint that gives a high-gloss finish. There are advantages and disadvantages to both.

Because oil-based paint takes longer to dry, a hands-off policy must be in effect until it's completely dry. Depending on climate conditions and paint brand, the process could take a couple days, which translates to keeping the painted area off-limits to children. Strong fumes are another disadvantage of oil-based paint although today's oil-based house paints don't smell as much as they once did because of reformulation. The odor of oil is noticeable, however, and takes longer to dissipate than that of faster-drying latex paint. To eliminate odors, it's important to provide good ventillation when oil-based paint is being applied.

Although more durable than water-based paints, oil-based paints require solvents such as mineral spirits (paint thinner or turpentine) for cleanup. For that reason, cleanup takes longer with oil-based products than with water-based paints.

On the plus side, however, oil paint has durability and smoothness going for it. If applied properly, the finish is level and doesn't show brush strokes. Because of their shine, high-gloss finishes are usually restricted to woodwork and not applied to walls.

As compared with oil-based paints, some high-gloss latex finishes have a tendency to be more "ropey" than others. It all depends on the quality level of the paint chosen. In other words, the better the quality of high-gloss latex finishes, the more forgiving it is of the stroke marks that a brush makes. An advantage to using water-based high-gloss paint is its lack of strong odor.

Latex paint comes in matte (flat); eggshell (slight sheen); pearl (semisatin) or semigloss (satin) finishes. It is extremely easy to clean up. If spotting occurs, it wipes up with a damp cloth. Soap and water are all that's required to remove latex paint from brushes.

Practically odorless, latex paint presents minimal fire hazard. It is also less expensive than oil-based products.

To stand up to the beating kids dish out, latex paint has been formulated differently in recent years by some manufacturers. They have developed a satin enamel product that produces the soft luster, or low sheen, of a flat paint, but performs like a gloss paint in washability. Look for those that not only claim superior stain resistance and scrubbability but back their claims with a warranty. Most companies also market eggshell enamel, satin enamel, semi-gloss enamel, and gloss enamel, all of which withstand sticky fingers.

Before deciding what works best in your home, ask paint store personnel about the texture and condition of the walls you're painting and whether they'll require a primer (base) or base coat first. Several factors may influence the kind of paint you ultimately choose. But do your homework before you head to the store. Know the surface you want to paint as well as its dimensions. Make note, too, of the condition, color, and type of its current finish so that someone knowledgeable can give you accurate information about changing it.

In response to environmental concerns over volatile organic compound (VOC) emissions from paint, paint companies in recent years have been reducing the amount of product thinner (i.e., solvent) that evaporates into the air. Although thinners are found primarily in oil-based paints, they occur in very miniscule amounts in water-based paint products. When thinner is removed, it must be replaced with a non-volatile oil or a resin. This reformulation is environmentally safer because it has lower VOC. Paint with low or no VOC ratings is generally marked on the top or on the label.

One further bit of wisdom to absorb before you make a selection: Flat paint absorbs light, creating the illusion of a larger room. Glossy paint reflects light and therefore tends to visually close in a room by making the walls appear closer together than they actually are.

BORDER PATROL TO THE RESCUE

What towers above a young child like a giant canopy? Go inside most rooms and look up. What you see on high is the answer.

While the standard 8-foot ceiling height is hardly earth-shattering information to adults, it's front page news to kids who may feel out of proportion to their surroundings. Considering this scale, it's no wonder kids seem to gravitate toward cubbyholes.

By using a little decorating magic, you can counteract that diminished feeling in your child's quarters so that the room height appears closer to his or her eye level than it really is.

An artistic A-B-C stencil border above a sponge-painted wall provides decorative and educational detail.

ABRACADABRA!

Just as trompe l'oeil art literally "tricks the eye" into believing a painting has spatial qualities, a decorative border encircling the room creates the illusion of a false ceiling.

Detailing that raises or lowers the visual height of a room is called a "dado." It can be created with paint, wallpaper, or other means. But more important in a child's room than the medium used to make it, is its location. If a dado is high on a wall, it's a visual cue to a child that this is a more adult space. Lower the border and the message changes.

One way to visually lower the ceiling and add punch is to detail the midsection of each wall by encircling the entire room with two or three horizontal stripes in varied colors. As discussed earlier in this chapter, pick a point on the wall a few inches above your child's head and begin the decorative dado there.

Don't limit creative expression to stripes alone. Animals, planets, flowers, and nursery rhymes are a few other ideas. But keep it simple since children's tastes are everchanging.

WHAT GOES AROUND COMES AROUND

For more intricate border designs, consider stenciling, a centuries-old craft that is enjoying a revival because of its decorative look and low cost. Sold individually or in kits, stencils are made from very thin sheets of plastic or Mylar which have been perforated or cut with a design or lettering. When paint is applied to them, an impression of the pattern forms on the surface beneath.

As simple or ornate as the stencil upon which it relies for pattern, stenciling calls for a special flat-topped brush to be dabbed onto the area to be detailed. Because stencils can be used over and over, it's possible to repeat a pattern for minimal expense. But exercise restraint in doing so. An overdone theme tends to become wearisome and unstimulating if it's the only decoration you view day in and day out.

Many stencil patterns are appropriate for a child's room. They range from educational designs such as the alphabet, to whimsical motifs such as teddy bears, to practical imprints such as a name or initials.

Although books provide do-it-yourself stencil directions, kits with precut, reusable patterns are an easier option. Some companies manufacture see-through designs with register marks that make pattern alignment a simple task.

STICK 'EM UP

For parents who like a wallpaper look but not the effort it entails, consider decorating kits with precut stick-'em-up characters.

Designed to transform wall space into a playful canvas, these kit designs combine sticker art with paper cutouts. Some are created by children's book illustrators and allow your child to create his or her own storybook scenes as diverse as the zoo, the prairie, and the sea. All come alive through a child's imaginative placement of characters.

What makes some designs particularly appealing is their adhesive backing, which allows for repositioning over and over. Because there's no right or wrong way to use this decorative dado, it fosters imagination and just plain fun.

FOREIGN BORDERS

Besides a little money, your imagination is the only passport you need to explore different borders. Consider the following three-dimensional objects as border material.

- **Kitchen and Bath Tiles:** Whether small mosaics or 4-inch squares, ceramic tiles make snappy wall borders when backed with double-sided tape so they adhere to the wall. First, use paper to map out an original pattern, which might include turning the tiles at an angle to form diamond shapes.

- **Decorative Bath Sponges:** Colorful sponges shaped like butterflies, barnyard animals, ducks, or dinosaurs create magic when they migrate across a child's wall. Masking tape or other adhesive secures them in place. To save money, use one or more shapes and dip them into different colors of paint to create a one-dimensional border. Look for them in craft stores and bath shops.

- **Miniature Flags:** Navigate the globe by encircling the room with self-sticking paper flags of many nations. Check your local flag store for 2 or 3-inch paper miniatures.

- **Calendar and Magazine Pages:** Pictures and photos of dolls, cars, and other collectibles fill calendars and specialty magazines. Full page favorites hung side by side form a one-of-a-kind dado.

- **Pennants:** Young sports fans can boast about their allegiances. Young travelers can keep track of where they've been. Pennants satisfy both interests and can colorfully trim a room.

- **Geometric Shapes:** A conglomeration of circles, squares and pyramids made of wood, cardboard, or fabric lend an interesting and educational dimension to a child's room.

IF THE WALLS COULD TALK

As quickly as children outgrow clothes, they shed interests. Encourage discoveries by being receptive once in a while to minor room makeovers that reflect new tastes.

Even the best border patrol experiences a changing of the guard periodically!

BRIDGING THE GENERATIONS WITH THE WRITE STUFF

Like a reassuring hug, discovering a written message from Mom or Dad makes you feel good inside.

When that message is posted in your room and changes regularly, it adds a comforting touch to the surroundings.

Whether by written or spoken word, it's important to keep the lines of communication open between you and your child.

Besides conversation, one way to encourage lifelong parent/child communicaiton is with a private message center. While a family bulletin board in the kitchen can be a place for schedules and reminders, other centers should be set up for each child, preferably on his or her own turf.

Maybe this can be a place for parent and child to share loving words that otherwise might be difficult to say. Or maybe it can be a neutral ground for siblings to communicate with each other. It might even be someplace for secret messages to surface from the Tooth Fairy or from an imaginary friend who visits only when your child is away or fast asleep.

A small chalkboard and a standard bulletin board turn this wall space in a boy's room into a center for communication.

COMMUNICATION CENTRAL

As reading and writing skills are being learned, create the message center in your child's personal quarters.

Finding a place for Communication Central is an easy matter. Choose the back of a door or the area under a window or some other free space on one wall where a writing surface will fit.

If two children share a room, set up two message boards, possibly by their respective beds.

Check the hallway outside your son's or daughter's room to see if the bedroom door can handle a clipboard or a mock "mailbox" made from a decorated shoe box or other small container. An alternative location that might work is a coat closet, the laundry room, or a mudroom.

Whatever place becomes the message spot, situate the center at your child's height or a hand's length above his or her head.

GETTING THE MESSAGE

Once you determine the best location, measure the area's dimensions. Many sizes and shapes of message boards are available, so it's wise to know limitations before going to the stationers.

Obviously, you don't need anything more elaborate than a pad of paper and a pencil to

Fuzzy fabric stretched to cover a foam core board serves as the ideal display area for flannel items. Even a wool blanket works.

See-through plexiglass protects the craft room wall it covers from project smudges, and provides a clever message area for parent and child.

exchange written words. But there are many interesting, inexpensive alternatives designed to captivate someone young. For example:

Marker Board: If your child is allergic to dust or chalk, this kind of board is ideal since it's made of plastic, melamine, or porcelain on steel. Because it requires erasable markers, it is often called a "dry erase" board. However, if used on other surfaces, these markers are permanent. Therefore, you may want to restrict their use to older children.

Bulletin Bar: A new twist on the old bulletin board standby, this space-saving message strip measures only $1\frac{1}{2}$ by $11\frac{1}{2}$ inches. Like its first cousin, it has a cork surface to which messages, pictures, and other pin-ups can be attached.

Flat or Flannel Board: Encourage creative expression and language skills with a board constructed from soft-nap surfaces to which cutout felt figures and shapes cling.

Magnetic Board: Unlock the secrets of magnetism with a board and magnetized letters of the alphabet.

Plexiglass Sheet: Create a see-through marker or art surface with a piece of clear plexiglass cut to fit a wall area or the back of a door. Marking pens and peel-off letters turn this into a message center.

Chalkboard: School comes home when you provide a miniature chalkboard with a tray. To break away from class tradition, get multicolored dustless chalk. Remember an eraser, too.

Tabletop Easel: When your young Picasso isn't painting away, leave messages for him or her on the art easel. Choose a fold-up version if permanent setup is a problem.

For versatility, get a combination board or easel with two different surfaces. Or team a few individual boards together on the same wall. By creating a message center with multiple features, you add interest to the area and expand the ways in which feelings and ideas can be expressed. Even when there are space limitations, you can carve out a message spot by integrating it within another activity station. A small notepad or marker board hung on a wall grooming center, for instance, provides an adequate way for written communication to occur.

OTHER HANG-UPS

Since a communication hub is a perfect place to remind the young about school dates and other appointments, make room for a clock and a calendar. If a friend is coming for a weekend stay or if a special outing is on the agenda, help your child count the days at the message center.

With regard to remembering dates, consider a write-on/ wipe-off calendar board or a day-by-day calendar with changing date cards. Since children love tiny objects, you can even hang a pocket calendar booklet like the kind many stationery stores provide free of charge.

If your child's message board doesn't feature a tray for markers, put up a catchall for writing utensils. Shoe-bag pouches are good for this. If space is at a premium, make do with a marker attached to a colorful piece of yarn hung along one side of the board.

SAY WHAT?

"Good morning!" "Welcome home!" "Good luck on your test!"

There are many things you can write to uplift a child's spirits especially if he or she is coming home to an empty house while you're at work. But go beyond the basics. Be creative in some of the following ways.

Informational Tool: Spell out details about fixing a special snack, doing a home project, or other activities.

By day, this chalkboard keeps the kids who use it occupied with pleasureable activity. By night, it flips over to show its other face—a bed to accommodate overnight guests.

As this combination grooming/communication center proves, you don't need much room to provide a place where parent and child can keep in touch.

Instructional Aid: Sharpen English and foreign language skills through word games that help increase vocabulary. Try simple crossword puzzles or anagrams designed for kids.

Family Interaction: Encourage brothers and sisters to communicate feelings to each other through the written word. When one of their teams wins a game, for instance, suggest that a message of congratulations be left. If one does a good deed for another, promote the idea that "thank you" take the form of a personal communication jotted down.

Decorative Touch: Commemorate year-long observances with holiday doo-dads draped on and around a message board. Pin up a flag on the Fourth of July. Hang a colorful banner on a birthday. Or jot notes with variegated pens denoting seasonal colors.

A WAY WITH WORDS? PASS IT ON

Just like an occasional note found in a lunch box, a written message at home from Mom, Dad, or another member of the family is an easy, affordable way to nourish self-esteem while supplying a comforting touch.

If exchanging thoughts and feelings becomes as everyday an activity as eating and sleeping, the habit could last all your lives. Who knows? It may even pass to the following generations.

HIGH HOPES FOR HIGH PLACES

As the first place your child views upon waking up and the last place seen before nodding off to sleep, the ceiling deserves more than the ho-hum treatment it usually rates.

Instead of thinking of it as a static site to which a single fixture is relegated, consider the ceiling in your child's room a blank canvas that can change as often as youthful interests do.

Whether it's an uncharted universe of twinkling stars or a field of fabric streamers, ceiling decoration can fuel a fertile imagination for hours.

If you lack inspiration for overhead decorating ideas, check day-care-centers, classrooms, and the offices of children's dentists. Chances are you'll find all kinds of suspended decor, from art projects and posters to mobiles and streamers. What enlivens the ceilings in children's public settings often will fit right in at home, too.

LOFTY ILLUSIONS

One easy solution is to paint the ceiling a different color than the walls. As simple as this sounds, it adds instant zip. Let your child choose what shade of the rainbow will cover his or her kingdom, but lend assistance in determining color intensity.

If the ceiling is high and needs to be lowered visually, opt for a dark color. But if the ceiling would look better raised, go with a light color. Keep in mind that a glossy paint finish will cause glare; a matte finish won't.

Does your child long to sleep in the Great Outdoors? Turn that dream into reality by dabbing white paint "clouds" on a solid blue ceiling, using a coarse sponge from a bath or art shop. Or turn part of the ceiling into the night sky by using glow-in-the-dark paint for the stars and moon and deep blue flat paint for the heavens above.

Turn out the lights, and this ceiling seems to twinkle— thanks to glow-in-the-dark paint.

Painted murals also can enhance overhead settings. If you're artistic and your child likes the circus, for instance, create an illusion of the Big Top with a striped ceiling pattern angled so it meets in the center. Or if a merry-go-round captures your child's fancy, paint a round disk-shaped medallion at the ceiling's midway point to give a carousel effect. With any mural, however, keep it simple so nothing major is involved when it's time for a change of scenery.

UP, UP, AND AWAY

For an interesting effect that helps absorb sound, hang several banners across the ceiling. Then, whenever your child lifts his or her eyes, the child's spirits will also be lifted.

Since banners literally come alive when touched by the wind, they provide added enchantment to a child gazing upward when a breeze comes through, a fan is in motion, or a heat vent is circulating air.

If you like to sew, create your own banners from fabric cut in different geometric shapes. Or forget sewing and look for pillowcases, since they are just the right size and shape for ceiling banners hung lengthwise. For a flowing look, lightweight material such as satin is probably best. To add interest to solid fabric, glue or sew on circles to represent the sun, moon, and other planets. Or applique other designs that appeal to your child. Keep appliques in mind when hunting through the remnant box at home or in a fabric store.

Cloth is also perfect for creating ceiling canopies. A large fabric square, suspended from the ceiling with nylon thread at each corner, may appear like a flying carpet to a young person looking at it from the bed below. Add some fringe, and it becomes a frilly overhang that may evoke an altogether different feeling. For a kid intent on being tented, these do-it-yourself fabric hangings are low-cost alternatives to a canopy bed.

Fortunately for those who don't sew, there are many ready-made banners. Some companies feature sets that build on a theme such as nature. Others include designs appliqued on both sides for convertibility. Often made from tough, translucent nylon taffeta, banners are usually sold in varied lengths, the longest ususally measuring 24 to 28 inches. Although meant for vaulted or other high ceilings, the longer banners sometimes can be adapted to hang from lower ceilings by being draped roller coaster fashion in a loop-the-loop effect.

Kites are another fanciful way to go in a kid's room. Whether a Chinese paper dragon with a long tail or a colorful cellophane box kite, what your child chooses to flutter across the ceiling will delight any viewer when a breeze passes through the room. Be cautious, however, if a kite shares space with a ceiling fixture. Make sure the bulb doesn't come in close contact with flammable material such as paper, and that the kite material doesn't interfere with the blades on a ceiling fan.

Windsocks, mobiles, and model aircraft can dress up ceilings, too. So can certain inflatable toys and wall hangings. If your son or daughter has a favorite plaything he or she would like suspended, make it airborne with clear monofilament fishing line that withstands weight.

CELESTIAL HANG-UPS

Wishing upon a star takes on special meaning when the galaxy your child gazes upon exists in his or her bedroom. That happens when glow-in-the-dark stars are positioned on high. Once the room is darkened, the ceiling turns into the night sky.

Young astronomers can create these phosphorescent constellations with kits that vary from plastic stars to cardboard planets the size of dinner plates. Designed purely for decoration, these heavenly look-alikes are backed with a self-adhesive that allows for easy rearrangement without ceiling damage.

In a room where two kids share a bunk, reserve a few stars for the underside of the top bed so the bottom sleeper can stargaze from a closer vantage point.

Besides being whimsical, bedroom solar systems are educational. As interest in outer space grows, allow more serious study to be pursued by attaching a map of the universe or a lunar calendar to the ceiling.

Other out-of-this-world ceiling items include:

- **Solar Mobile:** Make your own from paper or look for ready-made versions with planets scaled to teach their relative size and realtionship to Earth.

- **Photo Posters of the Planets:** Thanks to NASA, photos of space missions have been blown up as posters for sale through catalogs and retail stores.

- **Celestial Beach Balls:** Available at toy stores and other outlets, these plastic inflatables depict the universe.

LOOKING UP

Whether it is a skylight, a ceiling fan, a wallpaper pattern, or a field of neutralness, what a child looks up to every day and night either fuels or stifles imagination. Create something interesting to see up above, and provide not only added dimension to a room but inspiration for the one living there to reach new heights.

Swirls of variegated paint on a dark background transform an ordinary ceiling into a lofty look. The design is also reflected in the valance, a corrugated cardboard creation.

DON'T OVERLOOK
WHAT'S UNDERFOOT

Whether crawling on all fours, clowning around on both feet, or curling up in a corner, children claim floor space as special territory.

Playing hopscotch means going to your room, when the carpet is inset with different colored squares that invite activity.

Maybe it's because a child's first area of exploration is the floor. Or maybe it stems from the many play opportunities this space provides. After all, a floor accommodates all kinds of childhood activities from reading a book and cuddling a kitten to stretching out with a board game.

CHOOSING WHAT'S UNDERFOOT

Choosing the surface underfoot in a child's room depends on the child's age and specific interests. A budding ballerina, for instance, won't relish practicing on plush wall-to-wall carpeting, but an active tumbler will.

One of the best floor treatments for toddlers and preschoolers is a mix of vinyl and fiber. Simply divide bedroom or playroom territory into separate sections. Near sleep or rest space, create a soft area with throw rugs or carpeting. In the remaining section use vinyl, a surface reminiscent of the now-obsolete linoleum. On easy-to-clean vinyl, a child can pursue messy play such as fingerpainting, saving the textured space for other activities.

If you choose to carpet the entire floor, use common sense when it's time for activities that could create a mess. Cover a section of carpet with a painter's canvas, a thick plastic drop cloth, or a sheet of vinyl. A polyurethane mat, like the kind used beneath office chairs with casters, is another means of protecting a floor covering.

KEEPING IT SMOOTH

Durability, easy maintenance, and freedom for activity are the major advantages to vinyl flooring. Before deciding upon it, however, take note:

- Vinyl is cool to the touch and therefore may not be as comfortable as other surfaces for a child to play on.

- Composition vinyl is cheaper than solid vinyl but less resilient and less sound absorbent.

- Vinyl with a bit of texture will provide a bit more slip resistance, but it also may be more difficult to maintain because uneven surfaces attract dirt more readily.

- Vinyl tiles, available only in solid and composition format, may be cheaper than sheet vinyl and easier to install but not as practical, since dirt and liquids are easily trapped between individual tiles. Sheet vinyl is also softer than vinyl tile because of its special backing.

For cleanliness, a sleek vinyl surface may seem more sensible than carpeting. Like any floor covering, however, it does require upkeep—especially since scratching dulls the floor and traps dirt.

In weighing the choice of vinyl versus other options, consider the life span of each as well as the ease and cost of replacement, since you may not want the same flooring forever. Before shopping, also realize that installing sheet vinyl may cost as much as carpeting.

A SOFT TOUCH

To a child, a soft and warm floor covering gives as much cuddly reassurance as a comfy bed or a fluffy blanket.

But don't equate a need for softness with a need for plushness. Carpeting that's very thick snares dust and small objects and limits play. Building blocks, for instance, can't stand up on thick carpet nor can pull-toys glide easily over it.

A good choice for kids' rooms is either dense, low-cut pile or carpet having all tufts in a loop form of identical height. Called level loop, the latter may be woven or tufted and comes in a commercial grade designed for tough use and easier maintenance. Toys and furniture casters move more easily over low pile or tightly woven commercial carpets than they do over looser and thicker residential weaves.

To create a special touch, consider one of these alternatives to standard, solid covered, wall-to-wall treatment:

- In one area, have a professional carpet installer inset carpet squares in a mix of colors arranged in a hopscotch pattern that encourages motor skill activity.

- Along the perimeter of the room, let a professional install a wide carpet border of a different texture or thickness than the rest of the room. The dual-level effect fosters tactile awareness.

- Cover part of the floor in a variety of colorful carpet squares. These attach to the floor with adhesive and encourage familiarity with the rainbow. It is a reasonable alternative to standard carpeting, since a damaged or soiled square can be replaced easily.

Whatever carpeting treatment you choose, beware of sales pitches for loud-patterned carpets. Such designs not only visually close in a child's world and create a busy environment that one tires of easily, but also overpower a space. If you're intrigued by these wildly stimulating patterns, exercise moderation by using a small area rug rather than covering an entire floor.

FOCUSING ON FIBERS

Because children are active and prone to creating mess, consider durable carpeting made from 100 percent nylon.

Stronger and more stain resistant than natural fibers such as wool, nylon has built-in soil-repellent qualities. It allows for easy cleanup and withstands spills better.

A synthetic fiber, nylon comes in myriad colors and textures. Resilient as well as non-allergenic, it resists insects often harbored in natural materials. But thanks to technological advances, new treatments now counteract nylon's tendency to pill and cause static electricity.

Other synthetic fibers to be aware of while shopping for carpet include polyester and acrylic. Less expensive and softer than nylon, polyester wears well except in heavy traffic areas. Although it's also easy to clean and resists soiling, it tends to retain odors and is resilient only when pile is dense and the yarn twist is "heat set."

Acrylic, the most woollike in appearance of man-made fibers, is not only soft and non-allergenic but also wears well. On the down side, however, acrylic carpet fuzzes, pills, and has low resiliency. Like polyester, it is prone to static build-up which attracts dirt.

Whatever kind of carpet you choose, beware of unbelieveable bargains. Cheap carpeting that wears out quickly may cost you more in the long run if you have to replace it. Avoid level loop that's loosely woven or cut pile that exposes a considerable amount of backing when you bend it. From a wearability standpoint, the denser the better.

Also never cut corners in a child's room by eliminating padding. The extra cushioning it provides extends the life of a rug or carpet and may save the floor beneath from a beating. In addition, padding is an insulator and soundproofer.

With regard to installation, there are two methods professionals use. Carpeting is glued directly to the floor, or it is stretched between pretacked strips secured to the perimeter of the room. In the second method, a pad or cushion is installed beneath the carpet for comfort, insulation, and increased life expectancy.

The kind of padding chosen is important, too. Natural fibers, such as jute, may mildew and mat down. Rubber pad, on the other hand, may disintegrate in time, although is resists moisture better and initially is more resilient. Generally, a pad should not exceed $\frac{1}{2}$ inch in thickness, however, $\frac{1}{4}$ inch may be sufficient if the pad is dense.

On glue-down installations, foam-backed carpet provides some cushion.

Unless a carpet is being used as an area rug, it requires the skill of a professional to install. Consult one before placing your order, too, since it takes skillful measurement to determine the accurate amount of material needed to cover a floor. Ask the carpet installer's opinion about the most appropriate padding for your installation. In many instances, installers also sell carpet padding.

OTHER SOFTIES

If carpeting isn't feasible because of budget or other constraints, there are other "soft" alternatives.

For a child who plops down wherever play is suitable, invest in some small rubber-backed bath mats to create cushy islands around a room. Reasonably priced and readily available, bath mats are machine washable. Learning tools, too, they can be cut into circle, diamond, or other geometric patterns to help a child identify shapes.

Vinyl-coated cork tiles, available in natural tan, whitewash, and other natural colors, offer warmth, insulation, and soundproofing. Flooring grade cork—the only option worth considering—comes in different thicknesses. Avoid the cheaper wall tiles, because they aren't sturdy enough for this kind of application. Flooring cork is simple to lay and easy to keep clean if sealed properly after installation so that water won't penetrate. Even presealed tiles must be butted very closely together to prevent water seepage. Take note: the thicker the cork tile, the more sound absorbent it will be. Like any tile, however, it will attract dirt along the edges.

THE LOOK OF WOOD

Whether wheeling toys around or erecting playful construction, a wood floor free of grooves and splinters works well in a child's room.

Besides being attractive, wood is easy to maintain especially if it's coated with polyurethane to prevent scratches. But there are disadvantages to wood flooring. It does not offer much sound insulation from noise nor does it afford any padding for the young people sitting on it. Furthermore, if a wood surface is too smooth, it can be slippery for those tromping around in socks or footed pajamas.

On the plus side, a wood surface is ideal for hand painting or stenciling a checkerboard or other game pattern that amuses children. Interior designer Sandy Schiffman, *ASID*, *FIFDA*, often treats wood floors in a child's room as an artistic canvas for painting area rug designs. By adding details such as fringe that's slightly askew, her floor art looks like an actual floor covering in place. This kind of treatment works especially well in a room for a child with allergies to certain fibers in carpeting or the dust mites that collect in them.

For a child who uses a wheelchair, there are pluses and minuses to wood floors. As Cynthia Leibrock, *ASID* and Susan Behar, *ASID* point out in their book *Beautiful Barrier-Free*, textured wood floors in some oiled finishes offer good traction and don't require polishing. On the other hand, wood floors with polyurethane finishes offer limited traction and are especially difficult for people in electric wheelchairs. *(Other flooring options for wheelchair users are detailed in Chapter 6 in the section on children with physical challenges.)*

Make-believe starts from the ground up in this child's room, where the area rug is actually a design painted right on the floor.

CATERING TO AN OLDER CHILD

As a child approaches the teen years and forgoes play on the floor, a change of flooring may be desireable. Good options include area floor coverings such as cotton rag rugs or dhurries, or natural matting such as sisal.

Teens intent on making a bold decorating statement will enjoy the strong designs and colors of dhurries. One drawback, however, is that they need to be dry-cleaned.

Sisal, a grassy material used for floor covering particularly in tropical regions, is an interesting option available in both pile and woven designs well suited to today's natural look. It comes in varied sizes, including small area rugs. Although usually sold in its natural fiber state, it's easy to jazz up with acrylic paint. For a one-of-a-kind look, turn your teen loose to create colorful borders or overall motifs.

There are some downsides to sisal, however. Although inexpensive, it may be hard to clean. Also, it is flammable and tends to harbor insects. It has an open weave that may be backed for greater durability, but be aware that some matting sheds in spots and curls up naturally at the edges. To remedy the latter, use a nonskid pad underneath.

A local import store that sells cotton dhurries and sisal usually carries other kinds of inexpensive area rugs ideal for teens. Look for flat-weave kilims from the Middle East and woven rag rugs from a variety of foreign ports. The latter, also made in the United States, come in a riot of colors in solid, stripe, or plaid patterns. Any of these adds warmth to a hardwood floor and enlivens a setting. To prevent slipping, invest in a nonskid pad, usually available where these rugs are sold.

For a girl on the brink of adulthood, an area rug with an air of sophistication lends grown-up status to personal quarters.

A FLOORING FOOTNOTE

Grown-ups tend to take something as basic as the floor for granted. Kids don't. Their fascination with floor space never seems to bottom out.

Like Aladdin's magic carpet, whatever surface covers a child's kingdom will transport that child between make-believe and reality.

THROUGH THESE PORTALS
PASS THE PLAYFUL

Like multipurpose props, the doors in a child's room can be cast in myriad roles.

Dressed in vertical organizers, they serve as storage.

Outfitted with mirrors, they act as a grooming area.

Adorned with a chalkboard, they assume the role of communication center.

But such utilitarian ideas are just part of the doorway decoration drama. The passageways of childhood can also be fun and fanciful. With imagination and a little know-how, for instance, a doorway can be transformed into a play theater.

On the other hand, this area is also ideal space to promote worldly education. All it takes is a map hung at child height.

Distinctively treated, doors not only enliven surroundings but advertise in a big way the center attraction living there.

KNOCK, KNOCK

When it comes to decorating doors, a plan of action relies first on the door's location. Entry doors, because of regular in-and-out activity, are best left alone unless decoration doesn't restrict use. It's OK to utilize them, however, as a surface for display. The same holds true for a bathroom door leading into a child's room.

Closet doors that don't intrude upon the entry are usually good candidates for an activity center. But as the old "knock knock" jokes inquire, ask yourself "Who's there?" before plans to transform them get under way. Identifying the user's needs and interests help determine the best application.

If your child is artistic, for instance, his or her greatest desire may be a place to create or to show off creations. A door performs both duties in either of the following ways:

Door as Canvas: Hang a roll of paper on a heavy wooden holder with a nonserrated cutter. Keep markers nearby so it's also a message center. Or cut a piece of clear Plexiglas to fit all or part of the door's surface. Secured with screws at each corner, it's ready for crayon and marker drawings that wipe off easily. Peel-off stickers work well, too. For convenience, keep art tools accessible by hanging them with yarn on a door hook.

Door as Mini Gallery: Any door is an effective display area once padded with corkboard or other insulating material. For a finished look coordinating with the rest of the room, wrap tightly woven colored burlap or similar material around the backing. To ensure a snug fit, use a glue gun. For a young child, this is a convenient space to hang art; for an older one, it's perfect for displaying pop posters.

The menagerie who share this little girl's room serve as audience one day, "stuffed" shoppers the next. When it's time for a change of scenery, the precision-cut closet doors can be stored for the next generation and replaced with something conventional.

ACT 1, SCENE 2

For a child who revels in fantasy play, theatrics deserve a special theater. That's where a door or a doorway comes in handy.

Open the closet door wide, and in the space hang a curtain of sturdy canvas. Turn this into a puppet theater by cutting out a few small squares large enough to accommodate cloth characters and small hands manipulating them. Ask the puppeteer to stand behind the curtain so openings are made at the right height for hands and face. For effect, attach multicolored fabric flaps with Velcro or buttons. Or sew on pockets to hold props or playthings.

To secure the fabric between the door jambs, hang it from a tension rod after stitching a wide pocket seam in the material, just as you would in making a window curtain. Use enough fabric to fill the doorway top to bottom if you want to conceal storage.

A sturdier play stage than fabric is a door itself. If it's lightweight, it's easy to remove from the hinges so it can be detailed as a vertical prop before it's rehung.

67

Rhonda Luongo, *ASID*, the West Coast designer who acted upon this idea, turned her daughter's double closet doors into clever side-by-side facades. Delicately painted and trimmed with molding, little Kelsey Luongo's doors look like building fronts. Embellished with a row of precision-cut arched windows, they also feature flower boxes and decorative ornamentation similar to Victorian details.

A global-patterned shower curtain, cut in half lengthwise and hung on rods in place of the doors, turns side-by-side closets into more accessible alcoves and opens up a small room.

As with most pretend venues, customized closet doors like these entice a child to be imaginative. While they continue to hide the belongings stored behind them, they do double duty as a place to play store owner, bank teller, puppeteer, or other characters. Crafted by a handyman, the window openings promote group play as well as solitary activity. Behind-the-scenes details include fabric curtains attached with Velcro above the windows.

Aware that they beckon the curious to peek behind them, Luongo admits part of the joy of designing these doors was knowing they would entice a child to use imagination. An additional plus is the ability to remove and store them for another generation. Since they're standard (3 feet by 6 feet, 8 inches), replacing them with plain doors will be easy and inexpensive.

"In most spaces, doorways are subtractive elements, detracting from the space," says Luongo. "I like to make them additive and dynamic, tantalizing one to explore the space beyond."

If you like the idea of customizing doors but not the labor involved, consider painting, stenciling or wallpapering a design that can be undone very simply when a child tires of the look.

Doorway decorating takes on a whole new meaning when you remove a closet door altogether. In tight spaces, this is worth considering, because it visually expands the room's dimensions.

If exposing the closet's contents seems out of the question, take note. There are enclosures other than a door that provide privacy and decorative interest.

Vinyl bath curtains are one interesting alternative that also has educational possibilities. Choose a world map curtain, for example, and a doorway turns into a geography center encouraging world knowledge and foreign language skills.

Another decorative doorway treatment is one that the Japanese have used for centuries. Called a noren, it is a fabric panel slit with flaps. Typically, it hangs down 18 or more inches from the top of an exterior door frame, thereby affording privacy and protection from the sun. Often decorated with scenes and characters, a noren is used by the traditional Japanese shopkeepers and restaurateurs to welcome customers. It is also used in some homes. Besides being a playful element, fabric hung in the upper portion of a child's doorway is one way to visually lower the door opening to his or her height.

At Abington Heights School near Scranton, Pennsylvania, Dick Cook's Global Studies classes know firsthand how a noren changes a standard doorway. For several years, one has graced the entrance to their classroom. A gift from a former student who visited Japan, Cook says it draws the focus of anyone walking beneath it.

AN OPEN-AND-SHUT CASE

Whether using doors for display or for an activity area, help children to see exits and entrances as barriers to conquer. Transform them into magical portals and enrich a child's personal environment.

CHAPTER 3

FURNISHINGS
FIT FOR A CHILD

Back in the days when Little Miss Muffet sat on a tuffet, alternative seating probably wasn't too plentiful. Nowadays, it's a different story.

Today Muffy could plop into furnishings not only scaled to her size, but also created in her likeness—or the likenesses of many other nursery rhyme characters.

Were she snacking on curds and whey in this century, our little Ms. M. could relax in seating that ranges from a child's version of a traditional rocker or wingback, to a contemporary futon that flips open to become bedding. Then again, she might settle for a folding chair, a beanbag cushion, an adjustable secretarial seat, or a backless Scandinavian Balans chair with either a rocking or stationary knee rest.

If it all sounds too complicated to figure out, sit yourself down. There are ways to simplify the process, starting with a thorough examination of the space itself.

Like a road with many side routes, the path to just-the-right-kids'-furnishings leads in many directions. As you explore some of them in this chapter, prepare to expand your horizon beyond sleep, study, and storage units that are brand new. In the spirit of thrift, conservation, and just plain fun, you'll learn about recyling older furnishings as well as converting common items into unconventional kids' decor.

Curds and whey aside, Miss Muffet's modern counterpart has come a far stretch from the day when tuffets were in vogue. Who knows? Today, with all the interest in ecology, she might even befriend a spider who sits down beside her!

Slipcovered in sassy fabric, this plastic booster seat rates a place at the dining room table.

◄ *Bright splashes of paint and fabric add snap to a crisp white setting and help camouflage the little messes a little miss makes.*

71

A Matter of Measurement

Whether it's seating for a desk, the desk itself, or another bedroom piece, precede the furniture selection with exacting on-site measurements.

In taking dimensions, include the height from the floor to the ceiling and the width of each wall. Also figure out the window measurements and the distance between the frame and the floor. Plot the measurements, if possible, on a piece of $\frac{1}{4}$-inch graph paper to give you a visual layout of the space. Another useful tool for plotting space is a computer-aided design (CAD) program for home use.

Make a drawing of the space noting exactly where outlets, heaters, and vents are located. This eliminates the frustration of purchasing something that doesn't fit the space for which it was intended.

Besides arming yourself with measurements and any of the room's present or future fabric and carpet swatches, when you shop for your child's furniture bring your child along, too. Since he or she will ultimately use it, any piece being considered should reflect user preference and comfort or lack thereof.

Before embarking on a journey to Furnitureland, however, take several armchair travels through current home furnishings magazines and newspaper sections. Also check home and garden centers and other sources for how-to decorating books and videos.

In printed matter, study the ads as well as the stories. In so doing, you discover what's available and personally pleasing.

Whatever you find, share it with the junior decorator whose room is about to undergo a metamorphosis. Start a file of ideas and illustrated clippings that appeal to your child, making note of any features, such as a shape or pattern, that are not desireable. When the time comes to shop, the homework you've done will make the expedition that much easier. To make the most of your research and time, bring along the clips to communicate your wishes to a salesperson or in-store designer.

Also join forces with your child to compile a list of his or her specific wants or needs. Possibilities may include more shelves for books or drawers for art supplies or extra sleep space for a friend.

Cost, construction, and finish are all features that should influence a furniture purchase. You alone, of course, can establish the budget. If it borders on bare bones, set your sights on second-hand merchandise that can be rejuvenated. If your budget's moderate, stretch it further by comparison shopping during seasonal sales.

As for the framework of a furniture piece, consider more than shape, size, and appearance. Zero in on interior workmanship. If it seems flimsy, pass it up even at a bargain price. Cheap goods that are shoddy cost more in the long run when you factor in the replacement expense.

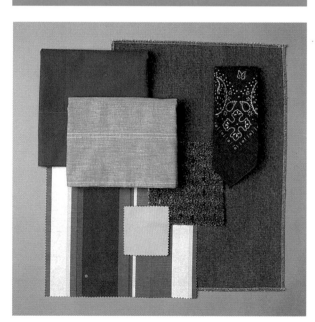

From fabric and floorcovering to kerchief and pillowcases, samples take the guesswork out of shopping for decor that coordinates with what's in a room.

One of the best ways to learn good furniture buying skills is to start at the top. In other words, scrutinize the "high end" lines first. Ask the salesperson to point out overall design attributes. Make a mental note of them. If you can't afford the very best, you can still shop the very best by setting your sights on lesser-priced merchandise with quality features.

As you narrow the choices for your living situation, also be mindful of these attributes:

- Hardware that provides easy use by a child.
- Furniture that performs a suitable function.
- Design that works now and into the future.

73

GETTING A HANDLE ON HARDWARE

Whether an old family chest of drawers or a brand new dresser, a storage piece meant for a child ought to be easy for him or her to manipulate.

But as obvious as that consideration may seem, many children's furnishings fail the accessibility test solely because the hardware is too difficult for a young person to use.

When selecting furniture goods outfitted with drawers or doors, scrutinize construction first. Ask yourself the following:

Color coding hardware helps children keep track of belongings which are easy to access when drawer pulls are in place.

✔ Can the hardware be grasped easily with tiny hands?

✔ Are the double handles on drawers close enough to each other for a child to manipulate with both hands?

✔ Will drawers weighted with belongings open and close readily if someone small is performing the task?

✔ Do heavy lids close slowly so as not to hurt an unsuspecting child's fingers?

If the answer to any of these questions is no, reevaluate the item you're considering. In some cases, that may simply mean changing the hardware so it meets the needs of a young user.

A SOFT TOUCH

When you begin shopping for furniture, keep in mind that a child's small fingers usually lack sufficient strength and dexterity to maneuver knobs.

As the reknowned educator Maria Montessori discerned years ago, one of the hardest tasks for a child to learn is using together the thumb, index, and middle fingers—the "pincers"—to grasp small objects. One very complicated hand movement for a child to master is buttoning, which simulateously involves the pincers on both hands. In comparison, activities such as zippering and tying are much simpler.

With this in mind, good hardware choices in children's furniture include:

- Drawer pulls positioned so that small fingers can wrap around them securely. Color code them to help a child differentiate a drawer's contents.
- Drawer glides that enable a drawer to slide in and out effortlessly when tugged lightly.
- Touch latches that release or lock a drawer or cabinet door with slight hand pressure.

IN THE GROOVE

Easy-to-use hardware isn't the only way to make furniture accessible to a child. Other options include furniture designed with either hand grooves or finger holes. Cutouts such as these on the furniture facing are easy for a young person to manage.

If a child has manual limitations, perhaps a better door handle would be the lever type. The advantage of such hardware is its maneuverability by a fist, a forearm, or an elbow. With just a little pressure on the lever, a physically challenged child can open doors to self dependency.

TESTING, TESTING

The best way to determine what hardware is the easiest for a child to use is to test it beforehand.

Most home improvement stores have comprehensive hardware displays meant for "hands on" examination by customers. Showcasing a wide range of handles and knobs, these displays include designs best suited for a child's grip. Naturally, the best way to tell whether hardware works for a child is to take that child shopping with you so he or she can manipulate it.

Armed with this information, you and your child are now ready to visit a furniture store together. Before allowing someone small to start testing the merchandise, realize that weight may alter the way in which a drawer opens and closes. For this reason, ask a salesperson to fill a drawer with phone books so it can be tested when it's full.

SAFETY FIRST

Good hardware is designed for safety as well as convenience. But don't assume that all ready-made goods fall into that category.

As you give furniture the once-over, be on the lookout for the following hardware features:

Storage with Locks: Since a toddler is likely to explore the nooks and crannies that open drawers and cabinets provide, be sure to invest in safety latches that keep them closed and therefore keep your child out of harm's way. If the furniture is large enough for a child to get into, dismantle or remove the lock so there's no risk of an accident ever happening.

Rolltop Desk: Make sure the slatted cover that rolls up and down has been engineered with hardware that prevents it from falling down on its own. A well-designed desk either will require human force to manipulate or will stop at a given point so there's no way for fingers to be trapped between it and the desktop.

Toy Chest Lid Hinges: Designed to protect against slamming, these hinges can be mounted on either end of a toy chest or in the center of it. If a lid is too heavy for single hinge support, install two or more. In any case, check periodically to be sure hinges are operating correctly.

Safety Grip Cover: An aid that keeps a child from opening a door and gaining unwanted access, this device slips over an existing door knob. It is made to accommodate the hand of an adult whose tight squeeze easily turns the knob. A toddler's hand is too small and weak to grip this device properly.

Safety Drawer Latch: Made to fit most drawers, this spring-loaded or tension device unlatches when an adult applies firm pressure. For added security, mount two latches per drawer.

One further note about safety: Because every child's physical abilities differ, the effectiveness of cautionary devices like these depend on developmental stage, inquisitiveness, and dexterity. Safety gadgets should never be a substitute for adult supervision.

In checking hardware, don't limit your investigation to new merchandise. On old furniture particularly, the hardware may be lovley to look at but dangerous in the hands of a child. Elaborate handles and other fancy details on heirloom furnishings can have pointed edges that may not only inflict pain but may also catch clothes. Adding new hardware may be all it takes to make an antique functional for a child.

AT YOUR FINGERTIPS

When a child's room is equipped with accessible storage, he or she is less likely to be frustrated in getting belongings or putting them away. What could have been an arduous chore instead has been simplified. The end result may be a happier child—and a tidier one!

TWO-FOR-ONE DESIGNS WITH KIDS IN MIND

In a child's room, furnishings with double functions rank right up there with an extra pair of hands. By doing more than one job, they lessen the work load on parents trying to provide their young with the right tools for sleep/study/storage.

But double-duty status isn't all that flexible furnishings have going for them. They save floor space that a child can use for playful activity by eliminating the need for extra furniture that swallows some of the square footage They save money, too, since it's usually less expensive to buy one piece of furniture than two.

Adaptable accessories in kid's quarters can be anything from bunks that reassemble as single beds to seating units that conceal storage. In other words, they're two-for-one design.

When home furnishings sales are under way in your area, decide what's best for your living situation by scrutinizing potential buys and asking how they'll serve the needs of young family members in years to come.

A CHILD'S FIRST CONVERTIBLE

Walk into a store selling nursery items, and chances are you walk into a wonderland of convertible furnishings.

Cribs that once served only as baby gear now do double duty by teaming with storage in a unit that breaks down to individual components designed for use by an older child. Configurations are as varied as styles.

If space is at a premium in your child's nursery, combination crib/storage units are convertibles worth a test drive there. Designed with multiple uses, they often feature a standard crib with rails attached at one end to a three-drawer side chest. Both crib and chest rest on side-by-side blanket drawers. When your little one outgrows the crib, sim-

Tucked along one wall, this built-in bunk bed unit provides sleep for two when the long bottom "drawer" is opened. Smaller drawers accommodate folded clothes while cabinets handle hanging wardrobe items. Out of camera range is the system's built-in bookcase, as well as a secret elongated storage compartment and steps leading to the top bed.

Once the bottom mattress of a trundle is removed, the cavity can be used for all kinds of storage—not to mention display space for special collections like a wooden train set.

ply remove the rails and the chest, and add the extension mattress and spring. (On some models, these are optional.) The result of this reconfiguration is a single bed with years of childhood usefulness and a freestanding chest good at any age.

Some chest-and-crib combos come with a detachable changing station on top of the storage. Styles vary from 30 to 40 inches high, so consider one that's a comfortable height if you opt for this arrangement.

AWAKENING TO ADAPTABILITY

Cribs that convert to youth beds are just part of the bedtime story in children's flexible furnishings.

Take a trundle bed, for instance. When your child is at the slumber party age, this roll-out sleep unit is pressed into duty as extra bedding. But it also affords other storage or play opportunities if there's no need for a lower bed. It becomes a perfect place for setting up either a wooden train set, dollhouse pieces, or other playthings. In addition, it's an ideal stowaway for large sports equipment.

Loft systems take top prize in the multiuse category since they're generally designed for more than sleep. Many have storage and study areas including a bookshelf and reading light. If two kids share a room in your home, a loft bed is a good space saver.

Another option steeped in convertibility is the foam futon, a lightweight mattress of Japanese origin. When your child isn't sleeping, a futon folds in half or thirds to provide cushy seating. Today, many futons are scaled down as pint-size recliners or sofas. Even a tenderfoot can easily flip the cushions. Kids' futons are often in loud, flashy fabric. Just recover with with a sheet to coordinate one with the rest of the room.

Traditional beds aren't known for convertibility, but some do fall into the double-duty category. Consider those with headboards that conceal compartments or extend up the back of the bed with shelves. In the case of the latter, limit what's placed on high to stuffed animals and other lightweights so no harm comes to a sleeper if something topples.

WHEN LESS IS MORE

Like your child's building blocks, modular furniture cubes can be arranged many ways, giving them the edge in the adaptable furnishings marketplace.

Used singly, cubes act as low display space or seating. Stacked upon each other, they turn into wall units. Fitted with doors, they change into closed storage. Stacked and bridged with a board, they complete the metamorphosis to desk.

Your child's height and activities will help you determine which cube arrangement works best. For ideas, look at displays in stores that sell them or peruse decorating books and magazines.

Modular furniture comes in a preponderance of inexpensive materials, from heavy-duty molded plastic and unfinished wood to plain particle board or particle board covered with laminate or a melamine finish. The latter is a process that begins by submerging decorative overlay paper in a bath of melamine liquid so it soaks through before being thermally fused onto particleboard or fiberboard in a second process. Plain particle board is usually the cheapest material, but its rough finish requires a few coats of paint.

With its ample dimensions and good storage space, an armoire is suitable for any age group. What houses clothes today can handle electronics tomorrow.

Dual-purpose furnishings come in many other disguises, too. The following might keep up with your child's growth spurts:

Armoire: Outfitted with shelves, it stores books, toys, electronic gear, etc. Reconfigured with a rod, this freestanding wardrobe accommodates hanging clothes.

Bookcase: Used against a wall, a bookcase houses reading materials as well as other treasures. Moved away from the wall and into the room, it gains an additional use as a divider, such as those in the library stacks. A bookshelf divider is very useful in shared quarters where it offers some amount of privacy.

Rolling Cart: Situated next to a bed or chair, a movable cart turns into a stationary side table. Used as intended, it makes an ideal art station with compartmentalized trays that hold arts-and-crafts supplies. As a budding artist's interests change, restock the cart with grooming aids, software, etc.

Toy Chests: Choose one with a solid, flat safety lid. When it's shut, this toy repository acts as a bench sturdy enough to hold parent and child or several small ones. With refinishing, chests fit into grown-up quarters as linen storage.

SPLIT PERSONALITIES

Flexible home designs come in many other forms that also make the stretch with a child toward adulthood.

Consider a secretarial chair with a flexible seat and back that allows for multiple positions. Readjusted, it will work just as well for your 16-year-old as it does for your 6-year-old.

Room accessories with split personalities include:

Sit yourself down when you want to use this window seat, or step aside and lift the lid to uncover a cache of playthings.

- **Reversible Comforter:** Select a cover with a dual look that coordinates. For example, choose a comforter featuring a pattern on one side that flips over to reveal a coordinated solid or stripe. Such bedding provides a quick room change at a moment's notice.
- **Retractable Lighting:** Because this ceiling fixture raises and lowers in height, it accommodates growth spurts.
- **Throw Rug:** Choose the tufted bathroom variety that can be redyed, and when the room color changes, the rug can, too.

A room's architecture can go the convertible route as well, if there's space for a window seat. It serves not only as a place to relax or read, but also as a storage spot if the seat lifts.

ROOM TO GROW

As your child goes through different phases, so should his or her personal environment. Support these changes with flexible furnishings, and help ease the growing pains.

OVERNIGHT
SUCCESS

Home Sweet Home could turn into Home Sweet Hotel once the joys of hosting a sleep-over are discovered.

Whether prompted by a weekend or by a holiday break, the possibility of inviting friends to spend an overnight eventually arises. If you're inclined to say yes, be sure you're equipped to accommodate a young guest.

Finding comfortable sleep space for company is often a challenge. When that company is a child, however, creature comforts take on new meaning.

A hideaway bed, for instance, may be fine for a grown-up visitor, but a child often prefers a sleeping bag just for the fun of it. And when a young guest is sleeping on the floor, chances are your own child will want to do the same.

The Japanese futon, another inexpensive sleep solution, is a light-weight foam mattress that folds in half or in thirds. When not used as a bed, it can serve as seating in a child's room or stack for easy storage. A removable cover keeps it clean.

If your home has a built-in cushioned window seat, it, too, can serve as an impromptu sleep space for a pint-size guest. Before you transform it into a bed, see that the cushion is wide enough and long enough for a child to stretch out. For added comfort, prop a few extra pillows near the window. If you're concerned that a small child might tumble during the night, cushion the floor to soften the fall.

This platform play space does triple duty. It affords space for sleep, play, and reading with plenty of task illumination and natural light near at hand.

DOUBLE DUTY OPTIONS

For a more conventional bed, consider a two-in-one sleep unit such as a trundle. It's designed with an extra bed underneath that pulls out like a drawer or collapses on a metal frame that rolls under the top unit when not in use.

Another double-duty sleep option is a custom bed with sleeping and playing features. Hinged to the wall on one side, this custom bed lifts up and secures to the wall to reveal the chalkboard on its underside. Reminiscent of a Murphy bed that drops down when it's time to sleep, this chalkboard/bed unit is ideal in limited spaces that need to accommodate playful activity, too.

If a young guest is spending the night, take precautions by covering the mattress with a plastic liner. Then you're prepared if spills or other accidents happen.

LIGHTS ON OR LIGHTS OFF?

Just because a child frequents your home in the daytime, don't assume he or she will remember the floor plan when it's dark. To be safe, put a night light where a guest is sleeping and in the hallway and bath. Those powered by photoelectric cells are energy efficient. When there's no light in a room, they're automatically activated. When there is light from another source, they automatically turn off.

Keep a flashlight near a guest's sleep area, too, just in case of emergency.

WHEN THINGS GO BUMP IN THE NIGHT

As exciting as staying at someone else's house may sound, not every child will adapt to the venture. If a young guest is unhappy because he or she misses parents or feels uncomfortable in strange surroundings, be prepared to end the discomfort by taking the child home. Assure him or her that it's OK to feel this way.

Aside from soothing an unhappy guest, console your own child so he or she doesn't feel rejection or blame because of a friend's unpleasant experience.

To guard against this situation happening, suggest that a child spending the night at your home bring his or her own pillow or other bedding. A soft blanket, a quilted bedcover, and other familiar fuzzies can do much to comfort a child.

MAKING ROOM FOR RELATIVES

While sleepovers may be terrific with friends, they may be disruptive if the roommate is an adult relative your child barely knows. Keep this in mind when out-of-town family members, including grandparents, descend upon the scene for a long stay.

Before altering your son's or daughter's space to accommodate a long-term visitor, explain the temporary arrangement. Ease the dismay of clearing room for a newcomer by letting your child help determine which drawers and shelves a guest should use.

ALL WASHED UP

Don't forget to allocate space in the bathroom for guest towels. Assign a different color or a particular towel bar to your overnight lodger. If it's difficult to empty a drawer for company use, provide a basket or other container for his or her personal items. Be sure to inform a guest where soiled towels and dirty laundry should go.

HAVE KNAPSACK, WILL TRAVEL

When your child is invited to spend the night elsewhere, discuss the visit ahead of time. If you sense slight apprehension, encourage bringing a favorite stuffed animal, blanket, or pillow. A framed picture of a parent may also soothe a child's fears.

Whether the hosts are grandparents or good friends, be sure your child is considerate of their family routine especially if it differs from yours. Find out what time the household goes to bed and gets up so their overnight guest doesn't disrupt schedules.

To promote independence, try to make each childhood journey a pleasant one. Join in the anticipation of an away-from-home adventure by helping your child pack clothes in a small knapsack or suitcase. Provide a little kit for a toothbrush and other personal supplies. Then, tuck in an upbeat note as a surprise.

LASTING IMPRESSIONS

Overnight outings are beneficial in many ways. They awaken a sensitivity to how other people live and instill an appreciation for family members left behind. Beyond that, they underscore the message that Dorothy learned in the *Wizard of Oz*—"There's no place like home!"

DESKS THAT MAKE THE GRADE

Whether homework means writing a report, doing a computer project, or reading a textbook, a child needs a good place to study.

That means providing a quiet area at home with an adequate work surface, comfortable seating, and good lighting. Depending on how well these necessary tools are supplied, a parent either fosters or frustrates the learning process.

A DESK OF MY OWN

Once a child is school-age, having a personal desk becomes increasingly important. Ideally, the desk and chair used with it should be suitable to your child's size. If they're not, then using them for any length of time may thwart the good study habits you want to instill.

Since your child is the best judge of what furniture feels right for his or her frame, let your son or daughter join in the search for a desk. Allow the opportunity for testing furnishings by taking a writing pad and pencil with you so that your young student can determine how it feels to work at different desks. Notice how far your child's reach extends. The right desk will have features accessible from a seated position.

There are many different types of materials from which desks are made, each with its own appeal. Wood, wicker, laminate and metal desks predominate the children's furniture market.

Designed to adapt to right- and left-handers, this reversible V-top home computer study station is spacious enough to accommodate equipment, including a printer, as well as paperwork. The chair adjusts to a child's size when it is flipped over.

- Wood has a traditional, warm look with natural beauty that usually lasts for years. If wear and tear take their toll, it's usually easy to do a face lift by refinishing or repainting.

- Laminate, an easy-to-clean waterproof surfacing material that comes in myriad colors, has a sleek, contemporary look. Because kids tend to be hard on furniture, it's a good idea to consider a desk with a protective surface such as laminate since it's usually resistant to most stains. A much less expensive option than laminate is melamine, which has a thinner "skin" because it's a fused paper coating on panel material. While melamine sheets are usually stocked in black, gray, white, and almond, melamine furniture is now being made in several other colors including red, green, blue, yellow, and neutral tones. Ready-made laminate furniture, on the other hand, comes in a wider range of colors, with custom pieces available in hundreds of colors and textures simulating wood, granite, reflective material, etc.

- Colorful metal, like laminate, adds a joyful element to a youthful setting.

- Wicker, a more fanciful choice, has a lighter look with feminine appeal. If the top isn't smooth, add plexiglass so it will be more functional as a work surface.

Whatever desk style you and your child choose, make sure the work area is large enough to handle the normal work load with enough room left for a desk light that illuminates the overall task area. Common sense dictates getting a desk with a larger-than-average work surface if your child likes to spread out projects or hobbies.

To childproof other kinds of desks, place polished plexiglass over the entire top. More than a protective measure, this see-through covering showcases projects, photos, and other mementos a child chooses to tuck underneath.

Desk compartments and drawers should be high on your checklist of important features to look for unless shelves, file cabinets, and other storage containers are nearby. A desk should have easy-glide drawers that can store paper, writing utensils, and other learning tools. Be attentive, therefore, to drawer depth as well as drawer handles. For young children, hardware should be easy to manipulate; for older ones it should also be sturdy enough to withstand quick jerks from opening and shutting.

BEYOND THE BASICS

Standard student desks suit most student needs, but there are a few other options to consider. These include the following:

Art/Drafting Table: A slanted work station designed for art-in-progress, an art/drafting table is suited for projects requiring ample space. Keep in mind this furniture usually lacks storage, so it may not work as a sole study area. If you opt for one of these, look for a model with adjustable height, and a groove that secures writing utensils.

Computer Desk: A desk designed for home computer systems normally comes equipped with shelves for disk drives, a computer printer and keyboard, and other gear. A well-designed computer desk will also include an auxiliary work surface, room to store related supplies such as manuals, and shelves that are within a child's reach. If there's a very young computer user in your family, consider a computer desk scaled down to the child's size. It not only allows for eye-level contact with monitors, but also puts the keyboard within easier reach than it would be on an adult-size desk. One further note: No matter the size of the computer desk chosen, be sure it has either an opening at the back to corral cords or another kind of feature that keeps equipment wiring out of harm's way.

Modular Desk: A modular desk has stackable components that permit multiple configurations of drawers, bins, and cabinets. A versatile system, it adjusts to different heights—a desirable feature if the user is a growing child. To cut costs, create your own modular unit by stacking two sets of file cabinets, storage cubes, or sturdy plastic drawers and bridging them with a cut-to-fit painted or laminated board or a door with a flat surface.

Rolltop Desk: A rolltop, the traditional study desk with a flexible sliding cover, conceals projects that need to be left undisturbed. It is usually larger than other desk styles, so room size is a consideration.

Custom Desk: Swivel surfaces, cubbyholes, and slide-out work areas similar to kitchen pull-out breadboards, are details that can be incorporated in a desk customized for the user. Well worth the cost for a child with limited mobility or other special needs, custom units should be thought out well before construction begins.

SIT YOURSELF DOWN

A study chair for someone growing up is a one-time acquisition if you buy a secretarial chair with an adjustable seat and backrest. This style offers mobility, too, since casters are standard features.

Two other desk chairs are worth investigating. The first, a straight-back chair, often accompanies a conventional wood desk. If you're concerned about the discomfort that might come from sitting on a hard surface, get a simple cushion to alleviate this problem.

Another option is the "balans" chair. Devised in Norway as an alternative to conventional seating, it eliminates back strain by contouring to the body. Uniquely shaped, it is meant to be rested "on" not "in," thereby allowing you to relax in a position of natural balance and good posture with minimal muscle use. The most popular design is backless with a knee rest on a base that rocks or remains stationary and adjusts to different heights.

TEAM EFFORT

In a shared room, each child needs a place to study undisturbed. A separate desk may be the only refuge from a roommate. For that reason, forgo side-by-side desks if children are at an age when close proximity would be counterproductive to study. In this situation, place desks at opposite ends of the room to eliminate distraction.

FRINGE BENEFITS

As serious as study is, not everything connected with it has to be. Desk accessorizes are a good example. Blotters, pencil holders, stacking trays, and other organizers come in many colorful choices that add a playful element to any learning station.

Like any other activity, learning is made easier with the right tools. Make sure the ones you supply pass the grade.

Home Settings
That Compute for Kids

No ifs, ands, or bytes about it.

Kids clamoring for computer time at home need an environment every bit as friendly as their hardware and software. And they need it whether using personal gear in their bedroom or family equipment elsewhere.

Before kids log on to do homework or fire up to play a game, the position of their monitor, the height of their chair, the light cast on their work surface, and other aesthetic concerns should be seriously addressed. Like rules of the road, they must be observed long before charging down any highway, even if it's paved with a gold mine of information.

Just as grown-up output relies on more than the machines being used, kids' performance is best when their overall comfort and access to learning tools are factored into the equation.

LOCATION! LOCATION! LOCATION!

Whether upgrading your child's old system or buying your family's first one, where you put it should be a primary concern. If the setting is going to be in a child's room, zero in on an area that takes stock of the surroundings just as you would at a computer station for a grown-up. Include on your checklist:

- **Electricity:** Adequate electricity is integral to an area for a computer, which needs an outlet for a three-pronged plug. It's also crucial to plug equipment into a surge-protector strip that prevents wipeout from a power surge.

- **Ventilation:** A computer needs breathing room because it's sensitive to heat build-up. Don't push equipment up against a wall or put it in a confined area such as a bookcase.

- **Lighting:** Natural light aids vision, so try to locate a study area near a window to take advantage of daylight. But components can't be in direct sun, because circuits can overheat. To be safe, hang blinds or window coverings that can close to block intense rays. Besides natural light, a child needs artificial illumination for when it's dark or dreary outside. An adjustable task lamp solves this problem by channeling light where directed.

HOLD EVERYTHING RIGHT THERE

Once the ideal area for a computer is identified in your kid's quarters, concentrate on the work station that will fit there. A student needs room for more than monitor, keyboard, and other gear.

"Ideally, equipment space shouldn't compete with study space," says Pacific Northwest children's designer Linda Runion, *ASID*. "If homework demands computer time, it's important for kids to be able to spread out, whether doing special projects or everyday assignments."

The mother of two young computer users with personal setups, Runion uses vertical space to handle the crunch technology imposes. If there's no room on your child's desktop for disks, manuals, and other essentials, she suggests adjacent shelves or a bookcase to accommodate them. Another option is a wall grid with accessories that can handle supplies. But be sure study aids such as dictionaries are within easy reach. Otherwise, you thwart the learning process.

If your child's existing work station is too small to handle a computer system, you'll need to invest in furniture that will work there. Measure the electronic gear, however, before hunting for furntiure.

Armed with dimensions of the computer and peripherals, you're equipped to shop intelligently. These are some questions to ponder:

Everything a young computer user needs is located in this corner station where homework aids are all an arm's length away. An articulating keyboard tray makes it easy for two people to share the system.

88

1. **Work space:** Will the worktop allow for homework sprawl? If not, would space open up sufficiently if a keyboard were placed under the worktop on an adjustable accessory pull-out tray? A tray that "articulates" (i.e., moves right and left), allows for two kids computing together—or parent and child—to share the keyboard more easily.

2. **Storage:** Is there room for software, manuals, printer paper, software caddies?

3. **Durability:** Is the piece sturdy enough to hold all your child's equipment along with reference materials? Does it have a surface such as laminate that is easily cleanable? If not, can a piece of Plexiglas be placed on the top to protect the surface?

4. **Safety:** Are corners rounded? Is hardware not only easy for small hands to manipulate but also devoid of sharp edges? Is there a hole for cable and cord management so kids don't get caught up in them?

SIT YOURSELF DOWN

Equally as important as the computer study station your child uses is the chair that interfaces with it.

It may be tempting because of budget constraints to assign any seating available, but resist the urge if the chair is not adjustable. For the same reason you wouldn't dream of pulling up a kitchen stool, a folding chair, or a straight-back seat to your office computer, you shouldn't let a child do so at home. After all, a hard edge hinders circulation and puts lower extremities to sleep.

"Kids must be able to look at the monitor straight on at eye level," says Carol Ellison, coauthor of *Parents, Kids & Computers* and education editor of *Home PC* magazine. "They shouldn't be bending heads way back. That puts stress on the neck."

The big advantage of an adjustable seat, Ellison points out, is its ability to grow with children as they stretch toward adulthood. The best position is angled so a young person doesn't reach too high or too low, which could pinch nerves over a prolonged time.

Because there are many design variables, take the user shopping with you. Only your child can tell whether a chair is comfortable for his or her frame and easy to adjust independently. As designer Runion discovered when buying a chair with 11-year-old son Brian, some adjustment mechanisms were hard for him to operate. And daughter Jenny, 15, found out chair backs that tilted back weren't right for her sitting posture.

Two other ergonomic aids also help the younger set:

- **Footrests:** Besides reducing fatigue and circulation problems and supporting legs and feet, this device, if height adjustable, encourages a child to maintain better posture because it removes pressure on the thighs that comes from dangling legs.

- **Lumbar Roll:** This aid to support the spine is user friendly, too, if it attaches with a strap to a chair back so it's adjustable to the sitter, thereby guaranteeing a snug seat.

If the idea of ergonomic aids for children seems a bit farfetched, consider a 1993 *CTD News* report that 1.89 million American workers claim to suffer cumulative trauma disorders (CTDs). "These are adults, many of whom have only been working on a computer 5 to 10 years," says Kevin DiLorenzo of Minnesota-based Ergodyne, a leading developer of ergonomic aids. "Now imagine a whole generation growing up with computers and working on them a lifetime."

With that in mind, DiLorenzo advises parents to inform kids of hazards associated with sitting at a computer for hours at a time, day after day.

Indeed, there's a high price to pay besides eye strain if using programs spells ongoing prolonged activity. CTDs, the National Safety Council warns, are directly related to repeated, long-term use of equipment including computers, or even repeated use of an uncomfortable (i.e., awkward) workstation.

To prevent young or old from experiencing this condition, the council suggests taking breaks in repetitive motion and changing the way a workplace is arranged. In essence, it recommends good ergonomics—adapting the workstation to the worker instead of forcing the worker to adapt to the station.

Finally, however, there is a repetitive motion even ergonomists can recommend. It's user-friendly software—a program automatically prompting you in 3-D every 50 minutes to stretch muscles at your workstation.

WHEN SCHOOL COMES HOME

Being concerned about high-tech hazards is certainly well timed in light of skyrocketing PC sales. As more and more personal computers come home and extend learning beyond school, parents become their child's at-home educators. If their residential classroom is safe and stimulating, it only increases the learning curve.

Computer Time?
Neither Food nor Drink nor Slime!

Like a postman undeterred by bad weather, nothing stops young children from being inquisitive about a piece of machinery, especially one they're allowed to use.

There are ways, however, to curtail curious kids from technically investigating a computer and causing serious or irreparable damage.

"Make your system as bulletproof as possible," writes Carol Ellison in the *Kids Computer Book.* The first rule of household computing should be "No food, drinks, Silly Putty or Slime near the keyboard," she says. "At a minimum, spills and mysterious oozes cause keyboard keys to stick. They can short out a system or cause other problems."

Ellison, the education editor of *Home PC* magazine, suggests the following additional rules for kids, with tips to parents on enforcing them.

- **Clean your hands before computing.** To cut down on accidental smudges, get a see-through keyboard cover. It allows a user to push keys without damaging what's underneath. Oversized keyboards with smooth plastic surfaces do the same.
- **Don't touch the screen with fingers, crayons, pencils, implements, or anything else.** Show kids how to point with keyboard arrow keys or a mouse pointer.
- **Keep away from disk drive openings.** If very young kids are at home, tape cardboard over the front panel to ensure that drive slots and reset buttons are out of sight and beyond temptation. Be sure it's plain cardboard; colors might attraction attention.
- **Don't play with floppies or handle them beyond the outer edges.**
- **Put away software and documentation.** Older kids should help label disks and make backups according to manufacturer's instructions.

Ellison's final tip for parents is to involve children in postcomputing cleanup.

"Don't let them scamper away and make you the computer Cinderella!" she quips.

91

Special Technology for Special Needs

The phrase "open sesame" takes on new meaning for special students when it's applied to voice-activated technology.

Thanks to specialized computer software and hardware that responds to spoken commands, kids with limited vision or limited writing, reading, or spelling skills can be on equal footing with others in average classrooms. Consequently, they can study on their own more easily away from school if this kind of setup is part of their home environment.

The way the technology works is simple. Any command or keystroke that can be performed on a keyboard, can be duplicated just by speaking into a microphone headset or hand-held receiver connected to the computer. The voice-responsive program Dragon-Dictate, for example, allows vocal users to work with text-based software.

If a sound board is used, computers can literally talk back to any users who ask to hear any text read. This feature makes it very easy for the visually impaired students to compete with peers who see, since a Braille keyboard will also accept the voice-activated program.

Already, optical scanners that scrutinize and record text, enable blind users—and those with reading impairments such as dyslexia—to listen to chapters read aloud by computers equipped with sound boards. At least one software program aids those who are legally blind, who have some eyesight, by enlarging characters up to 16 times the normal text point size. Called Zoom-Text, it is produced by AiSquared.

Although computers must meet certain specifications to use the advanced programs, many systems only need to be upgraded to run them.

Besides bringing academic success in the regular classroom within the realm of the impaired student, voice-activated computers may eliminate the need for private instruction once voice technology and software training are provided. As units become more affordable, it's anticipated they will revolutionize teaching methods on an international level.

"The most useful instruction would occur when a student has access to the technology both at school and at home," says Lowell Masters of Academic Achievement Center, a Las Vegas remedial center for students with learning problems who strive for lives of academic achievement.

For some seriously impaired students, the new tecnology may still require several drafts that are aided by spelling and grammar checkers. But in the end, the final product may look similiar to what's produced by nonimpaired students.

THE S.O.S. OF GOOD STORAGE

Like a character in a pop-up book, 10-year-old Nancy appeared to spring out of her surroundings—a topsy-turvy bedroom heaped with toys, clothes, magazines, and personal treasures.

In a storybook, this scene might have been comical. But this was real life, and Nancy's mess was no laughing matter.

If this kind of clutter and confusion describe your child's room, too, sound an S.O.S. call right away. That's S.O.S. for storage that's Simple, Organized, and Safe.

STORING ALL THAT STUFF

Dressers, closets, and toy chests may be the most common places to store childhood "stuff," but they certainly aren't the only ones. Alternatives include the following:

- Beds with built-in drawers or trundles, or beds with optional roll-out bins designed to fit under the frame

- Rolling plastic carts, like the kind beauticians use, that can store playthings for a preschooler as easily as they store paraphernalia for a teen

- Wood or plastic cubes that stack in various configurations to accommodate books, trophies, and other treasures

- Floor-to-ceiling space-saving shelves on adjustable poles designed for bathroom supplies but adequate for bedroom "lightweights" like stuffed animals and dolls

KEEP IT SIMPLE

Choose obvious places for childhood belongings. Books in a bookcase, shoes on a shoe rack, playthings in a toy bin, and so on.

Before assigning a permanent place for any storage, think about the kid who will use it regularly. Will shelf items be within the child's reach? Will dresser drawers open easily with their small hands? Children who struggle to get their belongings often act out their frustrations by cluttering the scene.

Keeping storage simple means keeping it accessible, too. In a closet, for instance, clothes rods should be placed low enough so someone small can easily reach what's hung there. Keep accessibility in mind, too, when you position closet shelves. If anything a child needs to reach is beyond his or her grasp, keep a step stool handy for the child to use.

Since a young child lacks sufficient hand strength to pull very large or very small knobs, look for scaled-down storage with drawers that feature one of the following: full-hand pulls, finger grips or holes, glides or touch latches.

Hardware such as glides and touch latches enable drawers to be opened and closed with slight hand pressure. They work especially well for a physically challenged child, whose limitations may also warrant open storage cubes or drawerless closets.

In all instances, let a child determine what hardware is the simplest to manipulate. Allow your son or daughter to test the hardware on store displays before purchasing the piece of furniture.

If shopping isn't necessary because hand-me-downs are plentiful, be mindful of a few considerations. Don't let nostalgia get in the way of common sense. Grandma's furniture may look pretty in your daughter's room, but it may not be the wisest storage choice if it's too high or its drawers are too heavy for someone young to manage.

KEEP IT ORGANIZED

Keeping a room orderly means more than having all the furniture neatly arranged. Whether toys, clothes, or school items, personal possessions should be organized and placed in designated areas that a child has helped to select. Remember: If a child invests time creating an environment, he or she is more likely to invest energy in its upkeep.

This custom art station, which adjusts to different heights, features individual holes cut to keep paint containers in place. An antidrip edge not only allows creative ones to apply paint liberally, but also limits mess and facilitates cleanup.

To encourage organization, store belongings where they most likely will be used. In the art area, for instance, keep crayons, markers, sketch pads, and similar items. Likewise, in the study area, file paper and other supplies in close proximity to the desk.

To help preschoolers keep their treasures orderly, try using inexpensive plastic dish basins for bulk items like blocks, beads, and small cars. Color code these or other containers and then label the contents with inexpensive peel-off letters available at stationery or art supply stores. This method promotes neatness while encouraging color association and language skills. It also personalizes a space.

KEEP IT SAFE

Never assume any furniture is safe because it's sold commercially. Before purchasing anything, make sure wood isn't splintered, paint isn't toxic, nails aren't exposed and hinges aren't unsafe.

Once the storage is in use, don't forget to check periodically for the following:

Shelves: Are things piled so high they could topple over with the slightest movement? If so, rearrange them safely.

Bookcases: Are books or other objects so heavy that they make the unit bow in the middle and therefore prone to tipping over? Securing the bookcase unit to the wall guards against this possibility.

Cubes and Other Stackables: Are they secured either to each other or to the wall? Either step offers security.

Toy Chests: Are lids designed with safety latches so they can't fall down on the head or fingers of a child hunting for a plaything? If not, take safety measures.

HIDE AND SEEK

Many parents mistakenly equate the need for order with the desire to keep everything hidden that isn't essential. While tidiness is an admirable trait, it's important to allow some of a child's treasures to be within view.

Seeing favorite objects that rekindle memories of events and people can reassure a child of his or her special place in the world.

PLAIN PIECES + PAINT + PIZAZZ = SPLASHY FURNITURE

A bouquet of daisies blossom on a footstool . . . A puff of clouds waltz across a carved headboard . . . Alphabet soldiers stand guard on a wooden toy chest.

As these images testitfy to all who see them, whether large or small, painted furnishings enliven a youthful setting. Just as they do when applied to walls, special finishes on furniture such as stenciling, spattering, sponging, and foam stamping jazz up a child's environment. Like other do-it-yourself touches, they add a dash of detail that transforms a plain piece of furniture into something snappy.

Detailed with paint, unfinished furniture acts as a canvas for myriad designs. If parent and child pool their decorative ideas, the result is bound to be meaningful. In the eyes of someone young, even a small hand-painted decal on furniture packs as much punch as personal art.

Because growing up means growing into different looks, furnishings that easily change face have longer-lasting appeal. With a little elbow grease and a colorful new decorative finish, painted furniture can assume as spirited or sophisticated a new personality as you want.

A SIGNATURE LOOK

Before deciding what furniture to paint in a room, consider the age and interests of its resident. For your preschooler who likes tabletop activities, detail a small table and chairs with a stencil design in his or her favorite motif. Once he or she is school age and doing homework, zero in on a desk or a big table suitable for projects and paint it in a color the student prefers.

The conversation is bound to be lively at this splashy table and chair set detailed with clouds, flowers, and squiggly lines. It's designed to spark imagination in the young people who use it.

In both scenarios, if the furniture is distinctively painted, it takes on special significance. On a desk, that can be accomplished by doing the drawers different colors your child prefers. Or it can be done by marbling the entire face. On a table and chair set, it could mean stenciling stars and planets on select parts. There's really no right or wrong plan of action as long as individual taste is reflected.

For ideas about painting furniture, visit museum furniture exhibits and folk art stores, or study painted dollhouse furniture, kids' clothing patterns, or books on Americana. To determine the best plan of action, look in the library for how-to books on painted furniture finishes by Jocasta Innes and others.

If you lack the creative flair to do a detailed project, take on something easy. In a room devoid of bold furnishings, even one object in a solid bright color pops out from the surroundings. Painting the handles of a dresser or desk in a contrasting color is another touch that doesn't demand special skill.

Both sponging and spattering are two furniture finishes with kid appeal. As they do when applied to walls, they lend a free-form look similar to fingerpainting. Sponging paint on a piece of furniture with a sea sponge gives a kaleidoscopic effect, depending on how many colorful layers are applied. Spattering paint creates random splash, too, once paint is flicked off with a wet brush. For a multicolored spattered look, add as many different colors as you like, but be sure each one dries before applying the next.

Foam stamps on furniture, like rubber stamps on paper, provide casual whimsy. Toy and bath stores sell high-density foam sponges that work well once acrylic paint is dipped on them and applied to the furniture.

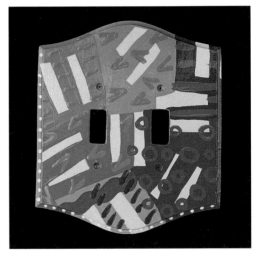

Three coats of nontoxic polyurethane cover this switchplate decorated in colorful acrylic and 3-D fabric paint. Besides being utilitarian, it provides decorative interest.

WANTED: BARE WOOD

After assessing the needs of your child and his or her room, it's time to find a piece of furniture that can serve as a "palette" on which to paint.

A store that specializes in unfinished goods is a good place to start if you want to unleash your artistry on something new. Besides chairs, desks, and dressers suitable for a person of any age, you'll see armoires and other storage geared for an older child.

As with finished merchandise, unfinished goods come in varied woods. If you plan to paint a piece, the wood chosen may seem inconsequential. It isn't. Oak, for instance, has a distinct grain that shows through paint. That's why stain is used as an enhancer.

For decorative painting applications, recommended unfinished woods include alder, aspen, birch, and better pine. As for knotty pine, be advised. In order for the dark knots not to "bleed" through paint applied over them, you'll need a base coat of shellac or polyurethane as a sealer. For guidance, consult an unifinished furniture dealer or paint store personnel. Do-it-yourselfers should also check how-to guides with step-by-step techniques for creating different kinds of decorative finishes ranging from antiquing to stenciling.

Another important consideration in choosing furniture to paint is also construction. Check the drawers, says Unfinished Furniture Association past president Randy Buck. On a quality unit, he notes, drawers are solid wood, not particle board made from sawdust chunks glued and compressed. Because kids tend to be hard on furniture, Buck recommends items that are solid wood overall. Be cautious of inexpensive veneers bonded to particle board. In general, he says, veneer isn't the best surface to paint because the wetness of paint may lift the veneer from material to which it's bonded.

If you want the look of hand-painted pieces but not the labor involved to create them, take note: Some unfinished furniture shops offer custom finishing. Naturally, it costs more.

ENCORE! ENCORE!

As appealing as something new may be, it's not the only game in town. Old furniture can be repainted in a zippy design that offers as much splash in a kid's room as a brand new decorative piece. In order for paint to adhere to it, however, you'll need to lightly sand the surface first. In some cases, old furnishings may require wood stripping. Consult a professional if you're in doubt.

Besides looking at home for relics worth camouflaging, check secondhand shops for finds. Overlook an existing finish in bad condition if something has good lines and construction. But think twice before buying a highly detailed piece of furniture. The more intricate it is, the more time-consuming its preparation for decorative application.

TWINKLE, TWINKLE, LITTLE DESK

There are many furnishings good for painted treatment in a child's world. They include:

Chests and Dressers: Because of their size and flat surfaces, both take large-scale design well. Simple yet striking is a combination stain/paint treatment, with the drawers and top painted a bold color and the sides and hardware stained. Painting each drawer a different color is yet another way to add interest.

Cube or Small Table: Paint a checkerboard pattern on top of either, and it turns into a child's game board.

Desk: Paint each drawer in a different color, or decorate each knob as a sports ball, such as a soccer ball, baseball, etc. Another idea is stenciling the desktop in stars, planets, or whatever else appeals to your young one.

Garden Bench: With some whimsical touches, this outdoorsy furniture takes a rightful place indoors as a rest stop for toys or tots. Use storybook illustrations as a guide for painting favorite make-believe characters on the bench back or seat.

Rocker or Chair: Beloved but battered rockers for adult or child are good candidates for revitalizing with special effects. Apply paint in bright colors to the spindles and legs, or stencil a storybook character to the seat. The adult rocker, like its child-size counterpart, fits right in, not only as a place for reading but also as a place for cuddling with a young listener. A child's plain wood chair also has possibilities for decoration.

Brilliant colors painted fancifully transform this rocker into a room statement.

Step Stool: This childhood helpmate is tailor-made for personalizing with a name or initials. For a one-of-a-kind touch, let your child imprint the furniture with a hand- or footprint. Dip his or her hand or foot in a shallow container with just enough latex paint to cover the skin. Make a small mark with a pencil where the footprint or handprint will go, and hold your child's wrist or ankle to guide the impression. Any paint residue will rinse off with soap and water.

THE FINISH LINE

As you furnish your child's room with a painted design or two, remember the fun part: Artistic expression follows no rules. Blend your child's ideas with yours, and the generational mix may be the best recipe ever for a kid's sensational quarters!

When Furniture Changes Face

A child's furniture can have make-believe qualities if it's painted with special effects. Depending on the illusion wanted, the following techniques are worth investigating. Check a paint store for kits and other how-to information.

Antiquing: Also called glazing, antiquing consists of painting a thin glaze of one color over a base coat of another. As it dries, the glaze is lightly wiped off, giving a two-tone effect.

Foam Stamping: Similar to rubber stamping paper with ink, foam stamping involves applying paint to high-density foam shapes and stamping designs on a surface, such as unfinished furniture.

Marbling: A painted finish resembling the durable mineral it mimics, marbling can be achieved with washes of latex paint.

Ragging: Ragging entails pressing a soft cotton rag on a wet painted surface to make a textured look. You rag on and rag off colors, but the effect depends on the kind of rag and how it's maneuvered.

Spattering: For a painted surface flecked with color, shower a dry base coat with a wet paintbrush dipped in another color. Flick it off the loaded brush either by tapping it against a stick or by flicking the bristles with your fingers.

Sponging: This faux finish of mottled impressions relies on a natural sea sponge. The result looks like fine or coarse granite, depending on the layers dabbed and the kind of sponge used.

Stenciling: As simple or ornate as the stencil upon which it relies for pattern, stenciling calls for a special flat-topped brush dabbed onto the area to be detailed.

100

No matter what technique you choose, cover the paint with clear finish to protect the design and the wood itself.

HAND-ME-DOWNS
WITH PICK-ME-UP

Imagine transforming chipped metal beds, a dilapidated school desk, and a small beat-up chair into furnishings fit for a kid's room on tour for admission.

Preposterous? Guess again. These post-war items highlighted a benefit showcase setting designed for two young brothers destined to occupy the space. Of course, by the time the bruised Forties and Fifties finds were permitted public scrutiny, they'd been refurbished to original glory.

Not all old furniture is face-lift material. What made these ideal candidates? Sturdy construction. Interesting shapes. Family history.

Designer Irene Sohm, *ASID,* of Santa Rosa, California, recognized the worthiness of her finds upon eyeing them in the attic of the home she was helping restore. With sanding, repainting, and minor renovating, the traces of time vanished. Ironically, the furniture's knicks and scratches were inflicted by the father of the two boys inheriting them; he grew up in the same room using the same furniture.

When they undertook this project, Sohm and her clients didn't view themselves as trendsetters. Now recycling is in vogue as a way to save not only money but also the planet from shouldering too many cast-offs. Similar success can be yours whether the hand-me-downs you target for pick-me-up are in Granny's basement, a stranger's yard sale, or a secondhand shop.

As you and your child search for used goods for his or her room, take pride in breaking the habit of a throw-away society.

Except for the hand-painted chests, all the furniture used by the brothers sharing this room was christened by their dad a few decades ago. Sanding and paint have erased any scars.

WHEN LOOKS ARE DECEIVING

Rummaging for finds to fit a kid's lifestyle takes more than common sense about what's worth salvaging. It takes time and know-how. For instance:

- Look past the existing finish, since it could be great once sanded, stripped, or repainted.

- Pay attention to good lines, good proportions, and interesting shapes.

- If it's wood, be sure it's solid, especially on the bottom of the drawers, which should pull in and out smoothly when a child tugs.

"If it's really beat up," Sohm volunteers, "beat it up more by whipping it with chains for a distressed look. Then go over the surface with a coat of paint or white putty that you wipe off immediately. What little remains in the cracks and on the surface is enough residue to give the piece a white-washed look that endures if covered with flat or low-gloss polyurethane."

To breathe new life into old pieces bound for kids' rooms, Sohm also recommends zippy paint finishes, too. Use two or more colors on the same item to give detail, she says, or use a technique like sponging, stenciling, or marbling. For specific instructions, consult a paint store owner or buy a kit with simple directions.

Hardware is easy to replace, so don't nix something with shoddy handles. But do think twice about trying either to resurrect furniture with unsafe construction or to repair an item that would be costlier to fix than replace.

ONCE MORE WITH FEELING

As any antiques dealer knows, old-fashioned upholstered designs can have new-fashioned appeal once TLC is given to them.

On worn upholstered pieces like chairs, an uplift obviously translates to fabric replacement. But don't get new material before pondering slip covers made from old sheets or bedspreads. In your quest for hand-me-downs, don't overlook the closet. Consider that ancestral staple—a patchwork quilt made with clothes outgrown by family members. For just a touch of nostalgia, do what our resourceful ancestors did—use remnants of curtains or other household furnishings to fabricate rag rugs, fabric dolls, or teddy bears.

Sharing family heritage benefits all generations psychologically, Sohm believes. "Parents like handing down a piece of their past as much as kids love receiving something their parents had growing up. It's tangible proof parents were kids, too," she says.

NOT-SO-INSTANT REPLAY

Playing the recycling game with hand-me-down furnishings may call for innovative strategy, depending on the piece in question.

What may have been used for one function a generation or two ago could be suitable today for an altogether different purpose. That cradle you slept in 30 years ago, for example, may be just the right repository today for the stuffed animal collection in your young one's room. Does a photo exist depicting its original use? Hang it in an old frame near the present setting.

If you can find them, other old discards worthy of adaptation include these items, which may rate reconditioning first:

✔ **Trunk or Footlocker:** Because of their size, turn these into storage compartments for athletic gear. As a precaution, disengage the lock and add a safety latch.

✔ **Kitchen or Other Tall Table:** Cut down the legs and create a low table for kids to use while seated on pillows.

✔ **Small Dresser:** If drawers are deep enough, stack art work in them. Depending on space, store supplies there in used, clean coffee cans.

✔ **Step Stool:** Let this do double duty as pull-up seating for someone small. It's also a good resting place for a special doll.

✔ **Mug Racks:** The hooks on this catchall invite all sorts of possessions from belts, hats, and scarves to jewelry and whatnots.

If you're limited to bits and pieces of your ancestry, such as photos, buttons, and so forth, create a collage of them in a shadow-box frame. Keepsakes like these in a kid's room instill a sense of family roots. As for present-day tiny treasures, encourage your child to set a few favorites aside in a storage box whose contents may inspire another collage down the road.

SENTIMENTAL JOURNEY

When you show a child how an old possession can be rejuvenated for current use, you teach appreciation for items with sentimental and historic value. Consequently, you instill the need to take good care of things so they never have to join the overwhelming refuse already heaped in the world's junk piles.

CONVERTING COMMON ITEMS INTO UNCONVENTIONAL DECOR

Many common objects, whether made for indoors or out, are often clever stand-ins for kids' traditional furnishings.

Proof positive of owner ingenuity or sense of humor, unconventional decor demonstrates what's possible when you develop an uncommon view of the ordinary. For instance:

- Garden planters and flower boxes become interesting stuffed animal storage when colorfully painted to coordinate with a child's room.

- White picket fencing finished with a smooth coat of varnish lends itself well as a youth headboard.

- Small fruit and vegetable crates make ideal closet containers for games, toys, and small sporting equipment. A giveaway at many markets, crates also convert to trophy and other treasure display cases once hung on a wall sideways so their opening faces out.

If you can see past the original intent of a design and imagine it in a different function, no telling what you'll devise. But don't ponder the possibilities by yourself. Involve children in the quest for unconventional furnishings to tap their fertile imaginations. In so doing, you'll likely tweak an interest in being resourceful.

ON YOUR MARK

Before you get set to go looking for possibilities, start this project with a lesson from experts like retail visual artists. Those with a knack for showcasing goods often do so by using familiar objects in unusual setups.

Besides studying window and department displays for ideas, expand your horizon by leafing through decorating magazines. Cultivate an eye for offbeat home fashions. Often contemporary design translates to unconventional furnishings that quite possibly could be appropriate on kids' turf, too.

Since necessity is the mother of invention, also turn to friends and neighbors. The decor they've already dreamed up may also be the answer to your family's needs.

As you contemplate what to do, visit building, restaurant, and other supply houses. Familiarize yourself with their distinct inventory.

A LESSON IN MAKE-BELIEVE

Suppose your child craves project space. Forget about a conventional desk. Think about other large flat surfaces like those available at a building supply center. For example:

Household Door: This old standby never loses its usefulness from one generation to the next. Generally 3 feet by 6 feet, 8 inches, a standard interior door can also be put to use on the horizontal. When supported by stacked cubes or any other sturdy base, a door is a workstation large enough for homework and projects as well as computer equipment.

Industrial Work Table or Retail Display Table: Salvage one of these large work or display tops and before cleaning and painting it, cut down the legs. The child-high surface you wind up with is good for spreading out puzzles, LEGO constructions, and so on. If a building center doesn't carry this kind of table, check newspaper ads for any company liquidation sales.

Melamine: This heavy particle board material coated with white plastic can be a durable work area for kids. Available where lumber is sold in 4- by 8-foot sheets, it's designed for cabinet interior use. At $\frac{3}{4}$-inch thick, it has a thinner skin than laminate but is still a smooth, durable, washable material, ideal for a person with occasional sticky fingers.

What better work surface for a future captain of industry than a table that once served industrial purposes. Unconventional touches also include a wall border made from outdoor house numbers, painted colorfully.

A building outlet has other materials for table interpretation. Paving stones and bricks, when stacked, create an older child's side table base that can be topped with safety glass or finished wood. If a teen's room has lounging space, let a new wood palette, used to transport warehouse goods, serve instead as a low table where feet can be propped without worry of furniture abuse.

Besides table and tabletop materials, building centers contain myriad other items worth viewing in a new light. Remember that picket fencing headboard? It's sold here in its raw state, along with garden trellises that afford a similar decorative look once painted. But check for rough spots that could splinter before installing either.

HOLD EVERYTHING

With all the things kids accummulate, finding enough storage containers, cardboard and otherwise, is a constant challenge. Let a kitchenware shop come to the rescue. What's cooking there is a potpourri of possibilities for comandeering clutter. Imagine this:

Colorful plastic dish basins labeled and filled with toys . . .
Mug racks draped with hats, belts, or costume jewelry . . .
A picnic basket stuffed with personal keepsakes . . .

Small, compartmentalized kitchen aids also have much to offer a child with tiny treasures. Ice cube trays, for example, easily house stickers, stamps, and other trinkets. So do muffin tins, which also accommodate marbles, beads, and other round things. Consider a recipe holder good storage for trading cards. A spice cabinet designed with an open box grid for bottles could just as easily display miniatures. Another kitchen organizer with kid appeal is a utensil grid, which welcomes calendars, clocks, and hangable school supplies.

PICK A LITTLE, SHOP A LITTLE

Expand your vista for unconventional furnishings at other specialty stores, including hobby and sports shops. Compared with traditional items, specialty merchandise often excels in design and quality. Geared for technical use, these items are made to be long-lasting.

Peek into a marine shop with your child. Many things work onshore, too. Foam boat cushions, for example, come in bright colors and make excellent soft, washable floor cushions for kids. For room accessories, check navigational charts, nautical plaques, boat lights, deck chairs, signal flags, and porthole-shaped mirrors. Some shops also carry or can order thick manilla hemp. It makes an interesting wall trim or decoration.

Look in airport shops that cater to private pilots for flight-related merchandise that may interest and educate your child. Usually located at small local airfields, shops like these sell area flight charts and satellite images, aircraft models and posters, including those of cockpit closeups. Some shops also carry a wall clock line with faces simulating instrument panel parts, such as the altimeter and directional gyro.

Auto supply and auto dismantler shops are other unconventional places to look for items with more than curb appeal to kids, namely, wheel hubs and tires. The former make interesting table bases; the latter make seating if you copy one resourceful architect who camouflaged tractor retreads by stretching elasticized fabric over them slipcover fashion.

A sporting goods store offers possibilities in the realm of storage. In the section for cyclists, check out bike baskets. They're dandy clothes containers in a kid's closet. In the fishing department, head for plastic tackle boxes. Their many compartments and handles rate high marks from kids who like to transport certain possessions.

Some do-it-yourself moving companies sell quilted pads used to protect furniture being moved. Large enough to be twin bedcovers, they have an especially funky look when decals, badges, or other decorations are added to them.

As varied in merchandise as all these stores are, they're merely a starting point. Look in the Yellow Pages, including industrial categories, for more ideas in your area. Or check library references such as the *Thomas Register*, a 26-volume directory of U.S. manufacturers, or *Sweet's Catalogue File*, featuring thousands of manufacturers' catalog pages.

But before contacting manufacturers, be advised. Many don't sell to consumers, although most will refer callers to dealers who do. As authors and design journalists Joan Kron and Suzanne Slesin pointed out in their research on industrial style when it first surfaced as a trend, buying commercial products isn't as effortless as buying soap in the grocery store, but it can still be done.

UNCONVENTIONAL WISDOM

Taking liberty with tradition by allowing unconventional furnishings to surface in a child's setting instills a lesson in ingenuity. Whether every search for something is successful or not is insignifcant. What matters is the tremendous value that comes in opening a young mind to new possibilities.

All This and Hardware, Too!

Today's hardware store has more than nails and necessities going for it, especially if you're bent on buying kids' furnishings.

Meander through the aisles at a slow enough pace and you'll probably find it difficult to visually take in everything you could actually take out for this purpose. If you need a little push to get your mind pondering the right possibilities, here's a checklist.

Heavy-Duty Boxes: Look past the nails at the triple-thick cardboard in which they're sitting. Durable enough to hold a child's weight, they make sturdy building blocks. Cover them in washable fabric after stuffing the insides with biodegradable packaging material to give some added weight. Since stores pay to recycle boxes, many owners gladly give empty ones away.

Homasote Board: Made from 100 percent recyled newspaper, a 4- by 8-foot sheet of this lightweight structural material can be covered in flannel to create a tackable board. Once covered, felt shapes cling to it. Lightweight items with Velcro strips attached also adhere to flannel.

Just because ironing board hooks are made for ironing boards doesn't mean they have to be used only that way. As this closet indicates, they're also ideal hang-ups for personal gear.

Ironing Board Hooks: Shoes, sports gear, and other bulky items rest well on this gadget's long tentacles.

Mailboxes: Use them as indoor message centers or decorations. The bare-bones aluminum model is downright cheap, and it's easy for kids to decorate with stickers and other personal touches. Let older kids store clothes and supplies here.

Metal Chain: Suspend a length of this from floor to ceiling and you've just installed a stuffed animal catch-all. Keep the menagerie in line with clothes pins or Velcro.

Outdoor House Numbers: Make these effective indoor decorations for a child learning to count by painting them differently so each number stands out on a wall.

Plastic Tool Box: Fill the compartments with arts, crafts, or other supplies.

PVC Pipe: Think of these white plastic plumbing pieces as erector set parts and you get the picture. PVC can be framework for shelves, bookcases, and other furnishings.

Clocks, bulletin boards, and childhood playthings all find a home on this "slot wall" system, similar to those used for commercial displays in stores.

If you crave more hardware ideas, ask the owner. In the line of duty, he or she has probably heard more than a few success stories they're willing to share.

109

CHAPTER 4

DETAILS, DETAILS

I t was the kind of conversation grown-ups savor and 10-year-olds soon forget. "If I asked you about a room's finishing touches," I queried Brian, "would you know what I was talking about?"

"Yeah. All the stuff you don't really need," he quickly answered. "Like the baskets and candles in the living room."

"What stuff would that be in your room?" I questioned further. His answer was a litany of childhood treasures.

"Ribbons. Trophies. Baseball cards. LEGO construction. Team pictures . . . "

"Sounds like everything! Isn't it OK for some of that to be in a keepsake box rather than on display?" I implored the fourth grader.

"No. It's not the same," he insisted. "I kind of like to just be able to look at it and see what I've accomplished so I can be proud about what I've done. If I put it all away I could only think about it. You look at pictures and other stuff, and can remember what you've done, where you've been, and who you've met, and they're a little reminder of who you are. It's kind of like a puzzle," he added wisely. "You put them together and boom!—you're there again!"

And so the ribbons, trophies, and sports certificates are put up where a boy and his buddies can easily marvel at them.

And the baseball cards and team photos are tucked under the clear top on his desk where a student taking a break can enjoy them.

And the LEGO creations are allowed to keep the books company on a top shelf where anyone can look up and admire them.

◄ *Relaxing comfortably comes easy in a setting personalized by favorite colors, owner artistry, and other individual touches.*

What amazing stuff kids accumulate. What a constant challenge to figure out what's worth displaying, not to mention what's worth keeping at all.

Come to think of it, the quandry isn't so different from what grown-ups face with their personal treasures. Just as they cherish objects and derive great pleasure from seeing them, so do kids. With finishing touches, I suppose, it's all a matter of who's been touched by what.

Try to reflect upon that as you help someone young show off memorabilia, whether ordinary days or holidays instigate the undertaking. What may be worthless in your eyes may be invaluable in theirs.

As for kids' room details such as window coverings and lighting, you're on your own when choosing what works best. Even so, consider a color your child likes, as well as a style that suits his or her age and needs.

And if some doodads are "stuff you don't need"? Take Brian's advice. If they mean a lot, make a meaningful display of them.

WINDOW
WONDERLAND

Like a blank canvas, a bare window in a child's room invites decoration.

But unlike the rest of the house, where style and taste often determine window fashions, in a kid's room what covers or frames the outdoor view should be more a matter of practicality and safety than just fad or fancy. And, if possible, it should also reflect a young person's color and taste preferences.

What works best in a windowed room for a toddler, teen, or in-between?

With so many styles available, there's no single solution. Options range from low-cost ready-made roller shades to high-priced custom shutters—not to mention other alternatives.

As you shop, be realistic. What solves a child's needs at one age may be inappropriate at another. Mother Goose curtains, for instance, may be cute for a preschooler, but the same person in junior high will be ready for more grown-up scenery.

Whether warding off cool or hot weather, reevaluate the window coverings in your kid's room. If they're no longer suitable or if use has diminished their ability to ward off weather extremes, replace them.

A VIEW WITH A ROOM

As with any furnishing purchase, it's easier to make a decision after seeing it in a setting. That's one advantage to shopping for window treatments—furniture shops, bedding outlets, and department stores all incorporate them in displays.

Before you and your child undertake this decorating adventure, gather carpet swatches and other samples from the room to coordinate with store textures, colors, and patterns. Be armed with measurements, too, such as length, width, and depth of a window casing and the distance between it and furnishings in close proximity. This precludes buying coverings that infringe on nearby items and ruin the appearance.

If overwhelmed by choices, shop where in-store decorators can guide you. Share measurements and samples. Show a room snapshot and a magazine photo featuring a style that appeals to you.

Trimmed with lace, gathered with tiebacks, and finished with a balloon valance, a frilly window treatment sets a sunny tone in this girl's room. Roller shades provide black-out.

THE GREAT COVER UP

Picking the right window treatment is an open and shut case if you choose any of the following:

Blinds: The mood is definitely contemporary with metal or wood mini-blinds. Reasonable cost and multiple colors influence many to choose them over other styles. But be forewarned: Cheaper brands bend out of shape easily and may be difficult to clean. Thanks to recent technology, however, aluminum blinds are now on the market that repel dust by as much as 50 percent or more. This feature is particularly advantageous in a room for a child with dust allergies.

Curtains: For an airy look, consider the lightweight cafe-style curtain gathered on a rod. Easy to clean when made of washable material such as cotton, it is often ready-made to match bedding. Fashion a set with coordinated sheets to keep costs down. For a feminine touch, gather curtains to the side with tiebacks. For a child with allergies, however, be mindful of fabric that collects dust. *(See Allergy-Free Kids' Rooms, Chapter 6).*

Draperies: Although impractical for a young child who may hide behind or pull on them, lined heavyweight draperies lend a sophisticated look to teen quarters. Designed for use with a traverse rod, they draw open or closed with a side cord.

Shades: Roller, Roman, balloon and stagecoach styles are common shade treatments for children's rooms.

A balloon window treatment in an arched window adds a touch of drama in a young girl's setting, where fabric makes an understatement about newfound sophistication.

- **Roller:** The least expensive option, named for the roller on which it's mounted, usually is made of paper or plastic. Roller shades come in many colors and textures and can be personalized with wallpaper, paint and fabric. Because it pulls up and down easily, this type of shade often tempts a playful child to tug and trigger the motion.

- **Roman:** Pleated like an accordion, Roman shades adjust at different heights to afford many light variations. To facilitate a child's use, mount its pulley system on the sill so the shade moves from down to up, rather than the other way. For safety in a room with very young children, use hardware that corrals the cord so it doesn't dangle. Also be sure to locate furniture away from windows so it's impossible for a child to climb and reach the cords.

- **Balloon:** True to its name, this style is made with billowy fabric that remains poufed at the bottom, where it's rounded. Feminine in appeal, it can be shirred at the top for a "cloud" effect. For a tailored look, choose balloon shades with inverted pleats that hang flat until raised.

- **Stagecoach:** These are made with fabric rolled and tied at the top either in the center or on both ends. The resulting look resembles the old stagecoach shade. Because of the way it is tied, it works best on narrow windows.

Shutters: Fitted movable louvers on shutters control the amount of light. Shutters are an expensive but long-lasting option if a quality purchase is made. Inexpensive do-it-yourself styles come in white and natural; custom-made shutters come in custom colors and finishes.

Valance and Cornice: A decorative heading above draperies or blinds that conceals window hardware, this finishing touch in a kid's room is a way to add an accent or to detail an otherwise plain covering. A cornice is a firm box-like heading usually padded or upholstered. A valance is a simple shirred or flat fabric heading without a hard backing.

Note: Whatever fashion is chosen, be sure the color of the back conforms with windows in the rest of the house if you want a uniform look from the outside.

ASSESSING THE SITUATION

Once you know the look you want, decide what features the final choice should incorporate. Use this checklist as a guide.

- ✔ **Cleanability:** In a setting where sticky fingers are common, choose window coverings that are either washable or treated with a fiber protector that repells soil.
- ✔ **Durability:** By nature, active children are rough on their surroundings. Select a window treatment made to withstand use.
- ✔ **Accessiblity:** For preschoolers on up, choose a covering easy to manipulate. This allows for some say so over their environment by letting them control the amount of natural light in it.
- ✔ **Insulation:** In hot and cold climates this is crucial. Besides installing storm windows, if draperies are used, add extra insulation with a layer of interlining between the material and the regular lining. Many home-sewing stores now offer classes for do-it-yourselfers on making insulated Roman shades. Ready-made insulated shades are also widely available.
- ✔ **Ventilation:** Because breathing fresh air is invigorating and healthful, a child's windows should allow good ventilation. An ideal covering is one that allows plenty of air flow.
- ✔ **Privacy:** Even a child's room with a view regularly needs to afford privacy. Make sure the covering selected does this.
- ✔ **Safety:** Curtain cords dangling low. . . Draperies dragging on the floor . . . Undoubtedly, these are unwise choices for a very young child's room. To avoid these and other dangers, consider safety measures at all times. Hanging cords, for instance, can be dealt with by wrapping them around a window cleat hung high.

LET THERE BE DARK

If drifting into Dreamland depends on darkness, then coverings that obstruct light are necessary where naps are the norm.

Where curtains are hung, use them in combination with a black-out shade or blind that darkens the room when necessary.

Kids who no longer nap don't need coverings that provide total daytime darkness, but if they enjoy black-out during play, don't remove such material without first consulting them.

A MEANINGFUL ACCENT

In a child's room, a window is a special link to the outside world. What covers it can be significant, too, as a way to make not only an impact but also an individual imprint.

Vertical shades keep kids cool in the summer and warm in the winter. Year round, they also block light during naptime. Unlike horizontal shades, these have no cords that could trip a playful child.

AN ILLUMINATING EXPERIENCE

Remember that old log cabin where Abe Lincoln tried to read in dim candlelight? As far-fetched a scenario as that is today, it's still possible to strain eyes by toiling under poor light. Find a child under covers reading with a flashlight and you get the picture.

Although any time is the ideal time to inspect home lighting, autumn and winter are times when it's particularly important to be concerned about it. That's because darkness falls earlier then due in part to that annual ritual in most parts of the country—the reversal of daylight saving time to standard time.

Besides cutting short daytime play, what standard time spells for a child is more indoor activity such as homework at night. Before that happens, bone up on the lighting available in the room your resident student occupies.

SHEDDING LIGHT ON THE SUBJECT

Since natural light aids vision, it's always good to locate work and play areas near a window to take advantage of daylight. Regardless of how much natural light pours in, there are times—overcast days or evenings—when artificial light is necessary. Some activities, such as reading, need direct light; others, such as exercising, need fill or ambient light.

To evaluate the lighting needs in your child's room, assess the basics:

General Lighting: Sometimes referred to as fill or ambient lighting, this is the main source in a room. In choosing it, look for an overhead fixture that provides not only a wash of soft light but also a diffuse spread of illumination.

Task Lighting: This illuminates an area where a visual task, such as writing, takes place. Lamps with movable arms directing light onto a work surface are ideal for students.

This preteen's room is illuminated in blue at the flick of a light switch when heat-resistant colored gels cover the track lights. Remove the colored filters, and the room is white.

Accent Lighting: Primarily decorative, this highlights "treasures" such as a prized picture or collection. Because it focuses only on a certain area, accent light isn't meant as sole illumination. Its dramatic touch, however, contributes to a child's sense of pride when cherished mementos are spotlighted.

MORE THAN MEETS THE EYE

Once you know what lighting is suitable, determine the amount of brightness needed by checking the light level in the room. This is affected by the room's predominant colors, ranging from decorations to coverings on the floor, walls and ceiling. A white space, for instance, reflects a larger amount of light than a dark space that absorbs light.

117

In other words, the illumination in a room with light walls is distributed farther and more evenly as the light is reflected from surface to surface until it gradually diminishes. Were you to paint a pale yellow nursery dark green, therefore, you'd need bulbs in higher wattage and/or more light sources to achieve the same light level as when it was yellow.

Texture impacts illumination, too. Matte finishes diffuse light, while smooth, glossy finishes bounce light directly away, reflecting it on other surfaces. A room with dark wallcovering requires brighter light than the same room would with painted walls.

BEWARE OF GLARE

Look directly at a bare light bulb when it's turned on, and you know what glare is and how discomforting it can be. Because it may cause headaches, avoid this kind of light when possible. To cut glare, avoid putting flat, shiny surfaces such as a mirrored table, directly under a light since they can deflect glare into your child's eyes. Repositioning a fixture may be all that's needed to remedy a glaring situation.

LET THERE BE LIGHT

Along with growth spurts come changes in tastes and habits. That's why flexibility is important when you choose lighting. The most adaptable fixtures in kids' rooms include:

- **Clip-on Lights:** Illuminating tight spots, a clip-on clamps to a shelf, the edge of a desk, or a headboard. The clip should grip firmly so it won't fall and pose a fire hazard. A clip-on may be ideal for sharing bedtime stories with Mom or Dad. It can also provide an older child with suitable reading light.

- **Dresser and Nightstand Lamps:** Decorative as well as functional, dresser and nightstand lamps suited for kids should be easy for them to turn on and off. Lamps with three-way bulbs on the high setting act as reading lights; on the low, they serve as night lights.

- **Gooseneck and Drafting Lamps:** These adjustable freestanding task lights adapt well to work areas. A budding artist can use a gooseneck to shed light on a drawing surface. When he or she matures, a gooseneck can then concentrate light on a study space.

- **Track Lights:** The most versatile light system, tracks come in varied lengths accommodating one or more fixtures ranging from round, square or rectangular cylinders to clip-on lamps and low-voltage spotlights. Because they tilt in any direction, they allow many illumination effects. For a younger child, they may be focused on a bookshelf that houses a rock collection. For an older child, they can spotlight a favorite poster.

Tracks can be mounted, suspended or recessed into a ceiling or wall. But take note: More than one track fixture means more than one light source using energy. Combat high-energy use with a dimmer switch a child can manipulate.

- **Retractable Lights:** A fixture on a retractable cord brings lighting down to child level. As growth and need dictate, it can be raised or lowered, whether mounted independently or on a track.

WATT'S THAT?

A bulb is as relevant to lighting as a fixture. Incandescents work with most fixtures, but heed the labeling. Use the bulb type indicated and never exceed suggested wattage.

For fixtures requiring fluorescents, consider a full-spectrum tube that duplicates as nearly as possible the natural spectrum of outdoor sunlight. It shows black, white, and colors more accurately than other fluorescent tubes and has tested in schools and hospitals with positive results.

For a quick change of environment or to evoke a certain mood, allow a colored bulb to be used on special occasions. Let your child pick the color he or she prefers, but limit use to playtime since colored light is inappropriate for work or study.

LIGHTS OUT!

Going to bed often holds no interest if the dark is frightening. For comfort and safety when it's time for sleep, supply a night light.

A dimmer is one way to help someone young adjust to the dark, if lights are gradually dimmed at bedtime instead of suddenly turned out. If bedtime means storytime, consider using a hand-held dimmer to indicate a story is nearing the end.

A flashlight also offers security in case of emergency, but check batteries periodically so there are no unpleasant surprises.

THE LIGHT FANTASTIC

Comfort, security, and celebration are a but a few roles light plays in our lives. Understanding these roles and their effect on an audience of children is very important.

"Light is so common, we forget how special and powerful it is," notes lighting designer Pam Morris, who says it can be as calming as candlelight or as agitating as headlights in your eyes. Because the young are receptive to its powers, she advises caution in determining what illuminates their rooms. "Too much light stimulates and can be a factor in overactivity," she points out.

The designer advocates using light as a means of instruction. A prism in a window, for instance, teaches color principles when light strikes it and causes a rainbow effect. Tracking shadows of window objects or "drawing" shadow portraits on a wall are other lessons that demonstrate light's many facets. What's more, Morris adds, "light is the single strongest element to evoke feeling." It can inspire or enthrall the viewer.

TIME FOR ILLUMINATION

No discussion of light is complete without mention of energy conservation. In homes, that often translates to dimming lights or using lower wattage bulbs than intended by the light's manufacturer. While conserving electricity is important, don't do it by sacrificing your child's health.

Poor lighting frustrates the performance of simple tasks such as reading and writing. Abe Lincoln knew all about that.

A PERMANENT PLACE FOR SHOW AND TELL

Like a late afternoon shadow, the desire to collect things sneaks up on you, even at a tender age.

Stumble upon a few seashells your first time at the shore, and the urge to find more instigates a journey of many footprints in the sand.

Discover a choice prize in a box of your favorite cereal, and the temptation to stockpile the rest in the series triggers a daily dose of the morning munchies.

Whatever the initial motivation, sooner or later children savor the experience of accumulating what they consider to be treasures: baseball cards and stickers, miniatures and dolls, stuffed animals and action figures. These are just a handful of items that a child of the Nineties might include on a "Most Wanted" list of stuff worth hoarding. Chances are, whenever additional collectibles arrive in your household, you wonder about how to herd all the new arrivals—not to mention the old ones!

THE MERITS OF COLLECTING

Fostering interest in your child's favorite objects by encouraging a collection of them is one way to teach appreciation for special things. Outdoor finds, such as rocks and leaves, provide a way to study nature and instill a respect for planet Earth. Collecting them on trips makes travel more adventurous, stimulating a child's wonder at new places and new pleasures.

Store-bought collectibles, on the other hand, teach children about the dollars and cents of everyday living. If acquired with their own spending money, such items instill not only the value of saving, but the satisfaction of owning something they purchased themselves.

AVOIDING THE CLUTTER

Just as exciting to a child as building a collection is showing it off. For this reason, it's important for parents to allow some treasures to be within view. Seeing favored objects rekindles memories of summer vacations or school friends, thereby reassuring children of the personal relationship they have to the world around them.

If display space in a child's room is already at a premium, Mom's and Dad's ingenuity can come in handy.

To avoid the possibility of clutter, let the cast of trinkets and trophies climb the walls! Even narrow space can be pressed into duty by cutting and fitting shelves to fit it, and filling them with tiny toys and other whatnots. Hang a mirror that reflects a display,

A collection of tiny trinkets, tucked on narrow floor-to-ceiling shelves between the closet and window, seem to multiply when reflected in full-length mirrors.

and you double the pleasure of a young collector who can now enjoy his or her possessions from several vantage points.

If vertical shelf space is out of the question, consider horizontal space. Like the plate rack that may have lined a high wall in grandmother's kitchen, a narrow shelf can work wonders in a child's room. Should you choose a wrap-around shelf for every wall or shelves just over the windows, special dolls and other doodads can dance around every side of the room. Since most of the items here will be out of the child's reach, however, be sure to consult the one who owns them to determine which possessions will keep the ceiling company!

SHOWING OFF SMALL THINGS

Stickers, baseball cards, and other small stuff that a child gathers may be too numerous to keep in sight. Yet not all of these goodies need to be tucked away in a shoe box or album.

Satisfy the urge to show off these acquisitions by allowing a child to select a few favorites. Arrange memorabilia on a desk or other flat surface, and cover with clear acrylic or tempered glass with polished edges. See-through coverings protect not only cherished mementos but the furniture as well.

For very small items, such as postage stamps, consider displaying a few in plexiglass box frames. This treatment enables a child to change the arrangement often and easily while still preserving valued acquisitions. For a rare stamp or two, a permanent frame may be more desirable.

When small treasures translate to a legion of stuffed animals, herd them together to minimize clutter. A big, open, flat basket that tucks into a corner is one solution. So is a hammock designed to hold toys when stretched between two corner walls. Another way to corral plush toys is to house them in wooden containers painted to match the rest of the furniture. That's what Michigan graphic designer Carol Jacobson-Ziecik decided to do in daughter Lacey's room. A menagerie of creatures now roam in the scalloped flower boxes her mother painted white to match the floor-to-ceiling bookcases that they top. Besides opening up the floor space, this storage solution adds a playful touch to an otherwise plain piece of furniture. Because her bed is elevated, the little girl can enjoy her collection from on high.

PICTURES AND POSTERS

Family photographs, school pictures, and celebrity posters often predominate a child's world. If that's the case in your home, consider these options for display:

- Turn one wall into a mini gallery by pinning up a piece of Homasote, a 4- by 8-foot lightweight structural board made from recycled newspaper. Available at lumberyards, it will need to be covered in material before rating pinup status. In order to diminish holes made by pins and tacks, use an open weave fabric such as burlap or wool. To keep costs down, look at remnants first.
- Hang corkboard or a large bulletin board on the back of a door, devoting it exclusively to snapshots and similar items. Make note: In a very young child's room, use the same space for a magnetized surface to avoid the danger of thumbtacks or stick pins that other boards require.
- Illuminate the gallery with a night light so that friendly faces provide extra security for a sleeper fearful of the dark.

ACCESSIBILITY TO THE RESCUE!

As an adult helping a young person map out his or her private territory, remember the need for easy access to belongings. If adjustable shelves are part of the scene, be sure they are placed within the reach of the child using them.

Whether grown-up or growing up, nothing is more frustrating than the inability to use what's yours because it's out of reach. Children who find it hard to reach their possessions will act out their frustrations, keeping things in disarray.

An exception to this rule is valuable treasures, such as antique dolls or toys, which are meant for admiring from afar. A see-through display case perched on high may be the answer, since it will prevent inquisitive hands from dissecting an heirloom and keep such treasures dust free.

A MATTER OF MAINTENANCE

Promoting a sense of order in a child's room is very important, but don't get so caught up in the exercise that you neglect to consider your child's wishes.

Letting young people decide exactly where certain collections go instills pride in them. It indicates that you value their judgment.

In the process of placing items "just so" on a shelf or elsewhere in a room, a child develops a vested interest in the display. An added benefit of being allowed to do this may be a tidier room.

Because a child's tastes are constantly changing, what he or she chooses to display may change constantly, too. As difficult as it may be for an adult mind to appreciate something that's not "picture perfect," try not to stifle a young one's creative bursts.

OLD VERSUS NEW

As old collections grow and new collections surface, space limitations dictate the time to retire some possessions from view. Parental guidance plays a significant role when this happens.

To ease the transition from spotlight to keepsake box, encourage regular spring cleaning. Let the start of a new year, or a new school semester, signal the time to store last season's ribbons and awards and make room for what the future holds.

TURNING SHEET DREAMS INTO SUITE REALITY

Just as comforting as favorite teddy bears are cheery fabrics that brighten windows and furnishings in a child's room.

When is a bed sheet not a bed sheet?

It sounds like a puzzler, but it isn't if you've eyed store displays, linen catalogs, or decorating magazines where sheets act as much more than mattress cover-ups.

Look closely, and they're swirling above beds as canopies or masquerading as skirts over tables or vanities.

Look again, and they're window draperies or doorway puppet theater curtains.

Pardon the pun, but to parents' ears, this should sound like sheet music. After all, linens literally refurbish kids' quarters lickety-split, whether the transformation is confined to the bed or encompasses other territory. And everything's easily washable.

Fortunately, you need not hire store display artists to duplicate their decorating skills, since many firms produce extensive sheet accessories right down to lamp shades and picture frames. Prices vary depending on workmanship and private label, so it may pay to take on do-it-yourself projects requiring little or no sewing. For guidance, consult company literature on decorating with sheets or quarterly magazines, since they showcase imaginative sleep settings and offer advice for copy-cat creations.

ADDING PIZAZZ

Besides visual impact, sheet make-overs enliven a child's room with color and pattern. But exercise restraint so you don't wind up with a cloth kingdom of colossal proportions. You know the offending look—layer upon layer of a favorite theme or character that overshadows everything.

You don't have to go overboard with dollars or details to do a good job decorating with sheets, since a little accessorizing can significantly impact a room and the child occupying it. The trick? Get sale, close-out, or irregular merchandise, and keep in mind that solid colors and store brands cost less than prints and name brands. But dye lots differ, so buy all you need at the same time. If you wind up with imperfections, disguise them as mix-and-match coordinates.

Before dashing out to winter white sales (a term left over from the era when whites prevailed), survey your daughter's or son's sleep area with its occupant. Judging by how dated or worn the bedding is, determine whether the room needs a little lift or a big one. For an honest evaluation of the room, take stock of your child's views, too. No matter how charming or timeless you think it is, it may seem otherwise to the one living there, especially if it dates back to nursery days.

To tap youthful interests, include your child in the shopping process unless it would overwhelm him or her to look at inventory. In that case, encourage home shopping via catalogs or store flyers. Or let the young person pick a favorite swatch or two from those supplied free by some firms in the bedding sections of department stores.

Listening to your child's likes and dislikes indicates you value his or her opinions even when they differ from yours. But be honest. If the family budget is tight, explain that affordability, availability and practicality might prevent things from happening all at once. Besides, gradual change may instill greater appreciation for the final conversion.

ACCESSORIES TO THE RESCUE

With so many bright patterns to pick from, sheets are a splashy way to provide minor pick-me-ups. Accessories that pack a lot of punch and pleasure in a kid's room include these:

Sheet and yardage remnants lend theatrical touches to the playful productions these sisters stage in a corner of their room.

Floor Cushions: When it comes to floor pillows, the bigger the better where kids are concerned. The largest you'll find in most linen departments is a 26-inch-square European style that makes a floor cushion super-size for a child.

Wall Art: Treat a boldly designed pillow sham or pillowcase as fabric art. On a free wall, hang it stretched on a frame or staple it over a bulletin board. For zip, turn it diagonally. You can also add wall dash for little cash by suspending satin-like pillow cases vertically from the ceiling as banners.

Braided Rag Rug: Recycle old sheets and enjoy your young one's helping hands by braiding a rug from fabric strips. A 24- by 36-inch rug requires three twin sheets and two to three spools of buttonhole thread, which is stronger but not costlier than the regular. Check a sheet decorating guide for instructions.

Table Skirt: Add punch in practical fashion when you drape a table with a sheet and top it with a smaller fabric square or round in a companion color or print. If no side table is available, get a low-cost particle board table or table round at a discount store or unfinished furniture shop.

Drape Canopy: One of many fabric effects to create over a kid's bed, a drape canopy calls for two twin flat sheets and a well-secured decorative pole over which to hang them. For a finishing touch, add tiebacks or ribbon.

A BIT OF WHIMSY

Every child's room should have some playful touches, and sheets provide the wherewithal for a few whimsical accents.

Fantasy play takes center stage in a doorway puppet theater that rolls up when not in use. A project that calls for simple sewing skills, it takes one twin sheet, one pillowcase in contrasting color, bias tape, a wooden dowel, and two spring tension rods. Decorating guides and sewing books include directions.

To create the effect of a magic carpet or a dragon kite, cut a double sheet into waves of fabric. For flair, use a patterned sheet on one side, a solid sheet on the other. To suspend this creation, you'll need 10 cup hooks, 10 plastic rings, and 5 wood dowels.

THINK BIG

Because of their abundant size, sheets extend an open invitation for undertaking large furnishing projects. Choose patterns with decorative hems and minimize the sewing required for special details.

To make a major statement such as a change in bed comforter, play the recycling game they do abroad. Don't shed the old one; get a new outer layer for it. Called a "duvet," it resembles a giant pillowcase and zips or snaps over existing bedding. For a more personal and practical touch, make your own duvet with two sheets. Choose a couple of patterns to make a reversible cover for shared quarters so a flip of fabric determines uniformity or separate tastes. Here are some other ideas:

- **Screen Divider:** Create privacy in a room siblings share with a free-standing screen paneled with fabric. Adding your own material requires one twin flat sheet per frame. Depending on the screen's design, you also may need staples and sash curtain rods.

- **Slipcovers:** Treat your child's room to a touch of "shabby chic," a relaxed and recent fad, when you slipcover an old upholstered piece of furniture. All it takes is one king size flat sheet per chair or two king size flat sheets per sofa, plus ribbon or cord. Tuck the material into the seat cushion crevices and secure with the ties chosen.

- **Padded Headboard:** Supply a young sleeper with a padded headboard made from plywood and 2- by 4-foot lumber covered in batting and a sheet that's stapled all around. The sheet size depends on the bed size.

Bold sheets set the tone and color scheme in this setting and complement the denim stagecoach shades and pillows. Clever touches include a pillow made from outgrown jeans.

IT'S A WRAP!

Today's sheet sizes, patterns, and textures make them a natural source for window treatment material. What works well in a child's room are Roman shades that fold like a pleated accordion, or swags that wrap around a rod or cascade over part of a window.

Because of the need for darkness at sleeptime, line sheets or use them in combination with shades that block out the sun.

Sheets and coordinating fabric dress up a room and add special interest when used in an imaginative fashion.

While weighing pros and cons of ready-made versus homemade window coverings, don't scout for ideas only in sewing and decorating guides. Check baby stores, too. If the pattern isn't too juvenile, a padded crib bumper, measuring approximately 12 by 153 inches, may be long and wide enough to be a valance in an older child's room.

Whatever covering you choose, be sure it passes the kid accessibility test and can be manipulated by small hands.

A TOUCHING EXPERIENCE

Like many parent/child decorating projects, a room make over with sheets teaches the young about color and texture. Soft or starchy, wild or plain, fabrics play a vital role in the development of tactile senses. A pleasant way for a child to experience texture is to enjoy the creature comforts that bedding provides.

Some Savvy About Sheets

Whether from sticky fingers or from grubby clothes, kids tend to leave an imprint on whatever is within reach—especially in their rooms where they spend so much time.

That's why decorating with sheets makes sense. Woven finely, they are durable enough to withstand repeated washings and still maintain color, quality, and strength. Sheets come in either 50/50 cotton/poly blend or 100 percent cotton, which requires more ironing. Keep that in mind when selecting sheets for decorative purposes.

To guarantee a long life for designs made from bedding material, follow these suggestions from Wamsutta, a manufacturer of sleep linens since pre-Civil War days.

- To prevent soil build-up, wash sheet decor often in warm water with mild detergent. In the washer, allow space for circulation so there's no overload.

- Minimize stains by treating home decorating projects with a stain-resistant finish such as Scotchgard Fabric Treatment. For stains that do appear, pretreat with a mild detergent or stain-removal product before washing.

- Tumble dry at a medium setting and remove as soon as the cycle is complete. Then fold or press immediately. If pressing, use a steam iron at a moderate temperature.

- To press large projects, fold them in quarters.

For complete care instructions on any sheet fabric, read the product label carefully!

CREATING ROOMS THAT CLICK WITH KIDS

If a picture really is worth more than 10,000 words, then imagine a child's feeling of well being when he sees his own image reflected all around the house.

Hanging personal photos of a child in his or her room continually reinforces self-image and helps instill a sense of identity.

Strategically placed, family photos are an effective way to reinforce your child's self-image and self-confidence. Visual reminders of school events, family trips, and everyday activities with friends are proof positive to a child that he or she has a place in life and relationship to others.

"It's important not only to be photographed in ways that indicate caring, nurturing, love and success, but also to see those images and take them in," says David Krauss, Ph.D., co-author with Jerry Fryrear, Ph.D., of *Photo Therapy and Mental Health.*

The Cleveland clinical psychologist, who often uses client photos in therapy, advocates going through family albums with children from time to time to give them a clear vision of growth and change, and to provide them with a sense of personal history.

But not every photo should be tucked away. Some should be displayed, Krauss' says, because kids who see themselves on view feel loved and valued.

The idea of a family photo gallery particularly appeals to Krauss. "What it says to a child is 'I'm important in this family to the extent my parents acknowledge and honor my presence with wall space.'" It also shows a child he or she belongs there and is meaningfully connected to Mom or Dad and others pictured.

Krauss believes visual cues in a child's room can enhance the feeling of safety or offer stimulation. "You want a room to be a safe place where interests, imagination and curiosity come to light." To him that means a room with images that not only document past joy and happiness but also showcase things that fascinate a child.

For a ready source of pictures, check the magazine rack for material your child likes. "Get down on the floor with your kids and cut out what appeals to them," the psychologist suggests. Then make collages to put on a bulletin board. This indicates parental interest and provides something to summon that memory later on.

MORE THAN MEETS THE EYE

When it comes to showing off at home what the camera captured, there's no right or wrong place, assures a University of Tennessee researcher who has spent several years studying the meaning and exhibition of family photographs.

"We need to get photos out and enjoy them more," says Anna Mae Kobbe, Ph.D., of Knoxville. Her doctoral studies convince her that photos are extremely meaningful in our lives, no matter if they're exhibited on the refrigerator or someplace else.

"Photos are especially important in a child's room," the family life educator says, "because they supply someone young with tangible security."

Through surveys and interviews, Kobbe discovered that images of the whole family enjoying life evoke a strong sense of self, and that a visible picture of someone close at heart but far away helps the viewer feel more connected to that person. Many kids live at a distance from grandparents and other relatives, she observes, and a child who regularly views shots of faraway loved ones feels more bonded with them.

As a society, the UT associate professor contends, we expect too much happiness from outside influences, including drugs and other people. "We really need to convey to children that contentment comes from within." Photos of good times get that message across, she says, since they help kids recapture moments of happiness even on dreary days. In other words, images can teach a child about inner contentment that comes from rekindling memories.

HERE'S LOOKING AT YOU!

Echoing Kobbe's opinions is child psychotherapist Stephanie Marston, whose seminars and books offer parents strategies for enhancing their child's self-esteem.

In *The Magic of Encouragement,* Marston suggests placing two pictures of a child next to his or her bed. One should show the child happily engaged in activity such as riding a bike, playing softball, or other pursuits. The other should show family togetheness.

"Why put them next to their beds?" she asks. "Research has shown the 30-minute time period just before bed is when children are more receptive—30 minutes when they

Putting family pictures by a child's bed creates a comfort zone that's always within reach.

listen and absorb more than any other time. That 30 minutes is the time just before bed. Put photos of your kids being capable and loved next to their beds," she deduces, "and these positive images are likely to be the last thing they see before they sleep and the first thing they see when they awaken."

Marston underscores her position by pointing to other studies showing that during sleep, the subconscious reviews the day's events up to 5 times except for the last 30 minutes. That half hour replays at least 10 times, she says. Her conclusion: Those two pictures by the bed help to reinforce a child's sense of being both loved and capable—the two keys to high self-esteem.

Encouraging a child to view, study and describe his or her own photo, Marston continues, is an excellent way to communicate that each person is one of a kind. She advocates attaching a photo to a piece of paper with the heading "I am special and loved". Beneath the words, let your child fully describe his or her physical characteristics, such as "I have brown curly hair with long bangs." Identical twins should focus on individual experiences and accomplishments. Once attributes are listed, Marston says, children realize they're unique. Show a child personal baby pictures to help alleviate jealousy of a newborn sibling.

Playing photo identity games with kids can begin as early as infancy. If babies see their own images, they get to know themselves. Place a picture of baby above the changing table, for instance, and amuse him or her by pointing out eyes, ears, nose, and so forth. Like looking in a mirror, when the baby recognizes the picture is him- or herself, it's a joyful moment.

San Francisco designer Ralph Frischman had that in mind when he co-designed a nursery with a series of the baby's portraits blown up and framed. "In a child's room," he says, "you don't need to be cutesy with wallpapers or themes. Photos can make it come alive and still be fun."

DEVELOPING A NEW VIEW

Besides enjoying and being comforted by images of themselves and their dear ones, children also derive great pleasure from taking and seeing their own photography.

"Displaying something you created with your eye adds to a sense of mastery," says Krauss, who thinks today's point-and-shoot cameras enable children to feel they can handle tools of the world and contribute to their sense of accomplishment by providing them with a product.

Thanks to recyclable single-use cameras invented a few years ago, children now explore photography at a much younger age. Of approximately 16 billion pictures taken in 1993, for instance, the Kodak film company estimates hundreds of millions were shot by kids photographing their family pets, football games, or friends. A 1992 photo essay targeted to specific teens, drew many entries. Those taken in teens' bedrooms showed memorabilia ranging from snapshots of friends to photo posters of celebrities.

Because watching instant photos develop is like magic to young kids, in recent years preschool teachers were asked to develop new teaching methods utilizing photos. One such program instituted by the Polaroid company encourages them to take candids of their preschooler classes to strengthen social skills with activities that explore emotions, expressions, and interaction.

Vocabularies of small children often fall short of their accomplishments. But a picture is all it takes to say, "Look what I did," "Here's my new friend," or "See what I learned." Besides capturing achievements to recall at home when school images can be viewed with parents, photos also serve as an educational tool. In both the classroom and his or her own room, a very young child who can't yet read can visually identify objects and belongings that are labeled with photos.

Another educators' program based on photos is a takeoff on the pen pal concept by bringing children "face to face" with others nationwide. It encourages kids to exchange photos with faraway peers on a variety of topics so the sender and the recipient can see into each other's world.

SMILE!

Whether formal family portraits or informal snapshots, photographs are mighty communicators about the people, places, and things that impact our lives. Share and cultivate the experience with a child and watch more than pictures develop.

Photos That Develop Into Decor

Framing photos for a kid's room is not the only way to show off images. Pictures can be made into myriad decorations, from calendars and trading cards to poster-size blowups and more. Check camera and film stores for more ideas or scrutinize the ads in photography magazines. For starters, consider:

- A wall border made with full-page magazine photos of cars, celebrities, etc.
- A back-of-the-door poster made from a personal photo enlargement.
- An under-the-desktop collage of snapshots.
- A ceiling mobile assembled with pictures hung on clear monofilament.
- A wall calendar featuring a dozen personal photo enlargements.
- A laminated personal photo cutout adhered to a stand-up base for tabletop use.
- A thick freestanding cardboard cutout of a favorite character in life size.
- A collection of trading card or other photos hung vertically on a door on extra-wide ribbon. Glue photos one by one, leaving some ribbon that shows in between.
- A room divider made with photo blowups adhered to lightweight 4- by 6-foot Gator board cut into three panels. Duct tape holds the back together; photo dry mount secures the enlargements.
- A ready-made decorative throw pillow embellished at home with a sturdy piece of clear plastic cut in the shape of a pocket. Stitch three sides to the pillow and store photos in the new pocket. Kodak calls this creation a "memory pillow."
- Photo-on-a-stick displays for plants, pencil holders, flower boxes, etc. Kids make them by cutting people and pets out of their photos and gluing them first to cardboard. The final step is gluing the cardboard to a Popsicle stick.

If none of these work for you, consider the easiest photo display option. Let your child arrange snapshots on a bulletin board.

GIVING CHILD SPACE A HOLIDAY FACE

Deck the halls, but don't stop there if you live with a child.

Whether celebrating Christmas, Hanukkah, or Kwanzaa, let home decorating spill into the rooms children occupy.

Besides the sheer joy they bring to kids, festive touches instill appreciation for decorative artistry, tradition, and different customs, particularly when some decor is international in flavor.

Set aside some "surplus" ornaments from the family treasure trove for your child, and teach a lesson in sharing, too.

Decorating a bedroom needn't be extravagant, since kids don't expect perfection. Downplay store-bought merchandise and concentrate instead on greenery, assorted household items, or a child's holiday artworks. Even one or two trimmings do the trick.

All this activity spells not only fun but family togetherness and special tradition.

'TIS THE SEASON FOR ARTS AND CRAFTS

When all those seasonal school projects come home for year-end vacation, designate them custom-made decor. Foster pride in accomplishments by encouraging your young Picassos to show off artworks on personal bulletin boards or in plain plastic frames.

Yuletide art—including crayon sketches, finger paintings, and drawings—also makes a festive wall border if lined up horizontally to ring the room. For foreign flair, create a "Happy Holidays" border in many languages. A computer banner program is ideal for this; however, homemade signs are fine, too.

Look to the ceiling for more decorative options by making mobiles, such as three-dimensional origami designs. Fold construction paper or old cards into shapes that dangle from bright yarn. Tinsel suspended from the ceiling is also kicky to a kid.

DECK THE DOORS

Once holiday mail starts arriving, so do ideal decorations for a door.

If your child doesn't receive many greetings, let him or her select favorite cards from those sent to the family. Or make homemade ones to exchange with each other. But whatever you do, keep old cards to make collages next year at holiday time.

Tape current greetings to ribbon secured top to bottom on the inside panel of any entry or closet door, or place the display around the doorway. For added frivolity, top each row with a big bow.

Is your child in a holiday pageant? Perhaps snapshots of it can be arranged on a bedroom door. A young person might also enjoy making a door "album" of old photos from past holidays, including a few pictures from Mom's or Dad's own childhood celebrations.

For a magical effect, gift wrap a door so it resembles a big package criss-crossed with ribbon and "tied" with a bow. Choose a brick pattern, and it becomes a chimney for Santa to investigate.

Simpler door decor includes a swag of greenery or a wreath, which can be festooned with small foreign flags or dolls. To avoid fire hazards, be sure greens remain fresh.

IT'S A WRAP

A table round provides many holiday dress-up ideas. Let the celebration dictate what kind of festive cloth or fabric remnant covers it.

In lieu of a small fabric square that often tops the large cloth on a table round, cut out a big piece of a child's favorite gift wrap to drape over the table. Don't worry if it clashes with the room's overall look. Nothing's too gaudy at holiday time.

Once coverings are in place, let your child choose something that merits top billing. Consider putting a festive ribbon around a favorite stuffed animal, or putting a tiny garland on a dollhouse, or a sprig of greenery over its door.

O CHRISTMAS TREE!

No matter its size or look, a Christmas tree holds special interest for a child. If there's a table or stool in your son's or daughter's room, place a tiny artificial or live tree there.

Otherwise, find a houseplant right for relocation and decoration. Besides being a perfect place for homemade ornaments, a child's personal tree comes alive with holiday cookie cutters, napkin rings, and other small objects. Supplement these with leftover family ornaments or distinctive gift-wrap trims salvaged from previous holidays.

A string of safety lights is the most common way to finish a tree, but it's far from the only option for a child. Other youthful garlands are popcorn, a paper chain or a colorful jump rope.

ONCE UPON A TIME . . .

The Polar Express, The Nutcracker, The Night Before Christmas—what child's holiday would be complete without hearing one of these classics? Yet as wonderful as these tales are, they can be augmented by other holiday stories describing customs in other parts of the world. This increases both global awareness and understanding.

Ask a librarian, teacher, or bookseller to guide literature selections. Then add them to the holiday bookshelf or prop them on a bed next to favorite dolls the night they'll be read. Youthful yuletide music can add sounds of the season to continually lift young spirits and fill children's rooms.

The children's book *Kwanzaa* by A.P. Porter describes the December 26 to January 1 holiday when African-Americans celebrate their culture. Although it honors black people and their history, Kwanzaa is an opportunity for kids of all races to learn about those of African descent who shaped our nation. Porter's book details the items needed to observe it. They include corn, a woven place mat, and the red, green, and black bandera flag.

Whether tradition calls for singing Christmas carols such as "Silent Night" or lighting the menorah during Hanukkah, religion provides a child with historical background about these holidays.

Holiday stories nestled in the hands of favorite dolls, wrapping paper used as a tablecloth, and seasonal school art projects transform a child's room into a Yuletide setting.

If only to widen a child's view of the world, read books and play music about sacred rituals. Also teach age-old religious customs by displaying a crêche, playing with a dreidel, and so forth.

WINDOW WONDERLAND

So many storefronts and home windows twinkle during the holiday season, it's only natural for children to want lights in their own windows. If that meets parental approval, use lights that adhere to safety requirements.

If lights are taboo, let kids create window scenes with vinyl press-on decorations that can be reused.

A window is also a good spot to suspend little ornaments or handmade designs. Paper snowflakes are always good candidates.

Another effective room treatment is a colored light bulb that washes a room in holiday colors visible through the window when the lamp is on.

CELEBRATE THE MEANING

Allowing a child to decorate personal space can be a very meaningful holiday experience. It not only underscores how special this season is, it enables someone in the midst of development to test creativity in a nurturing environment.

A child's bedroom corner takes on a seasonal look with a display of their arts and crafts projects. Even a birdhouse lends a festive touch once plastic holly decorates its doorway.

Star Bright, Star Bite?

Glittery tinsel and shiny colored stars hanging within reach were more than a precocious 1-year-old could resist.

Mesmerized by the tree's sparkle, I chomped away unseen by parents or an older brother. Only carpet residue told the tale.

The result? A trip to the doctor who was flabbergasted that the incident caused no internal injury. Fortunately, only my ego suffers each season as the story is repeated at family events.

Even today holiday sights can spawn holiday frights, unless precaution prevails. Let these tips guide decor in a kid's room or elsewhere at home.

Lighting: Use only lights with an Underwriters Laboratories (UL) mark. Be advised—fire, electrocution, and other hazards are posed by conditions ranging from faulty wiring and cracked or broken plugs, to frayed or bare wires and loose connections. To eliminate concern about electrical lights, use battery-operated lights.

Candles: While candlelight's glow adds a cozy aura to holiday scenes, it also risks danger. Never leave burning candles unattended or where children can reach them. Be sure Hanukkah, Kwanzaa, or Christmas candles are not placed near flammable materials such as curtains, draperies, or holiday evergreens.

Ornaments: Don't use ornaments resembling candy or foods that will tempt kids to eat. Also, don't place breakable ornaments or those with detachable parts on lower branches. Little ones may choke or cut their mouths on them.

Greenery: Place greens away from any heat source, including vents. When they become too dry, remove them. This also applies to natural trees. Also, whether live or artificial, a tree may topple and hurt someone small if not properly anchored.

When doubtful about a decoration, discard it.

139

CHAPTER 5

SOMETHING
SPECIAL

With marker pins systematically placed all over it, the large map from a distance looked like the kind executives hang when plotting major strategy.

But this was Jenny's map and plotted lifelong dreams. What it covered was a big portion of the wall in her room, where a Civil War relief map was also displayed. Besides teaching her about North America, the flat map served another grand purpose. It reminded the 14-year-old of where she had been and where she hoped she was headed.

The different colored marker pins, placed in cities near and far, were described clearly on a card. It was tacked just below the geography chart, presumably so a viewer like me would understand the pins' significance.

"Green is for where I live. Orange is for where I've been. Yellow is for where I know I'm going. Pink is where I want most to go."

On this day, the yellows highlight Gettysburgh, Pennsylvania, Orlando, Florida, and Yellowstone National Park. Who knows what they'll pinpoint tomorrow?

In Jenny's private world, tracking past accomplishments and mapping future goals on this paper view of part of the world is extremely important. It signifies she's the one doing the plotting. Like any other young person, she needs to explore daily the person she now is and the person she may become. Just as she learned to feed herself to survive, she must discover her own personal path. Her parents, however, are the expert guides.

◄ *A plain sketch pad, a few marker pens, and a budding artist turn this wall space into a center for artistic expression.*

Miniature tea service, a collection of pint-size books, and a couple of special toys turn plain shelving into interesting accent pieces.

What makes Jenny's room a model for others? It reflects her interests—not Mom's or Dad's. That's what any kid's room should do.

Tailoring surroundings so they mirror the child living there calls for individual areas within the room that foster science, art, fitness, or whatever else intrigues the resident. These "learning centers" help channel curiosity and encourage active participation in a world that too often finds kids passive in front of TV.

To stimulate a young person's imagination, "co-design" learning centers with their help. Let them voice their thoughts about what these specialized areas might be and where they may be located. Once kids see they can affect their surroundings, they'll cultivate positive feelings about mastering the world around them.

After all, a child spends more time in his or her room than anyone else and should cast the deciding vote about the way that space might look. As an adult overseeing the action, especially for a very young child, add or subtract centers as interest dictates.

As you join forces with your child to create learning stations like those described in the following pages, keep this in mind: Allowing freedom to choose doesn't mean granting license to do everything at once. While you want your children to feel free to express all their ideas about their rooms, you also want them to be realistic in their expectations. As a practical parent paying for this transformation, it's your task to figure out the essential elements, compromising or modifying the rest to achieve satisfactory results.

To guide the creation of localized areas, zero in first on your child's favorite activities and continuing interests. Let them be a springboard for fostering others down the road. As with Jenny, who knows where the first educational journey will lead?

Learning About The
Learning Curve

To enhance rather than hinder the learning process in a child's room, more than his or her personal preferences must be taken into account. Developmental and educational needs as well as learning style must be factored into the equation.

"Children and adults have different learning styles with various strengths and weaknesses that define the way they learn," says language and speech specialist Rhonda Luongo, *ASID*. "Some are primarily *auditory learners* who gain knowledge best by listening to and storing verbal information. Others," she says, "are either *visual learners*, who absorb data best by processing graphic information, or *kinesthetic learners,* who acquire skills by *doing.* They need to be actively involved in the learning process.

"Each of us utilizes all these learning styles but some styles are more dominant than others," adds Luongo, who left the educational field after 15 years to pursue a career in interior design, specializing in environments for children. A member of the American Speech-Language-Hearing Association, she is also affiliated with the American Society of Interior Designers.

To drive home her message about the importance of tailoring a setting to kids' specific needs, the former educator zeroes in on organizational skills, pointing out that while all children need to learn orderly traits, they process information differently.

"Learning to categorize information and organize data are fundamental building blocks to language development.

"For younger children," she explains, "organization and problem solving skills can be enhanced by providing bins to sort toys by color, shape or type. For older ones, it can be fostered by providing filing space for personal data and research projects and plenty of shelving for books, collections and other belongings.

"A child's language enrichment—a critical component in the learning process—is enhanced with practice in fluency, elaboration, and originality," Luongo continues. To foster these skills, she recommends that space be provided for open-ended creative play. With young children, that can mean anything from areas that allow for puppetry to building LEGO cities to playing store. For older kids, it can encompass room for theatrics, science experiments, or other avenues of self expression.

The teacher turned designer also notes that some children find the process of acquiring skills blocked by interference relating to visual or auditory perception problems. Such a child will benefit from living in a space taking that into account.

Let's say a child experiences difficulty focusing on auditory input. This child who "just doesn't listen" may need a room with sound insulation to help screen out miscellaneous auditory stimuli. By providing this, you help him or her stay focused on the task at hand.

Now take the child with visual perceptual problems who may experience difficulty discriminating shapes and patterns. In order to concentrate on the activity at hand, he or she may need an "uncluttered" setting with softer, low-contrast colors to minimize visual distractions. For this child, a patterned wallpaper may be visually fatiguing.

A child with visual acuity problems (i.e., poor sight) will need a setting with bolder colors and strong visual contrasts in order to place him- or herself in the space and utilize it to the greatest benefit. In a monochromatic room, for instance, a visually impaired child may literally bump into furniture and walls and get lost because he or she might not perceive, for example, where the walls intersect or where the tan carpet stops and the oak desk begins. A dark floor covering in contrast to a lighter wallcovering will help the child "see" the intersecting two planes.

As Luongo emphasizes, knowing what's best as a "living and learning environment" for your child means understanding his or her personal educational skills and styles. If you aren't aware of them, consult teachers or other professionals with whom the child comes in contact. Then try to provide a home environment that enhances chances for education.

Creating A Station
For Imagination

Creating learning centers takes careful thought and planning.
As a parent, don't let your own personal tastes or preferences influence what goes into your child's special interest areas. Provide the opportunity for his or her interests to develop even if they're not the same as yours.

Learning centers need not be expensive or expansive, but they do need to be within a child's reach. Rethink a room's physical limits and you'll find all sorts of possibilities for stretching them. Consider:

Dance practice is made easier in a room with wood floors, a ballet bar, and a mirror.

The Closet: Remove the door, add sufficient light, and look what happens! A closet now resembles an alcove that invites reconfiguration beyond storage possibilities. Turn one side into a Hobby Center by installing a few shelves that accommodate collections and other special treasures.

The Walls: Transform this site into a Grooming Center by simply hanging a mirror on the lower half of a wall where a child can look into it. If it's full length, the site becomes a Dance Center once closet rod brackets are attached to the wall on either side of the mirror and a single ballet bar is secured in place. Hint: A thick wooden dowel is all it takes to make a dance bar that nurtures a budding ballerina's talents.

The Doors: Make an Art Center for self-expression on any bare door in a child's room except the busy entry. Simply mount within a child's reach a chalkboard or clipboard with a sketch pad.

145

On a standard door, an 18- by 24-inch version works well. To corral markers, crayons, chalk, and other art materials, hang an ordinary shoe bag near the drawing area.

Windows: Promote firsthand understanding of the seasons by devising a Weather Center near a window that's within a child's view. Outside, suspend wind socks, hang wind chimes, and mount an exterior thermometer or rain gauge. If a window is too high or too awkward to use, let tabletops and walls accommodate items such as a barometer or a hygrometer. The former measures atmospheric pressure; the latter, humidity. Before you equip this kind of learning center, however, be mindful that exposure to sunlight, rain, and wind is crucial for certain instruments to function properly.

Open Shelves: Establish a Math Center that's entertaining and educational by comandeering an open shelf or two. Outfit the shelves with familiar household items such as measuring cups and spoons, a postal or food scale, funnels, and a tape measure. Add pint-, quart-, and gallon-size clean, unused paint cans that cost no more than a few dollars total at paint stores professionals use. Label these according to volume with inexpensive peel-off vinyl numbers or letters available in most stationery stores. Don't forget to include metric equivalents! Such tools provide the building blocks for a maturing mathematician.

Tabletops: Open a child's mind to the marvels of nature by creating a Science Center on a tabletop or desktop. Rock, shell, and leaf finds are ideal for this area. So are special pets such as hermit crabs and goldfish. To further acquaint a child with Mother Nature, hang botanical prints or relief maps and place nature books nearby.

Before investing time and energy to establish any learning center, however, consider the following:

- Never force an activity on a child that he or she isn't interested in pursuing.

- Narrow the number of learning centers to interests a child favors most, keeping an open mind about how many to incorporate in a room. One or two centers supplying hours of discovery in activities that a child loves are better than a half dozen that a parent randomly selects for a young person who may or may not like them.

MAKING ROOM FOR THE YOUNG AT ART

From finger paintings of plump turkeys to pencil sketches of dinosaurs, student artistry thrives.

Because imaginative exercises like painting and drawing are important childhood undertakings, don't confine them to the classroom where learning a lesson is usually the goal. Let them flourish at home, too, by designating some space as an art area. That way there's ample opportunity for spontaneous expression of personal interests that may not be fostered at school.

By using imagination in an artful way, kids experience the joy of creating something uniquely their own.

DON'T OVERLOOK WHAT'S UNDERFOOT

From a practical standpoint, the floor is your first consideration when deciding where to position an art station.

Easy-to-clean vinyl or ceramic tile provides a good surface on which to allow messy play; therefore, you might want to restrict this activity to the kitchen, laundry, or another "safe" area where a portable easel or art center can be situated from time to time.

Even carpeting, however, can be safeguarded so that novice artists don't accidentally damage it. Good cover-ups include:

- **Canvas Drop:** This heavy covering comes in assorted sizes, including runners. Professionals use these when painting.

- **Child's Paint Mat:** A durable plastic drop usually in a playful design, it's sold in specialty arts-and-crafts catalogs.

- **Linoleum Remnant:** Scrap sections of linoleum for small jobs are sold in many flooring outlets. For easy storage, choose one that rolls up, but be sure to put it away so the top side faces out, thereby allowing it to unroll in the right direction.

- **Vinyl Cloth:** Check out a fabric store's thick-ply vinyl yardage, or a variety store's vinyl kitchen or picnic cloths.

Whatever flooring is underfoot, encourage cleanup. Caring for materials and work space is part of the artistic experience. Start the lesson with a reminder to wear a paint smock before the masterpiece gets under way. Also prevent messes by providing no-spill plastic paint cups with tight lids.

ARTIST IN RESIDENCE

Devising a special art nook in a child's room is not complicated or costly. Nor does it need to be space consuming. Besides paper and markers, all it requires is one of the following:

- **A Closet Door:** Let an aspiring Rembrandt unleash his or her talents in this vertical space by hanging a roll of butcher paper on a heavy duty wooden holder. For safety's sake, get a dispenser with a feeder bar that has a nonserrated paper cutter. Look for a holder with a flat side so it can also be used on a tabletop or on the floor if a door isn't available.

- **Open Space:** What better way to feel like a grown-up artist than with a freestanding easel—even if it's set up only part time. Look for one that features a shelf or plastic trays to hold supplies, adjustable work surfaces that adapt to different heights, and/or multiple panels that allow for different kinds of expression—from finger painting to marker-board sketching. If your home includes two budding artists, a double-sided easel may be preferable since both can work simultaneously.

- **A Horizontal Wall Strip:** Creativity is within arm's reach when there's a chalkboard mounted on the lower portion of a wall. To save space and money, spray a wall area, or a thin piece of wood that can be hung there, with several coats of chalkboard paint. It has the same erasable properties as the real thing. What also works well as a writing surface is a wide horizontal strip of white or colored butcher paper. Tack it up and position it so your child can draw comfortably while standing.

- **A Vertical Wall Strip:** Parent and child can join forces in a special way at a vertical art center that hangs from the wall like a loose piece of wallcovering. From the ceiling, rig a pulley that will support a large roll of butcher paper on a holder with a thick dowel. This will allow the paper to drop safely against the wall. Secure it top and bottom with strips of wood. Choose a vinyl-covered wall, or secure a rigid sheet of acrylic to the wall for protection. In either case, be sure to limit creative bursts to washable markers.

- **Table or Desk Top:** Art is easy to do on a flat surface, too. Besides being good to draw and color on, tables and desks can accommodate a tabletop easel. To turn this space into a multipurpose art center, find an easel with interchangeable sides, such as a chalkboard and a write-and-wipe surface.

IT'S AN ORIGINAL!

Experimentation and discovery are not the only pleasures derived from art expression. Sharing and showing off originals thrills an artist of any age.

Allow children to marvel at their own abilities by displaying some personal creations in their bedrooms. Encourage pinning one or two up on a bulletin board or in inexpensive box frames. Don't forget to hang works at child eye level and to have the artist sign all orginals!

Because parental approval is important to novice artists, look beyond the bedroom for show-and-tell opportunities. Perhaps a few art pieces can be part of an ever-changing gallery in the hall. Maybe others can literally be pressed into duty as kitchen place mats. Just stick clear contact paper to both sides of the art and press down so that the wrinkles come out.

Encouraging children to make gift wrappings and greeting cards is a good way to spread their artworks among family and friends.

Cork wallcovering provides hanging space for a 5-year-old's important projects, art work, and memorabilia.

FROM THE HANDS OF BABES

To a child, one of the greatest values of art expression is communicating in another way besides words. Becoming skillful doesn't matter. What does is showing grown-ups how life appears from a pint-size perspective.

What better way to see the world through a child's eyes than by viewing it through the artwork created with his or her hands?

SETTING THE STAGE FOR FANTASY PLAY

Dressing up in costumes on Halloween and pretending to be someone else is one of childhood's greatest pleasures, yet it need not be restricted to that day only.

Any time of year, to a child, is the right time to practice being a doctor, astronaut, or magician. All it takes are a vivid imagination, a few props, and a place for fantasy play.

These theatrics encourage a child not only to be expressive, but also original and creative.

A PORTABLE PLACE TO PRETEND

Turning an area into a nook that inspires make-believe is easy once you realize the setting need not be elaborate.

Children have healthy imaginations, and for most it's effortless to play a game of pretend with a minimal backdrop.

Whether indoors or out, a playhouse adds a special dimension to a child's life, stimulating magic in everyday situations. As a center for imagination, this miniature dwelling can change function regularly. A store, an office, a hospital, and a fire station are a few possibilities.

A simple way to create an indoor playhouse is to drape a card table with fabric. For durability, use canvas or other sturdy material. In a pinch, a sheet will do. Slit each side the length of the table leg to make "door" flaps for easy entry. Use bias tape to bind the cut edges and reinforce the corners.

Permit your budding actor or actress to stage performances by cutting several large "portholes," making sure again to reinforce openings with bias tape. For decoration, add appliques, stickers, or other artistry to the "stage curtain." Since fostering your child's creative expression is your ultimate goal, encourage his or her involvement and decision-making in every step from choosing the fabric color to the details that embellish it.

A more portable setting for pretend play is a large appliance box. Scissors and simple ornamentation convert it quickly into a play structure. Let your child determine where doors and windows go, but assign scissor duty to yourself or an older brother or sister.

Junior decorators can dress up their corrugated kingdoms on the outside with colorful poster paints, felt-tip markers, or contact paper. On the inside, let them decorate the walls as they wish, too. If the box is strong enough, hang their art in lightweight frames on adhesive-backed wall hangers. Otherwise, encourage your young interior designer to draw window curtains, clocks, even a TV screen, right on the walls. Glued-on buttons and knobs also add a "real life" touch.

Move in a child-size chair or two, and the playhouse is ready for habitation!

DOORWAY PUPPETRY

Little Red Riding Hood and Cinderella, Kermit and Miss Piggy, dragons and other fearless creatures: Hand and finger puppets foster both language and communication skills by inspiring productions that deserve a special theater. That's where a doorway or closet comes in handy.

The first place to consider creating a puppet theater is in your child's own room. At the top of an open door frame, hang canvas or other sturdy material from a tension rod suspended between the door jambs. Stitch a wide pocket along the top so that the rod will slide through.

For a tidy look that conceals closet storage, get enough material to fill the entire doorway top to bottom. Ask the puppeteer to stand behind the curtain so that openings can be made in the right places to accommodate a child's hands and face.

For special effects, attach multicolored fabric flaps to the openings with Velcro or buttons. This provides a variety of colorful backdrops.

To cut costs, create a closet theater with less fabric by hanging the rod down at your chlid's height. Or use a playfully patterned vinyl shower curtain as a stage drape.

Attach large fabric or glitter stars to any of these play areas, and the stage is set. While the performers rehearse their parts and don costumes, make popcorn and prepare for showtime!

Unfinished bunk beds take a bow at playtime, thanks to a hand-painted plywood facade attached with screws to one side. When the sisters grow up and are ready to change the scenery, it's a simple matter to remove the design.

COZY ENCLOSURES AND TEMPORARY STAGES

For those living in cramped quarters where no space exists for puppet theaters and play-houses, a bed tent may be the ideal solution to a child's longing for a special hideout. A child fascinated by tepees, igloos, and cubbyholes will enjoy the coziness of a bed tent, which forms a fitted dome on top of the bedcovers. A side zipper permits entry.

Like other cocoon shelters designed for kids, bed tents appeal to the young because they offer a secret retreat for daydreaming.

If there's enough space in the corner or along one wall, create a small platform where theatrics have a stage. It needn't be elaborate to provide special effects for the one who will be using it. When your child's room won't allow space for a permanent miniature dais, consider a small, temporary setup that can be moved into place for special productions and stored under the bed or elsewhere between performances.

A PLACE FOR PROPS

Props are just as important as a place to perform. A grown-up's cast-offs, including clothes, shoes, and jewelry, make ideal costumes. Before discarding anything, consider the second life it could have as theatrical garb for your child.

Hand in hand with collecting props is finding a place to store them. This can be a big box labeled "Dress Up" that fits under the bed, or a laundry basket that tucks away in a closet. If you want the container to be something special, find an old suitcase or trunk. For safety's sake, dismantle the lock.

ENCORE! ENCORE!

If you find yourself becoming absorbed in your child's fantasy play, don't be surprised. Make-believe casts a spell regardless of age.

Enjoy the parent/child interaction this activity sparks. After all, it's never too late to have a happy childhood!

WIDENING A CHILD'S WINDOW ON THE WORLD

Small sticker flags lining window ledges . . .
Colorful ethnic dolls adorning shelves . . .
Interesting, exotic creatures peering from posters . . .

While these touches demonstrate decorative ideas for kids' rooms, they more importantly underscore simple ways a home setting can open up a child's young eyes to the world at large.

Why make global knowledge a priority in a home environment? Because young people need more than a casual grasp of events here and abroad to compete in economic, environmental, political, and social arenas that are all based on geographic context.

Becoming geographically literate takes more than focusing schoolwork on the world around us. It means rethinking a child's living situation so that curiosity about planet Earth is nurtured at home.

PLOTTING A ROUTE

Hanging maps in a child's room is one of the best ways to guarantee that the world will make daily impact. With so many sizes and colorful types to choose from, you and your child will have no problem finding something educational and decorative.

To advance global knowledge near and far, get local, national, and world maps with pinup possibilities. Let age, preference, and budget guide the purchase of varied maps, which can be spray mounted for stability and padding on a lightweight piece of foam board. Using this backing keeps map plotting pins from marring the wall.

Different kinds of display maps to consider include:

- A flat street map of your city that is easy to mark, with significant locations such as homes of relatives, friends, and your own family. After acquiring such a map from the Chamber of Commerce or another local source, let the one who will be using it find

Maps in kids' rooms do more than teach about the world and geography. They help a young person intent on exploration plan distant travels.

bright markers or stickers at the stationery store to signify specific sites. Older children may enjoy using plotting pins designed with colorful pinheads for this purpose.

- A flat national or world map big enough to plot vacation routes. Once destinations are known, encourage young travelers to acquire tourist bureau addresses from the library so that they can write for maps, and other materials. A temporary display of this information will add to the excitement of travel while broadening knowledge of unknown places. For a good selection of maps, check auto clubs, book and map shops, and catalogs like those distributed by Rand McNally and the National Geographic Society.

- A three-dimensional map with raised topographical features makes various regions come to life, since mountains project above the plains. Molded vinyl maps invite a child to "feel" the geography in many regions of the United States and elsewhere.

For a different approach, get less conventional maps, such as multi-colored corkboard versions of the United States or the world, or maps with repositionable vinyl stick-on states and important facts about each region. Or use geography board games such as "Where in the World Is Carmen SanDiego?" and "Take Off!" to promote education in an exciting way if exhibited on a wall when not in use.

Hang another map or globe in the TV room so the nightly news is a family activity time. Challenge viewers to find sites mentioned, including those where favorite sports teams are on the road.

WORDLY HANG UPS

Maps and game boards aside, there are many other opportunities for giving wall space international flair. Consider these:

- Transform one wall into an adventurer's paradise with a world mural that goes up like strippable paper in eight panels. Sold through Rand McNally, it is 8 feet, 8 inches by 13 feet and can be trimmed to fit smaller walls.

- Turn shelf space into a foreign study center with a display of ethnic dolls or other playthings.

- Create a wall-to-wall international look with flag stickers of many nations arranged in a row at child height.

- Decorate part of a wall with posters or calendar photos of faraway scenes or exotic animals.

- Let a wall-hung chalkboard become a language center by writing a new geography term or foreign word on it regularly.

- Transform the ceiling into a learning lab on high with inflatable globes or paper flags suspended as mobiles.

- Cover all or part of a door with foreign postcards, advertisements, or flat souvenirs.

- In place of a closet door, hang a drapery rod that supports a vinyl shower curtain depicting a world map.

O GEO MIO

Foreign lands aren't so strange when you become familiar with their customs. Devote an area of a room to pursuing this knowledge, and you establish a center for global study.

Like any other learning station, equip this one with books and materials related to the topic. Foreign stamps and coins are ideal acquisitions for this specialty area. For display purposes here or elsewhere, encourage your child to create a collage of foreign items that can be hung in a simple box frame or shown off under a clear desktop. If there's room and the objects aren't too big, place them on a wall map to indicate where they came from.

Global awareness also comes home with a display of imported foods and other household items. Let your child hunt for these in the kitchen cupboard.

Globes, nature finds, a microscope, and other treasures turn these shelves into a combination science/geo center that enhances knowledge about the world around us.

CULTURAL KNOW-HOW

A great way to introduce another culture is to learn about personal ancestry. Encourage someone young to ask older relatives about family history so a genealogy tree can be made for display.

Photos of family ancestors foster pride in lineage, too. So do foreign souvenirs or domestic items with a faraway country's heritage depicted by a flag or other motif.

Ideal opportunities for learning faraway customs present themselves on holidays like Chinese New Year or Cinqo de Mayo. To celebrate them, suggest reading books about these traditions or visiting a numismatist's shop for cancelled stamps from the land being commemorated. A party goods store is also worth exploring for appropriate holiday decorations that can be displayed on a bulletin board in your child's room.

To reinforce the value of knowing "roots," challenge young TV viewers to use the map in the television room or elsewhere to find sites mentioned on the nightly news, including those where different ancestors came from before settling here.

DISCOVERING THE WORLD

Stirring children's curiosity about the world by steering them toward geography has many elements of intrigue, from foreign travel to exotic customs.

Feed youthful fascination about the global community through an engaging home environment, and nurture a lifelong interest and understanding of the world.

T U R N I N G   N A T U R E
O U T S I D E   I N

Rain or shine, children enjoy playing games with Mother Nature. On sunny days, that translates to climbing trees and picking wildflowers. On wet ones, it means splashing through puddles and making mud pies.

But what if the weather outside is miserable? Must the bond between child and nature be broken?

The answer is definitely no if you invite the outdoors inside all year. With the preservation of natural resources so crucial an issue, it makes good sense to instill a concern for nature's treasures in your child. Such understanding nurtures a child's love for the planet as well as a respect for his or her place in it.

There are many ways to learn about the earth in an indoor setting. A room that promotes this interest allows a child in all types of weather to investigate nature.

PLANTING THE SEEDS OF LEARNING

One way to encourage firsthand knowledge of the world around us is to allow your child to care for a small houseplant. For a lesson in the life cycle, take a cutting of a philodendron or other plant already in the house. Put it in a water-filled container in the room so its growth can be charted.

If there's space on a sunny shelf, tabletop, or window sill, devote it to a small indoor garden. Besides plants, recommend that your resident Green Thumb nurture an avocado seed, a potato, or sprouts. All of these grow quickly in water, so their vines and shoots yield daily discoveries.

Many succulents and herbs, including parsley, chives, and oregano, grow well indoors, especially in pots on a sunny window sill. But no matter what part of the house an indoor herb garden occupies, involve your junior gardener in its watering routine with a small watering can and, if needed, child-sized garden gloves. For scaled-down implements, check plant or hardware stores or specialty catalogs.

Inside or out, real flowers and vegetation convey the message that life thrives all year. A local nursery is a good place to introduce the young to many flower varieties. Look at flower beds first; then examine seed packets with colorful pictures of specimens in bloom. Even if it's not the right time for planting, purchase some packets for bedroom pinups. In bleak weather, these small hangings lend a bright touch to the surroundings. Place them in a row on one or more walls and presto! A brilliant bouquet blooms day and night through any season.

For children with a serious interest in nature, a greenhouse window brings the outdoors in on a grand scale. With a step stool nearby, a child can tend to plants that grow here. Store a cleanup cloth within reach so that watering doesn't trigger problems.

GROWING CONCERNS

As for any subject worth cultivating, build a library of nature materials. Include books, binoculars, magnifying glass, flower press, and weather instruments. If possible, arrange them on a single shelf or in a particular drawer to create a focused interest area.

Here are some ideas you might consider:

- Hang botanical prints or nature posters on a bulletin board or wall. Include your child's own art, such as drawings of plant life or collages of nature discoveries.
- Mount a calendar with nature scenes on the wall or the back of a door so that the year unfolds through rich color photos.
- Arrange glow-in-the-dark stars on the ceiling to look like the constellations in the night sky.
- Create a display area for rocks, seashells, or similar treasures. Let individual finds become desktop paperweights, and gather larger collections in baskets or other containers. Small baby food jars can show off sand collected during trips to various beaches. Label the contents with the location of the find to teach a lesson about the variety of elements in the earth's outer layer.
- Play prerecorded cassette tapes of different outdoor sounds. Nature's "music," such as the sound of mountain streams and waterfalls, is soothing and inspirational.

COME RAIN OR SHINE

Because climate controls nature's disposition, it's a good idea to promote an understanding of it by setting up a small weather station. A child's bedroom window is a good location for this, since it affords a view of what's happening outside. Offer the opportunity to understand climate changes by hanging a rain gauge and thermometer outside within a child's view so that regular weather checks are easy to do. Indoors, place a barometer where it, too, can be read easily.

If there's a tree near your child's window, claim a branch for a birdhouse or feeder. Do-it-yourself versions work just as well as ready-made models. Building one from spare wood or Popsicle sticks is a great rainy day project.

A playful and practical canvas floorcloth creates an ideal balcony nature station for a junior gardener intent on cultivating an interest in growing things.

COUNTRY FRESH

As adults who love potpourri know, nature's sweet scents are too good to remain outdoors.

Teach an appreciation for fragrance by encouraging the collection of dried pine needles, lemon and orange rinds, lavender, and more.

Long after picking, these aromas linger. Close your eyes, inhale, and you're in the forest—or at least the backyard!

To give children's clothes an enduring fresh smell, keep some aromatic wood blocks in dresser drawers or closets. Visit the lumberyard or a carpenter's shop for scraps. Depending on where you live, offerings might include pine, redwood, cedar, and oak. For safety reasons, sand the blocks and round the edges to prevent splintering.

To give clothes an enduring fresh smell, foster the idea of keeping some wood blocks in drawers or closets.

A GARDEN OF MAKE-BELIEVE

While nothing replaces the actual beauty of nature, there are ways to reflect the seasons in your child's room. If allergies are involved, illusion may be the best way to foster an appreciation for the outdoors from a safe distance.

To create the illusion of spring or summer, look for material that follows a nature theme. Linens and spreads become large garden patches when fabric patterns blossom. With your child's help, pick sheets or material with a plant or floral motif to "plant" in areas of the room. With such touches, a child's world becomes a tropical rain forest, a wildflower preserve, or a country landscape.

Silk flowers and floral fabric create the look and feel of spring indoors even when nothing's blooming outdoors.

Add to the imitation garden effect by decorating the window sill with inexpensive flower boxes, such as long plastic floral containers filled with dried, silk, or handmade paper flowers and greenery. Secure the container to the window sill with double-sided tape. To reinforce seasonal changes, periodically change the contents by "replanting" it.

OUTSIDE IN

A room that conveys the look and feel of earthly delights encourages an appreciation for the environment. Today's nature lovers could very well be tomorrow's conservationists!

159

MAKING YOUR HOME ONE FOR THE BOOKS

Pillows propped behind them and light overhead, mother and child read a story chosen from the bookcase placed low by the bed, where a young reader has access to his library.

From a baby's initial look at a colorful vinyl book to a teen's exploration of unknown worlds in sci-fi novels, the desire for kids to further their knowledge depends heavily on how well such behavior is kindled at home.

Parents should test their child's room—along with the rest of the house—for reader-friendliness. The start of a new school term is a good time annually to check the place where you live for its reading potential, since homework often means doing that.

Whether an area is set aside for study time or story time, it should be quiet, comfortable and well lit. In tight spaces, that may translate to a nest of pillows on the bed. In spacious surroundings, it may mean a reading loft. In any case, the success factor hinges on whether or not the setup welcomes relaxation and concentration.

For inspiration and ideas, visit bookstores, libraries, or toy shops with children's reading corners. Or look through decorating magazines for window seats and alcoves that have been designed as seating areas that invite reading.

While you needn't sink big money into creating a custom haven for reading, you should put big thought into how inviting and accommodating it regularly will be for one or two readers. That's because you need to invest time in reading to your children in order to stimulate their interest, imagination, and language development. Let them also see you reading alone to demonstrate that grown-ups enjoy this activity. As studies continually show, homes that foster reading play a lead role in promoting literacy.

CHAPTER ONE

As basic as books are to reading and as enjoyable as building a personal library is, good reading environments don't depend on how many volumes are owned. A source of vast information, the library lends materials without charge. And millions of books are available annually from Reading Is Fundamental, an agency that enables young readers to pick the prose they prefer.

To live up to its reading potential, a room must have literature not only handy but accessible. A bookcase in a child's room ideally affords such availability and is important because it enables children to go there by themselves when they want to read. Keep it low if the one who will be reading is too short to reach high shelves.

THE THREE Bs

What else constitutes an environment conducive to reading? When polled by author and educational consultant Jim Trelease, lifetime readers indicated several similar traits.

Besides owning and regularly using a library card, what bookworms had in common were as vital to education as the 3 Rs. Described by Trelease as the 3 Bs, they are Books, Baskets (or boxes) to hold them, and Bed lamps. About the latter, be advised. Reading in bed may be the most important night school a child ever attends.

As every teacher knows, good readers aren't born that way. They develop the skill through interest fueled at home. Even the comics can fire that interest, according to research indicating that 90 percent of the top readers indulge in the funnies.

READER-FRIENDLY SETTINGS

Since a child's relationship with books often begins on a parent's lap, a big overstuffed chair or rocker is high on the list of furnishings that make reading pleasureable. But there are alternate arrangements that work just as well. Consider these:

- **The Bed:** Prop up some pillows and set the stage for a nap or bedtime story session, letting your child choose what's read.
- **The Floor:** Use pillows, futons, carpet squares, or bath mats to build a reading fortress or "island" on the floor.
- **Storage Cubes:** Stack them so it's easy for you and your child to read sitting side by side on cushions.

No one is ever too young or too old to be read to, insist child development specialists. Books may change, but the experience remains the active ingredient.

A NOOK FOR BOOKS

Part of the joy of reading is curling up with a good book and momentarily leaving the world behind. One of the coziest places to do that is a window seat like the kind in old houses.

A wonderful tuck-away, a window seat seems tailor-made for a grown-up and child eager to snuggle up to the delights of children's literature. Situated apart from everyday activity and cushioned for comfort, it's especially tempting during the day when natural light streams in. When filled with man-made illumination, it welcomes young readers at night or when it's dreary outdoors.

If your child's room lacks a window seat, look for an alcove a handyman can convert to a reading niche. Consult do-it-yourself storage guides for plans on building reading cubbies. Then choose a design with enough shelving for dictionaries and reference books so that a window seat also becomes a learning center.

To achieve the same effect without much expense, place a loveseat or overstuffed chair or stool in a window recess. If space allows, put shelves or a table next to it for reading matter. What also works in some alcoves is a flat trunk or chest padded so that a child can sprawl on top to read.

Well-lit corners throughout a home promote reading if comfortable seating is available and literature is handy.

NOVEL SITUATIONS

Imagine the lure of a loft where you look down upon a world you usually look up to. With little effort or money you can create this kingdom in the upper recesses of a child's closet.

Remove the closet door. Replace the upper rod with a sturdy shelf that supports a small child's body weight. Secure a safety bar for protection and a ladder for climbing. Then add the final touches—a good light and a padded foam mattress.

Loft beds and bunks also offer interesting possibilities as reading refuges. If only one sleep area is used, turn the other into a hideaway restricted to kids and storybook characters.

THE REST OF THE HOUSE

One of the best ways to foster continuing interest in reading is to keep diverse reading and writing materials all over the house. Even a bath and a kitchen should contain litera-ture, experts say, since captive moments alone often moti-vate one to pass the time reading. A couple other consid-erations include:

- **The Family Room Sofa:** Turn off the TV and gather the clan to the sofa for a reading pow-wow. Get extra comfy with afghans.

- **The Breakfast Nook:** As cozy as a window seat, this spot does double duty during non-meal hours as a reading retreat.

READING PROBLEMS

While you cultivate reading as a pleasureable pastime, bear this in mind. As with any developmental skill, chil-dren learn at different rates. If your child seems to have trouble reading age-appropriate material, it might be wise to have him or her evaluated for possible learning disabili-ties. Early intervention may prevent reading and school-work from becoming burdensome.

A BEST-SELLING PLOT

Like a beacon that draws ships in the night, comfortable, well-lit areas in a home invite all who pass to linger a while with a good book, a magazine, or other material. Beckon a child to curl up here and read, and watch the plot thicken in the next generation's life story.

A sturdy bookshelf positioned within reader reach encourages bookish behavior when good literature that interests a teen is stored there.

Nurturing The
First "R"—Reading

Introducing children to the wonders of reading involves more than decoding words and mastering their meaning.

It's an ongoing process that's dependent on how well you also keep them engaged in writing and other language skills.

To help motivate kids to read when they're away from school, experts suggest the following ways to create a home environment that's rich in words:

- Post personal notes for the kids on home bulletin boards.
- Put a special message in the lunch box to read at school.
- Let younger family members maintain the grocery list.
- Label objects in pictures and display them.
- Encourage joining a book club and/or becoming a pen pal.
- Subscribe to a magazine on a topic your child fancies.
- Look at newspapers together and comment on photographs.
- Play family word games at home and in the car.
- Give gift certificates to a bookstore on special occasions.
- Foster the idea of trading books with other young people.
- Audiotape your child reading favorite stories or poems. Played back, it will bolster language development and confidence.
- Buy or rent prerecorded tapes of children's stories. (Word to the Wise: Don't force your tastes on the listener.)
- Encourage beginning or developing writers to keep journals.
- Write a letter and let your child add a postscript.
- Limit TV viewing to free up time for reading and writing.

164

DECOR THAT SCORES BIG IN A SMALL WORLD

To a sports-minded kid, cheering home teams or school squads means more than watching games or yelling at every win and loss.

It means waving pom-pons and pennants, sporting team sweatshirts and caps, and amassing a conglomeration of treasures.

Whether players or spectators, kids collect memorabilia. If not personal ribbons, trophies, or athletic pins, it's professional posters, pennants, photos, or other paraphernalia.

Sports spawning all these items seem to grow in number like Olympic feats. In fall, it's football, soccer, and cross-country. Come winter, it's hockey, basketball, skiing, and ice skating. In other seasons, it's baseball, softball, tennis and track. Add year-round sports such as gymnastics, racketball, and swimming, and all the equipment and collectibles particular to each sport, and it starts to add up to a mountain of memorabilia.

How can a room reflect all the rah-rah regalia without setting records as a packrat's paradise? As with athletic games, it requires some rules and strategic play. Team up with your child to set them in motion and enjoy input and interaction.

FOR FANS OR FANATICS?

Recognizing the obsession that many have with sports, merchants have glutted the market with decor, many of it targeted to kids.

In myriad stores and catalogs, you'll find accessories galore, from phones shaped like helmets and lamps made with baseball bats, to youth beds modeled after racing cars. With so much available, it would be a snap to turn kid space into sports mecca.

Regardless of your budget or motivation to do so, resist the urge to create a mini sports kingdom. The reason? An overall theme time locks a setting. A child's ever-changing tastes guarantee a look will be outgrown long before items portraying it wear out. Once interest wanes, a theme room will annoy the very one it was meant to amuse. Besides, as a child cultivates other interests, there should be space for them to surface, too.

165

ZONING IN

For a young enthusiast bent on a sports motif, there are ways to satisfy cravings without bombarding a room with doodads. Focus on a special spot such as one wall or the closet door. Transform that area into a large bulletin board that continually changes with pinned-up ribbons, team photos, and other decorations.

An effective way to show off posters, art projects, and other large paper-thin memorabilia is to back them with foamboard, a lightweight polystyrene material that comes in easy-to-cut 4-by 8-foot white, black, or colored sheets. Available through craft or stationery stores, foamboard adheres to items spray mounted to it and gives a three-dimensional look once in place.

Besides foamboard or corkboard, pinups can also be mounted to a sheet of Homasote, a lightweight structural board. If you choose the latter, cover it in an open-weave fabric, such as burlap or wool, chosen by your child. To show off partisanship, narrow the choices to a favorite team's colors.

To create a zone that accommodates flat collectibles, cover a desktop with a sheet of $\frac{1}{8}$-inch clear acrylic. Now the underside can be used for display purposes. Items that may rate on-view status here include trading cards, sports photos, or ticket stubs from athletic events. To keep each piece of memorabilia in place, put a small piece of double-sided clear tape on the back.

In shared quarters, when siblings have separate tastes, avoid rivalry and hurt feelings by allowing each child to individualize a different zone. To a grown-up, the result may look like a crazy quilt of uncoordinated possessions, but to a young person this hodgepodge is his or her personal imprint.

CLIMBING THE WALLS WITH TEAM SPIRIT

For fun, function, and flexibility, designate sports treasures as art and hang them on a free surface at child eye level.

Plaques, helmets, and other sports mementos often make ideal wall decorations. Hang large

Helmets, plaques, and other sports decor tell the life story of the budding athlete who claims this room as private territory.

items individually but group small ones together, especially if they are similar. Huddled together, they form a collection that fosters pride in earned acquisitions. As a custom touch, attach a grouping to a paint- or fabric-covered board. Or arrange items interestingly in a plastic frame that comes apart easily. This makes changing or rearranging contents simple when new victories earn a budding athlete new awards.

Think "posters" if you want to make a big impact on the wall. But don't limit the choice to what's available in sports catalogs or stores. If there's a good photo of your child playing a game, have an inexpensive blowup made through a camera store.

One further note about posters: If limited wall space prohibits putting them there, turn your sights upward. The ceiling not only provides ample room for posters, but also allows a young person to gaze at something besides empty space when lying down.

Shelves do a good job, too, of accommodating sports items. If vertical space is at a premium, consider horizontal. Like the plate rack that may have lined a high wall in Grandma's dining room, a narrow shelf rimming the upper recesses of a child's world can work show-and-tell wonders. Choose a wrap-around shelf for every wall, or just over the windows, and allow trophies, autographed balls, and other treasures to signal home base for a sports faithful. Since most of the items here will be out of a child's reach, however, consult the one who owns them to determine which possessions will keep the ceiling company!

SPECIAL PLAYS

Plenty of other ideas pack a sporting punch. Consider:

- A row of pennants draped on a rod above a window or door.

- Caps or helmets placed on a hat rack or on decorative hooks.

- Toys or gear stored in a metal hoop-shaped wastebasket.

- Walls or accessories trimmed with wallpaper borders of professional team insignias, or one-of-a-kind borders or splashy magazine spreads featuring sports celebrities or events. Placed side by side, these pages add contemporary dash to a kid's room.

Placed on high for all to see and admire, these hard-earned ribbons and plaques, along with trophies not shown, rate the special status they deserve to encourage achievement. Treasures of another kind are housed in a custom wall cabinet for collectibles.

TIME OUT

As with team play, the desire for a sporting environment must come from your child and not from you. That's because the child's room should reflect his or her interests—not yours.

If sports or sporting events hold little or no attraction, don't force the issue. Instead, encourage nonsports activities that make your child feel good and bolster a developing ego. Promote displays of nonathletic treasures and underscore their importance as well as your approval.

Even when parent and child share sports enthusiasm, allow the emerging athlete or fan to make the call about its emphasis, or lack thereof, in personal quarters. A young person may or may not want to show off treasures such as ticket stubs or programs. Instead, he or she may prefer keeping small mementos in a box of "valuables," pasting them in a scrapbook, or tucking them away in individual vinyl pocket pages punched to fit a three-ring binder.

A WIN-WIN SITUATION

Personal space that reflects sports interest or ability can be as beneficial as a healthy dose of fair competition. It not only contributes to well-being if it mirrors a child's accomplishments, it also builds interest in worthwhile activity—whether amateur or professional performance.

A NEW SLANT
ON PHYSICAL FITNESS

Burning off youthful energy comes naturally outdoors where playgrounds, athletic fields, and open spaces invite physical activity.

But what about an indoor home environment? How can it serve a child who needs to flex growing muscles?

Considering the declining stamina of youth gauged in recent years from endurance runs and fitness studies, regular exercise needs to supplement school and extracurricular physical education programs. That's where home can play a significant role. If the environments where children live encourage exercise, they will motivate young people to change their sedentary lifestyle and spend time away from computer games and TV.

With simple equipment, minimal expense, and a little effort, a child's room can function part-time as a small-scale exercise center.

Encouraging workouts at home for 6-year-olds and up fosters positive self-image and a sense of achievement in comfortable, noncompetitive surroundings. Such a program provides a regular opportunity to release tension and develop coordination, with parental guidance.

Instilling the desire to stay fit emphasizes the important connection between a healthy body and a sound mind. If your kids aren't members of athletic teams or don't play sports because of physical limitations, then all the more reason to provide a home arena for fitness.

As with any exercise program, consult your physician first. Once the green light is given, prevent exercise-related accidents and unwanted doctor visits by requiring that warm-ups precede workouts to prevent strains, pulls, and cramps.

A mini trampoline keeps this young exerciser active. Positioned near adult equipment, it also encourages a family fitness routine.

HOME TRAINING

Whether a corner of a kid's room or a basement gym, the area where exercise takes place should feature the following:

Comfort and Quiet: Exercise rids the body of stress, so a relaxing atmosphere is important. If the only available spot is not peaceful, and soundproofing is out of the question, let audio or video workout tapes or appropriate music stifle unwanted noise.

Good Ventilation: Ideally, fresh air should circulate during workouts, so open a window, weather permitting. Otherwise, a portable fan can keep the air flowing.

A Safe Space: If one area of a room can't be permanently designated for fitness equipment, the space cleared should be away from furniture or sharp objects that could cause injury if your child slips or falls during exercise. To be on the safe side, check equipment periodically to be sure bolts and springs are safely secured and not broken.

A Laundry Area: Keep a hamper nearby so sweaty clothes can be discarded for the wash. Be sure there's a dry towel nearby, too, so a child cooling down after exercising can wipe off perspiration from hands and equipment.

STRETCHING IT

To channel some of a child's energy safely and promote flexibility, provide a padded floor mat especially if the floor is not carpeted.

A vinyl mat with a cushy foam core softens the bangs and bumps of a would-be gymnast and is an ideal surface on which to stretch and do other exercises. It also keeps the noise level down.

For easy storage, buy a mat that folds up to fit under a bed or in a closet. Considering the action this equipment will endure, invest in a tough nylon tear-resistant binding.

KEEPING IN STEP

For budding dancers intent on developing balance and coordination, home practice is a good way to keep limber.

Inside a closet door or against a free wall, establish a ballet area with a dance bar made from a simple wood dowel like the kind that serves as a bannister. Within viewing range, hang a long mirror so a dancer can observe his or her progress. An ideal setup would be to mount a standard closet rod and shelf bracket on each side of a mirror. Be sure there's enough space between brackets for a 2-inch dowel at least 3 feet long.

As endurance levels increase, add a mini trampoline to build lower leg muscles in the same way a jump rope would. A child may find trampoline activity pure fun, but it is extremely worthwhile from a health standpoint. For safety's sake, however, set some guidelines so no one attempts any circus antics. When not in use, this lightweight equipment, about the size of an inner tube, can be stored under the bed.

Once everything in this special corner is in place, alert the performer: Turn on the music. Put on dancing shoes. Feel the rhythm of aerobic exercise!

STRENGTHENING GROWING MUSCLES

Just as important as a home fitness curriculum encouraging flexibility is one fostering muscle strength. By the time a child reaches preteen years and outgrows simple gymnastics, he or she may be ready for more challenging equipment such as a slant board.

Designed for sit-ups and other exercises that strengthen stomach muscles, it literally slants against a wall at different angles. Minimize cost by making a do-it-yourself version. Buy a 2-foot wide solid wood plank that's long and thick enough to accommodate your child's height. Sand, smooth, and finish it. Then, at one end of the board, drill two holes that will fit over two strong utility hooks anchored to the wall 18 inches from the floor. Twelve inches down from the same end of the board, attach a soft vinyl or leather strap to snugly hold the exerciser's ankles in place during sit-ups. This same strap allows a child to do other exercises, incuding knee tucks and leg raises.

Let body weight dictate when it's time to replace a homemade slant board with a ready-made, heavy-duty freestanding model.

If there isn't enough space in your child's room for a slant board, a sit-up board is an alternate option. A free door is all it takes to assemble this simple device with a padded bar and mounting bracket that attaches easily without tools under a door. This equipment allows for a range of exercises from basic sit-ups to double leg raises.

Upper body exercises are within arm's length with a horizontal pull-up bar specifically designed for doorway installation. Sporting goods stores sell the solid chrome, adjustable kind that expand to fit securely between door jambs. To ensure stability, buy one with safety catches and easy-to-install support brackets. But set some ground rules. A pull-up shouldn't be used for horseplay or by more than one child at a time. Nor should it be used by an adult exceeding the mechanism's weight limit given in the directions.

When it's time for a workout, this teen takes off for her closet to use the pull-up bar permanently installed between the door jambs.

CHASING THE CLOCK

As fascinating as fitness equipment is, it might not interest a child with a busy schedule. Parents concerned about their child staying in shape can help by joining in the act.

Establishing a family fitness routine is a good way to encourage participation by the younger generation. Along with purchasing equipment and setting up the fitness area, this joint project strengthens the bond between siblings and parents while providing an active, enjoyable means for family members to interact.

FOREVER FIT

As important as fitness is, it's crucial to see that your child doesn't overdo exercise, since injury could result. While a workout should be challenging, it should not be painful. Make sure your child knows to tell you if he or she feels pain or exhaustion.

Getting in shape requires time as well as commitment. The ultimate reward is good health not only during childhood but throughout adulthood as well.

CHAPTER 6

SPECIAL CHALLENGES

Children with special challenges.

It's a phrase often used to describe kids that are physically restricted. But if that's the only image conjured, you're seeing only part of the picture..

Young people face all kinds of special challenges. Often they are as inescapable as physical limitations and as unpredictable as the weather. Consider these situations that may induce thunderous turmoil for millions of kids every day:

- Like a sudden downpour, a new sibling storms into the world. Ready or not, the arrival may mean adjusting to a brother or sister cohabiting a room that was once private territory.

- Like a tornado, a family move puts a household in spin cycle. Besides being uprooted from familiar surroundings, the change of address may translate to cramped kidspace or to plain, uninspired rental space where modification is out of the question.

- Like an earthquake, parental split-up cracks a home into separate residences. In the aftershocks of reestablishing living situations, a child hopscotches between both sites.

- For some kids, the weather alone is a challenge to conquer. Allergic to mold and mites caused by climatic conditions, they cope with what's indoors as well as what's out.

◄ *Ladderlike redwood bars support shelving and the small ones who head for this hideaway, an oddly located closet cubicle otherwise inaccessible.*

173

And all young people, including those inexperienced with any of these situations, face the challenge of growing pains. By the time the teen years hit, the Battle Against Babyhood means conflict with any vestiges of childhood days. The struggle then calls for tactics to convince the world of fledgling maturity.

Coping with childhood's special challenges takes more than grit on the part of the one experiencing it. It also takes gumption, especially for parents eager to ease life's real or imagined burdens for the person they brought into the world.

What's the solution to these problematic situations? In part, perhaps it's for parents to cushion their children's personal environments, since that's where they spend the most time and where they recharge their fragile egos. In some cases, it takes only a few helpful aids—personal photos strategically placed or private nooks established—to eliminate "bumps in the night," or in the day, for that matter.

As you and your son or daughter weather together the storms that sprinkle childhood, consider the shelter afforded by the ideas in this section. They may be what enables someone young to conquer a barrier and go forward in life.

ELIMINATING THE SQUEEZE IN TIGHT QUARTERS

It's no secret that the smallest bedrooms are usually consigned to kids.

But while confining, cozy quarters can certainly be just as functional and enjoyable as larger ones. It all begins with ingenuity—either yours or someone else's.

In the stretch to accommodate a child in a tight living situation, there are courses of action worth investigating. Sometimes it takes a skillful closet organizer to create efficient storage solutions. Or sometimes it calls for a proficient designer to plan the space. Whether you or an outsider masterminds the solution, however, it often requires two-for-one strategy so that a single furnishing performs two functions.

Easing the frustration in a room that stifles work and play also may depend on a visual trick or two. But more on that later.

OUT OF THE CHAOS

Finding sufficient storage is the biggest hurdle to overcome in a squeeze situation. To survey the scene at its maximum potential, remove all clutter to another location. Before stuffing everything back into original resting places, stretch your imagination by considering the following stowaway options. All of these can promote orderliness—quite possibly an easier task for kids if they help decide what goes where.

Light, airy furnishings help open up these cramped quarters for Raggedy Ann, Raggedy Andy, and their young human friend.

Under the Bed: So much childhood play takes place on the floor, why not put dead space under a bed to work by keeping playthings there in containers? Deep plastic basins or cardboard boxes work fine, but the easiest containers for a kid to use are roll-out bins made for this purpose. Sold at furniture stores, bins come in varied sizes. Since some may not fit under your child's bed, measure available space first before investing in one.

Behind the Bed: Depending on its design, a headboard with closed storage compartments can house everything from extra bedding to books and a radio. Above the headboard, secure narrow shelves for stuffed animals and other lightweights that can't harm a sleeper if toppled.

Up the Wall: If there's no place to go but up the walls, climb them! In other words, take advantage of vertical space by comandeering them for shelves. For an interesting effect, stagger them on the wall. To maximize space near the ceiling, hang a shelf on high for trophies, ribbons, and other items that rate prominence but not day-to-day handling or access.

By the Window: In a window alcove like a bay, have a handyman build a lidded enclosure and use it as storage space. Cushion the top, and it becomes a seat.

Behind a Door: Many household organizers fit behind doors and can corral kid stuff just as easily as everyday items. One catch-all that's fun and functional is a hanging shoe pocket used for school supplies and whatnots.

Odd Nooks: Is your child's room under the eaves? Turn that slanted cranny into open storage with shelves angled to fit. Are there a few inches between an entry or closet doorway and the wall? Put them to good use with narrow floor-to-ceiling, made-to-fit shelves just right for storing tiny treasures.

THE "OTHER ROOM" IN THE ROOM

Look to the closet for more hidden space opportunities. Remove the door, revamp the insides and discover a gold mine in usable space.

Budget permitting, consult a space organizer to make the most of this area. Otherwise, take matters into your own hands after scouring magazines and books for ideas.

A doorless closet opens up a room, but if it's too chilling to contemplate open storage in a child's room, rest easy. With a pull curtain on a rod or vertical blinds, contents can be hidden when necessary.

To make a closet space-efficient, consider these details:

- Two adjustable clothes rods hung 30 inches apart and raised as dictated by your child's growth.

- Storage drawers lined along the floor.

- A closet divided in two with split-level clothes rods on one side and stacked adjustable open shelves on the other. In a double closet with sliding doors you might allocate half the area for the dresser. This frees main floor space in the bedroom.

For a very young child, the closet is enticing play space. Lower and reinforce the top shelf, and it becomes a play loft once you add a cushion, safety bars, and a ladder with sturdy dowels. Take advantage of loft storage possibilities by keeping stuffed play pals here. Under-the-loft space-saving ideas include a study area made by bridging storage units with a painted or laminated board.

DUAL-PURPOSE DESIGNS

Put twofold furnishings to work for more breathing room.

Like building blocks, modular units assume split personalities, depending on configuration. Used singly, they act as low storage; used one upon the other, they turn into wall units.

A high bookcase or two placed well become a room divider. To make them sturdier when placed side by side, bolt them together.

A series of custom bookcases staggered in height to form steps show another alter ego—a play staircase. When there's a loft above, this may be an interesting alternative to a ladder. As easy as it is to achieve custom stairs with standard bookcases of varying height, make sure a furniture unit is designed with that purpose in mind. If bookcases are used this way, be sure to bolt them together for safety in climbing.

Other dual-purpose designs include:

- Futon chairs that flip open as sleep units or padded tumbling mats.

- Low chests and trunks topped with a pad for seating.

- Free-standing cupboards like armoires that serve myriad uses, from storing belongings to accommodating electronic gear.

- Loft beds with built-in study areas below, or platform beds supported by storage drawers that are ready-made for multi-use.

- Murphy beds that fold into storage cabinets, allowing floor space to remain open when they are closed. These provide a unique solution to the problem of multi-use space.

WAVING THAT MAGIC WAND

Practical considerations aside, there are whimsical ways to deal with this issue.

A few decorating ploys, such as art that appears three-dimensional, fool the eye into believing a room is bigger than actual size. In tight spaces, they spell relief as well as magic!

What looks like a closet facade actually keeps a Murphy bed hidden and the floor open for daytime activity. Open shelving, including some that wraps around the corner, also lends a spacious look to this otherwise confined space.

When placed so most of the area is within view, reflective material appears to double a setting's dimensions. In the same way that a mirrored wall in a restaurant "enlarges" a site, full-length mirrored closet doors visually expand the space they reflect. Place treasures within range, and double the number of collectibles seen when looking at their mirror image.

Color also creates a sense of spaciousness if the walls, woodwork, window and floor coverings all match. Paint furnishings the same color, and the overall monochromatic effect increases the optical illusion. Keep in mind that light colors give the impression of open space; dark ones do the reverse.

A wall of floor-to-ceiling windows, minimal furniture, and a light color scheme all contribute to the openness of tight kids' quarters carved from a one-bedroom condo's living room balcony. Besides limited space, there was limited time to complete the project for two young boys moving in with Dad on a post-haste basis following divorce.

To convert the balcony to living space, ever clever New York designer Joan Halperin quickly enclosed the $6\frac{1}{2}$- by 12-foot area with glass and finished it as an interior room with

Like a small cabin of a seaworthy vessel, this balcony-cum-bedroom functions by utilizing every square inch. The sleep units accommodate storage, and the walls handle books and display.

When space is tight, decorating tricks can ease the situation. A monochromatic scheme like this one expands the space visually, as does using one side of the closet for dresser storage.

heating, gypsum wallboard, and recessed lights. Using a ship's cabin as inspiration, she built two beds to fit an "L", with the smaller one suspended over the longer one. Three deep drawers were tucked into the side of the high bed's platform and under the base of the other bed. Bookshelves on high provided more storage. To create homework surface without bulk, a desktop fitted with drawers was suspended at the opposite end of the long balcony.

Overlooking the Manhattan skyline and Hudson River from the New Jersey side, the Halperin remodel is breathtaking at night. "With its dramatic view of city lights and twinkling stars, it looks like a sky-box in space," the designer remarks.

Another urban highrise setting shy on space was transformed into spacious-looking teen quarters by Anita Goldblatt, *Allied ASID*. Besides adding built-ins that hug the walls, her ingenious solution for opening up the room was to draw the eye upward to the setting's new focal points. These include open shelving that wraps around part of the walls and a custom Murphy bed that is topped with an architectural pediment cut with a central hole for added interest. By using fabric-covered cork to cover part of the remaining wall space, clutter is kept to a minimum and the teen's posters, charts, and papers needn't vie for pinup status.

STRETCHING THE LIMITS

Obviously, the illusion of spaciousness doesn't dent the problem of confinement. But it may prevent the feeling of claustrophobia.

As the balcony conversion proves well, having a small room doesn't have to be a limiting experience. Face the problem head on with your child as a joint challenge to conquer, and learn together a lesson in ingenuity.

Keeping A Kid's Room
Clutter Free

When it comes to cramped quarters, a kid's room requires constant spring cleaning.

The best way to fight overcrowding is to establish a regular routine for eliminating discarded, broken, and outgrown items.

Let the annual school book benefit or community clothing drive for the homeless signal times for children to weed through personal libraries and wardrobes. This not only underscores the need to rid their lives of clutter, but also instills the humanitarian value of contributing regularly to those less fortunate.

To encourage someone young to make room for what the future holds, keep lesser-used belongings out of the room on a revolving basis. Child development specialist Susan Isaacs explains the exchange system in her book *How to Organize Your Kid's Room.*

"When a child doesn't use something but doesn't want to give it up," Isaacs explains, "put it in the exchange system box. When one toy is put back in the room, another has to be put in the exchange system."

For efficiency, a rotation schedule is suggested at intervals you decide upon and mark on your calendar.

"Don't fight with your child about throwing out or keeping items," the mother of three further advises. "If he wants to keep something, let him. But if he is ambivalent, set up an exchange system or storage place. If there's no spark of interest when an item rotates back, you can be certain your child has outgrown it."

179

WHEN THE ROOM I CALL "MINE" IS REALLY "OURS"

Four walls.

Two children.

One challenge—design a room that works for more than one. Whose tastes surface? Whose tastes remain submerged?

In the ideal situation, a room accommodating two or more young people reflects each one's character. With children, that often translates to private quarters with a split personality where one child's area may be methodically organized and the other's haphazardly arranged.

Parents trying to comprehend a jumbled childhood scene might do well to realize that children, whether rooming together or apart, deserve the chance to develop in their own distinct ways. In other words, sharing a room doesn't mean sharing the same needs and desires.

ONE BY ONE

Take each child aside separately to discover his or her preferences.

Start by asking questions about sleep and study areas, keeping the absent child in mind throughout. For instance, after asking the one at hand, "Where will you sleep?" then add, "Where will your sister (or brother) sleep?"

Take time to reinforce the message that final decisions will depend on joint approval, including yours.

Once each child has had a chance to visualize and verbalize privately about the room of his or her dreams, bring both together to share their thoughts and consider compromises. On areas where they agree, compliment them for having the same good idea. Where they differ, guide them in negotiations.

If both want to sleep on the top level of a bunk bed, for example, work out an arrangement whereby both can. Simply divide the year into alternate months and allow each to have top billing in the time assigned to him or her. By tactfully offering tangible solutions that allow each to win and neither to lose, you not only avoid sibling rivalry but also hurt feelings.

DUAL IMPRINTS

Ultimately, in a shared room, each child wants to know that somewhere his or her personal imprint is taking hold.

To a young collector, this may mean simply propping a mountain of stuffed animals on a bed.

To a budding artist, it may mean displaying personal creations on one particular wall.

In a child's mind, each visual image creates impact. Therefore, the differences in a room two share make all the difference in the world.

Parents may view their children's mutual quarters as a hodgepodge of possessions and a crazy quilt of tastes and interests. But in their children's eyes, the fact that this space caters to both personalities is what makes it work on a daily basis. For that reason, try to be open minded about allowing a mixture of furnishings that don't necessarily coordinate. Or, if you prefer, take measures guaranteed to satisfy all sides, including yours. Here are a few ways to do this:

For the triplets who share this space, individuality surfaces on and behind their beds, where color preference and initials tell the story of each distinct personality.

Reversible Fabric: Mix or match bed linens for the roommates in your household by acquiring two reversible bedcovers or comforter covers that match on one side and are different on the other to indicate each child's choice. When the room is occupied, allow those living there to determine which side of the cover is face up on their respective beds. Otherwise, keep the look uniform.

Colored Light Bulbs: Individualize parts of a room with colored light bulbs that respond to each child's preference. An inexpensive touch, they

Painting a room in half horizontally to reflect individual taste gives each bunkmate a sense of self. Keeping bulletin boards by each sleeper's bed also differentiates territory.

also help to evoke a certain mood during holidays or other special times. Be careful how often you allow this kind of lighting to fill a child's room. While enjoyable at playtime, colored bulbs should be replaced for study so that reading and writing are done in appropriate light.

Paper Capers: Tell a tale of two dwellers by lining the bottom of storage containers and dresser drawers with patterned paper reflecting the user's taste. To keep costs down, consider decorative wrapping paper as lining material. When storage is closed, the look is consistent, but when it's open, it's an altogether different story.

COLORING THEIR WORLD

Just as a room for a single child should show off that child's color preference, so should a room for two cater to both children's preferences.

If the same shades of the spectrum don't appeal to those sharing space, simply divide the room's color scheme, perhaps by painting the lower half one color and the upper half another. This treatment works especially well for those with bunk beds who can surround themselves at naptime with the part of the rainbow they favor.

If your budget is limited, concentrate on a smaller area. Encouraging your children to select their own sheets is another way to allow individual color preference to surface. The pleasure that comes from creating a customized comfort zone may add greatly to a good night's sleep.

Colored blotters, area rugs, and small throw pillows provide additional ways to delineate territory without spending much money. They also emphasize what belongs to whom—a message that can be carried through in the bath with washcloths and toothbrushes color coded for each child.

A PLACE TO BE PRIVATE

Just as adults need quiet time alone once in a while, so do children require solitude periodically. Carving out private space in a room two share is possible in many ways, starting with a room divider.

Decorative folding screens offer a simple solution to the need for divided space. If you can't afford one, make your own from trellis material, stretched canvas or large pieces of scrap plywood that can be painted or wallpapered to look more attractive.

Still other ideas that afford privacy include:

Sliding Screens: Reminiscent of oriental shoji panels, sliding screens provide as much privacy as a child desires. When moved along on a track, panels can stack to one side to open up the space, or line up to close it off. Besides using wood panels or a wood frame covered in fabric, you can achieve this effect with sturdy translucent material similar to the white rice paper used in shoji screens.

Stograge Cubes: The modular, stackable variety act as an ideal partition, creating nooks and crannies where open space once existed. Filled with books and other personal belongings, they act as barriers that offer some seclusion when desired.

Curtains: Just as hospital curtains do in a room for two patients, fabric hung along a rod can transform open space into sectioned quarters. As sleep or personal needs dictate, areas may be cordoned off to shield them from intrusive eyes. One inexpensive way to make these fabric dividers is with king size sheets.

Closets: As an alcove for work or play, a closet can provide a reprieve from a central area and from another person. In a room that demands closeness, a closet may be just the retreat for a kid seeking a bit of privacy. You can create a haven by removing the closet door and raising or removing the lower clothes rod to accommodate a low storage unit topped with a cushion. After stacking belongings on high shelves, be sure to add light.

Solving the privacy needs of two when space is designed for one calls for clever tactics. One solution is to create a divider that either keeps the space open and airy when the mood calls for camaraderie, or separates room dwellers when quiet time is preferred.

If none of these ideas appeal to you, look around elsewhere for space your children can use. Attics, enclosed porches, recesses and nooks formed by dormers and eaves might be ideal settings for spillover childhood activities. Used this way, such locations welcome child's play and child's work.

Beyond these measures, there's one other alternative to solving the occasional need for privacy. Set aside time regularly for each child to be in mutual quarters alone. If both parties agree, time alone could be spent playing music, spreading out playthings, or just enjoying solitude.

A SPECIAL BOND

Coexisting in a room with a brother or sister is rarely an easy experience day in and day out. But the bonding that may result from sharing common ground can endure a lifetime and inspire everlasting role models.

HOW DESIGN CAN BRIDGE THE DIVIDE IN SHARED CUSTODY

Whether shared custody means dividing the month evenly between parents or splitting the arrangement otherwise, it's not easy to smooth the wrinkles for a child caught in the strands of divorce.

Even in the best of times, a transitory existence for someone young can mean confusion and insecurity. When caused by a family split-up, the stress factor escalates— unless there is love, understanding, and continuity.

With so many issues, such as school and activities, coming into play, a child's personal space may be overlooked by parents. Considering how much environment influences development, however, surroundings are extremely important, especially in a home setting where kids spend the most time.

What can be done in dual residences to foster continuity? How can topsy-turvy feelings be quelled while shifting homes?

Some psychologists and educators believe comforting touches can cushion the experience of being uprooted. How soothing creature comforts are, however, depends on parents' attitudes and behavior, which heighten or diminish the trepidation of continual change.

CONTROLLING THE EMOTIONAL CLIMATE

Since no two families are alike, there are no clear-cut rules to smooth the wrinkles of coparenting. But there are guidelines.

"Kids can adjust to a lot if parents respect each other and there's no conflict between them," says Rosemarie Bolen, director of Kids' Turn, a San Francisco Bay Area agency dedicated to alleviating the anxiety of kids in family breakups by teaching parents to cooperate.

"When there's coordination and cooperation," Bolen emphasizes, "kids get better accustomed to different family structures like dining in both homes even if one is vegetarian and the other isn't."

A child's clothing is one issue divorced parents would do well to coordinate, Bolen maintains. "It's better when kids don't have to drag clothes back and forth; it saves a lot of arguing."

Shuttling other belongings, however, is a different matter.

"There is a comfort level when you have things nearby that belong to you," says psychologist and news commentator Dr. Joyce Brothers. "In the same way older people like to take some favorite belongings to a nursing home, so do children."

Objects that comfort kids, Brothers explains, can be as ordinary as a pillow or as special as scented soap. "Smell is very close to your emotions," she says, "even your own scent." Regarding soap, she comments that it's a tiny expense to absorb so that a child can use it in both homes to derive some comfort.

To facilitate moving things from place to place, allow a child to transport preferred items in a small carryall such as a backpack. But don't place unreasonable restrictions on what those items can be or even make suggestions about them.

"Stay out of it," Dr. Brothers advises. "Let the child choose. If it's a gift that belongs to the child, be enchanted that they think it's so special, they want to take it with them."

Not surprisingly, some kids want to share the journey between Mom's and Dad's respective homes with a four-footed friend. "It's a companion you can cuddle," explains renowned psychologist Dr. Judith Wallerstein of the internationally recognized Center for the Family in Transition. Because it's important that a child's interests be taken seriously, she recommends that parents consult with their young ones about these matters.

"One 8-year-old always talked about his bird. It was his closest ally," she confides. "His central concern during the divorce was 'Where would the bird go?' " Another child she recalls made parent-to-parent treks with the same houseplant in tow.

Distance and the pet or plant in question dictate whether or not it can be transported. If there's doubt about the former, check with a veterinarian before investing in a proper carrying case.

Whether animal or plant life, a living thing that accompanies a child back and forth, Wallerstein reasons, is a companion. "It's symbolic but real," she maintains, "and if it's an interest of the child, it should be taken seriously.

"Allowing a child to carry something back and forth—not a new toy but something that has emotional feeling—is a way to provide a sense of continuity," adds Wallerstein. Having counseled more than 6,500 children of divorce since 1971, she's convinced that objects to which a child has emotional attachment instill a feeling of security that may lessen stress.

"Help a child feel at home and comfortable," Wallerstein continues, "and you won't get as many symptoms (headaches, stomach aches, edginess, etc.) that often come with transition."

To ease adjustment to double living situations, involve your child in decisions about his or her personal quarters in each home. "Children often feel very peripheral and like an intruder," says Wallerstein, "especially if there is a child or children in the household they're going to." For this reason, she says, it's extremely good to involve the transitional child in what that child wants to put in his or her personal space. "Divorced children have a real loss of 'Who am I?', a feeling that they're gypsies. Being able to recognize themselves and their room therefore has its advantages," Wallerstein explains.

Concurs Brothers: "If you can, let a child choose the room color." Or at least consult with children, she suggests, about what they'd like in their environment. Letting them participate in these matters may contribute to their level of comfort, says Brothers.

GETTING PERSONAL

Because divorced people often remarry other parents, unrelated kids often become part-time roommates. To prevent the transitional child from feeling like an invader when he or she lives in shared territory, experts offer the following tips:

✔ Set aside a shelf, a corner, or another area that conveys the notion of private territory that can be left undisturbed.

✔ Let treasures be stored in a box that locks for privacy.

✔ Display a child's artistry in both locations.

✔ Pick a place where a mess can be made without disruption.

✔ Hang a drawing of the route between Mom's and Dad's homes with familiar sites so a child formulates a mental map and knows he or she isn't at the end of the earth on drop-off days.

✔ Duplicate a pattern or color on each bed or another area. It can be as general as stripes or as specific as a particular Laura Ashley print. But let your child select it, says Laura Ashley designer Judy Mashburn, whose experience proves that kids often pick a more adult pattern than a parent would choose for them. A tip: If fabric chosen for one room has matching wallpaper border, repeating the look is as easy as putting a tiny strip of the border around a visible keepsake box.

SEEING IS BELIEVING

If a young person in a move-around lifestyle feels like a nomad, viewing photos of them-selves with others may offer a context of belonging. One educator suggests putting two photos by a child's bed; one with the family and one alone but happily engaged in activ-ity. The effect? A lasting impact of being loved and capable.

"People use photos at times of change to cope with crisis," says University of Tennessee family life educator Anna Mae Kobbe, who is researching the meaning and display of fam-ily photos at home. It's important, she believes, for kids with two families to view photos of themselves with each group to feel a signifi-cant part of each.

Kids' Turn director Bolen agrees.

"Pictures of both parents in both homes give the message to the child that the parent whose home they're in, values their relation-ship with the other parent and the other par-ent's relationship in their life." She adds: "It doesn't have to be a family picture of them all together nor does it have to be anywhere except in the child's room."

If friction might occur should certain images be displayed, simply allow those pictures to be kept in a wallet or a locket.

TURNING LEMON INTO LEMONADE

As disruptive as shared custody is to a child, it needn't be destructive. Like so many other happenings that affect our lives, it can be a growing experience.

"It's hard at first. You have to make adjust-ments," Brothers concedes, "but in the long run going from one household to another can teach a child there isn't just one way of doing things."

Meaningful playthings such as a keepsake box decorated in a familiar pattern, help cushion the ongoing transition from one parent's home to another's when identical boxes are kept at both sites.

A Game That Guides
Children Of Divorce

Whether heading over the river and through the woods or across town into a high rise, kids on the go between one divorced parent's house and another's often feel lonely and uprooted.

That's no surprise to Dr. Judith Wallerstein. Her landmark 15-year study on effects of family breakdown on children shows lingering stress, a jarring finding considering the assumption that time heals all wounds.

"I was startled 10 years into the study to find how green, vivid and powerful children's memories still were," says the psychologist and author of *Second Chances*. The book reveals that 10 and 15 years after divorce many kids deal with the pain even if parents don't. Why? Parents may find new spouses, but children can't find new parents and don't want to.

To help young persons cope with the confusion and fear that divorce initially causes, the Center for the Family in Transition, which Wallerstein directs, developed a board game as a communication tool between parent and child. The Visiting Game is geared to 4- to 8-year-olds and parents looking for ways to discuss new realities. It may be played with up to four children.

The game's 38 cards cover a range of issues, including changes in routine and other post-divorce family challenges. Repeated play, the Center claims, may help kids overcome anxieties.

For more information about the game, contact the Center for the Family in Transition, 5725 Paradise Drive, Builiding B, Suite 300, Corte Madera, CA 94925.

A favorite pillow, game, or pet cat can be a reassuring travel companion for a child living a transitory existence between two homes.

A ROOM FOR A CHILD FACING PHYSICAL CHALLENGES

Turn back the pages of time to your first grade classroom and envision it.

Chalk-smeared blackboards . . .

Ink-smeared notebooks . . .

Dirt-smeared faces fresh from play . . .

As you recall specific images, enlarge the picture. Include your student perch—that big, bulky school desk so deep and high your feet can't touch the floor.

Now flip the pages of memory forward to the day you returned all grown up to that same classroom. Gazing around, your eyes fall once more on the weathered seat you once occupied. How small and confining it seems now, doesn't it? How could you ever have fit your frame into that desk and chair? Imagine trying to use it now.

As you reenter the present day, reflect on the previous picture. Fuzzy as it may be to you, it's very much in focus for physically challenged children. Every day they ask themselves, "How will I fit in that space or that piece of furniture structured for someone free of handicaps?"

Fortunately, the picture is changing. Today kids with physical limitations have a good chance of conquering an environment built without them in mind. With the passage of the ADA (Americans with Disabilities Act) in 1993, they can now look forward to accessing all public places, including those not previously considered barrier free.

But what about overcoming obstacles in their personal settings? Since private residences needn't conform to ADA, is it worth the expense to tailor a home for someone with special needs?

Without doubt, children who face physical challenges require special consideration. Nowhere is this more important than in their own bedrooms, where they probably spend the most time.

DESIGN WITH A DIFFERENCE

Just as a child with no handicaps flourishes in individualized surroundings, so does a child with physical challenges. Whether temporarily restricted by an accident or permanently confined to a wheelchair, a child will undoubtedly thrive in settings fostering independence and self reliance.

No one knows this better than Florida interior designer and author Susan Behar, *ASID*, a national leader in the movement of design that's accessible to all without looking utilitarian or different from what's standard. As a parent of a child who uses a wheelchair, years ago Behar witnessed firsthand how frustrating most residential design can be for the physically challenged. Her commitment to alter restrictions in daughter Jessie's private world drove home a powerful message upon completion. An enabling environment can open the door to independence wider for the disabled than many, including disabled people themselves, might believe possible.

"It's important not to predetermine limitations," Behar says. "People go beyond what we feel they can do."

To heighten the abilities of her clients in their immediate surroundings, Behar dedicates herself to providing details that make a difference. A music-oriented child with multiple disabilities, for instance, was enabled to control a radio for the first time in her life when the designer located a toggle switch in her bedside security niche. Not surprisingly, its installation initially instigated the sound of music long into the night!

Sensitive to the limitations a wheelchair places upon someone continuously seated, Behar is very attuned to widening a child's life experiences from that position. Residential features she has provided for kids in wheelchairs include windows and aquariums placed at eye level; roll-out toy bins situated under window seats; raised garden areas provided on adjacent balconies, and extra wide closets with recessed doors and clothes rods lowered for completely unrestricted access to belongings.

Attentive to caregivers, too, Behar values the importance of design that not only facilitates the role of the

A change area that resembles a window seat, and a safety railing that looks like wall art, add comfort in an attractive way to this setting for a child with physical challenges.

caregiver, but also looks attractive. In the home of a child with multiple disabilities, for example, she designed the change area with a wood railing that prevented accidental falls. When not in use, the ladder-like design hangs Shaker style on the side wall, where it looks more like a piece of art than a functional object.

"Very few ever dream about what can occur when barriers are removed," Behar points out. "People want to make life easier for children facing barriers. They don't think of it as a fun project, yet it's all that and more when design opens the door that provides the first step towards independence."

SAFETY FIRST

From the location of the outlets to the height of the furnishings, design is a critical factor in a room for a special child.

To identify problems that might exist, begin with an overall room check. Be on guard for furnishings and architectural details that could hinder or endanger your child, such as unmanageable hardware and slippery floor coverings.

Next, observe your child's daily routine from dressing and bathing to playing and getting ready for bed. Watch how easily or not-so-easily these activities are done. For example, if a wheelchair is used, take note of the following:

✔ Is there trouble clearing doorways and rotating direction?

✔ Is it easy to grasp doorknobs and light switches?

✔ Are cabinets too deep to access what's in the rear?

Once you know what problems exist, decide what improvements could be made to facilitate tasks.

To prevent continual frustration, see that everyday items are within hand reach. Height, distance, and grasp are crucial if a room is going to work for a child facing physical challenges on a regular basis. If the room doesn't work, it becomes yet another day-to-day obstacle to surmount.

There are several easy ways to promote self-reliance:

• Lower all the shelves.

• Lower all the clothes rods.

The challenges to a girl who uses a wheelchair are diminished, thanks to thoughtful design features. Besides an extra wide closet with recessed doors, the setting has glue-down carpet in a level loop that's flush with the tile in the adjacent bath for ease in mobility.

- Remove the closet door so belongings are easier to obtain.

- Store toys and clothes in bins that wheel out of the way.

- Buy furniture with easy-to-handle drawer pulls and glides. Other features to look for include pull-out surfaces that readily accommodate a user of a wheelchair whose equipment may not fit under a traditional opening such as that of a standard desk.

Custom-made furniture is another option for a child with restricted mobility. Bookshelves, storage cabinets, and countertops can be customized to accommodate a wheelchair or other special gear a child uses regularly. Before you hire a handyman or carpenter, however, consult an interior designer with expertise in special needs design. A professional's knowledge of resources and skill in using them are worth tapping.

Regarding wheelchairs and motorized scooters, take note. The equipment itself dictates certain space requirements. In general, a wheelchair necessitates a 36-inch wide doorway and a 60-inch clearance on either side to provide a 60-inch radius in which to turn around. Motorized scooters, on the other hand, may vary in dimension. The best way to determine space demands is to check with the manufacturer and keep the information on file in the event of a move.

Besides allowing room for equipment to be mobile and removing obstructions that would impair this, provide space near the bed for its storage during sleep time. This is not only a practical consideration, but also a reassuring measure of safety for both parent and child, especially in case of an emergency.

OVER AND OVER AGAIN

In a home with a wheelchair, flooring also demands special attention. One option that provides ease of wheelchair movement is a solid vinyl floor with a nonskid surface. Vinyl is suitable in most areas, but it may not be preferable in a child's bedroom where texture plays a big part in providing a cozy atmosphere.

Undoubtedly, carpet is more difficult to wheel over, yet riding over a padded surface is much more comfortable. Besides cushioning any childhood falls, it also lends an element of warmth, insulation, and sound absorbency.

If you opt for carpeting your child's bedroom, look for carpet styles with a low, uncut loop pile commonly described as level loop. Carpeting with a high density—originally designed for commercial use—can stand the heavy use like constant wheelchair movement.

In their book *Beautiful Barrier-Free*, Cynthia Leibrock, *ASID*, and Susan Behar, *ASID*, note that carpet used with wheelchairs should not exceed a $\frac{1}{2}$-inch pile height, although people who lack strength may require $\frac{1}{4}$-inch height pile. "Use an uncut or tip sheer in a high-density pile for an easy traverse," the authors recommend, explaining that "cut pile may pull the wheelchair in the direction of the nap."

To make traveling on floor covering easier, eliminate padding in favor of glue-down installation. It prevents rippling caused by wheelchair use and affords a more stable surface on which to ride. If glue-down installation isn't feasible, choose a firm, resilient hair pad, since it is resistant to the constant crush of wheels. For ease in negotiating, however, you may want to apply latex rubber to both sides of the pad.

If the bedroom is next to the bath, install bathroom floor tile flush with the carpet so that it's easy to maneuver from one area to another. Take note, however. Deep joints between the tiles of a width greater than $\frac{3}{4}$ inch, may hold the wheel of a wheelchair.

FOSTERING INDEPENDENCE

As you strive to instill independence in a child with physical limitations, take advantage of technology geared for independent living. For example:

- Levers, like the kind used in place of doorknobs in public buildings, are much easier to use at home for someone who lacks grip strength or has limited manual dexterity.

- Light switches at standard height become accessible to those who can't ordinarily reach them when simple gadgetry is installed. Pressure or "rocker" switches, for instance, are easier to operate than standard toggle switches. More elaborate remote control systems enable someone from any location to turn on wall switches, lamps, and even appliances from a hand-held controller. One of the least expensive devices turns on and off with a hand clap; however, other loud noises may activate it, too. There are also lamps on the market that work just by tapping them lightly at the base to control the intensity of illumination from dim to bright.

- Intercoms, when placed bedside, allow for easy communication by a child with mobility problems.

- Electronic devices that control computers and telephones are ideal for those with severe physical limitations. The Touch Talker, for example, enables a nonspeaking person to communicate by means of a tongue switch requiring little movement to activate.

With regard to lights themselves, hang them carefully to avoid viewer glare, which can be a problem for someone seated in a wheelchair. Track lighting or "down lights" may eliminate this problem.

Many of these devices are available through hardware stores or electronic shops, however, there are firms that specialize in this type of gadgetry. Look at the ads in magazines targeted to individuals who are physically challenged or consult with rehabilitation specialists aware of state-of-the-art technology.

BREAKING DOWN BARRIERS

Encouraging strengths and strengthening weaknesses—that's what a room should provide for a child with special needs. Beyond that, however, private quarters for someone young with limitations should also reflect that person's tastes and interests. In that sense, it's no different from what an environment should be for a child without handicaps. After all, anyone's domain should be pleasant and pleasurable—not just practical and accessible.

A Barrier-Free Bath

Details. Details. That's what a bathroom designed for someone with limited mobility demands.

If that someone is a child in a wheelchair, plan to incorporate the following:

- Grab bars next to and above the toilet, and above the tub. For safety reasons, choose the easy-to-grip rigid nylon bars over metal or porcelain. Also be sure to reinforce the walls before installation.

- Towel and toilet paper holders located where they're easy to reach.

Wall-hung lavatory fixtures and nonskid flooring aid the person in a wheelchair in using this bath unassisted. A setting that works for all individuals, it shows how good looks don't have to be compromised for special needs.

- A storage cabinet mounted beside the sink at counter height. This increases visibility of contents and makes items accessible.

- A mirror lowered behind the sink to counter height or hung at a downward tilt for better viewing by a child looking up from a chair. An extendable mirror on a flexible arm is another good choice.

- Levers instead of standard faucet handles. With just the palm of a hand, they permit water temperature and pressure to be adjusted. Be sure to install anti-scald valves on all faucets, including the sink, shower, and tub, where water fixtures should be offset closer to the front edge for accessibility.

195

If you're adding a new bath or renovating an old one for a child with a handicap, use this checklist as a guide for aids worth installing:

✔ Nonskid ceramic floor tiles with narrow grout lines that allow for a smooth ride when wheeled over.

✔ A wall-hung sink or a standard sink in a cantilevered counter. Both allow room underneath for easy wheelchair roll up.

✔ Shallow cabinets that permit someone seated to reach into the back section.

✔ A bath/shower unit featuring a removable transfer seat, so that a bather can sit down and swing his or her legs over the tub edge instead of stepping into it.

✔ A shower floor that's sloped and not curbed, because a curb can cause tripping. The ideal setup is a very gradual slope that allows the entire bathroom to drain easily.

✔ A bath/shower area without glass doors, which limit access and can create a barrier. Shower curtains allow more flexibility for entering and exiting bathing areas.

✔ A toilet with a raised seat designed for someone with limited mobility.

✔ A ceiling fan that helps circulate heat for someone at wheelchair height.

Because the bathroom is a high risk area in the home, it's a good idea to install a telephone in case an emergency arises. The toilet area is usually a good location, however, be sure the phone is placed low enough so that it can be easily reached by a child from a sitting position.

CREATING A TEEN SCENE WITHOUT THE GROWING PAINS

Once the teens years hit, take a good last look at kids' rooms with circus stripes and other cutesy touches.

Like getting a driver's permit, revamping personal space goes with the territory of being a teen. It's as if those emerging hormones pulled up childhood stakes to establish residency in a new, mature setting. Under yesterday's roof, all that mattered was bedroom space for sleep, study, and storage. Within today's shelter, there must also be room to socialize.

If your resident teen's quarters look OK to you, be advised. Chances are the one nesting there is ready to shed any vestige of babyhood. Creating a grown-up environment helps a person on the brink of maturity establish a firm footing in adulthood. Just as you wouldn't expect a 4-year-old's clothes to fit a 14-year-old, don't expect a setting fit for a younger child to suit his or her needs 10 birthdays down the road.

Given the interests and activities that occupy many young adults, an exercise in redecorating their childhood setting may call for more of everything, from extra seating to increased display space to expanded storage.

But "more" needn't be costly. By exercising creativity and ingenuity, teen space can be designed with minimal outlay—especially if the renovator is into recycling. If that's the case, of course, the finished look may translate to a funky mix of finds. The trick to blending them? Imagination, basic know-how, and an open mind for eclectic looks.

CHARTING A COURSE

Before a metamorphosis gets under way, the decision maker responsible for these changes should assess the situation. Encourage your teen to tap his or her needs and interests by pondering the following:

Wall-to-wall storage for a teen's clothes, books, and other belongings keeps clutter to a minimum. When space is needed for floor activity, the Murphy bed flips up and out of sight.

Function: List what areas the new room should contain. A place for grooming? Room for exercising? A place for relaxing with friends?

Furnishings: Be reasonable. Can old pieces be updated with paint or other touches? If the bed is in good condition but looks too juvenile, for instance, let a new headboard and covers lend grown-up status. Or if there are low modular pieces currently in the room, stack them in a more adult configuration such as a high bookcase.

Once you know what can stay, make a "wanted" list. Comfy seating for more than one . . . a bigger desk with a larger work surface . . . more storage—all might be considerations.

Budget: Get a clear picture of the finances that can be expended on a renovation. To make the most of the resources available, think about ways to stretch them. Shopping for sales is one way. Staging sales is another. By that I mean if there's a need to replace existing furnishings, sell them and add the profits to the kitty for refurbishing.

Color: Last but not least, this final consideration influences all major buys. But no matter what palette is picked, don't bombard the site with it. Even used sparingly as accent, color makes a distinct impression. Used all over, it makes a bigger statement that will be enjoyed or endured for a long time.

SCAVENGING FINDS

For fun and funky looks, turn to secondhand merchandise. Grandma's attic, a yard sale, or a secondhand shop are good places to search for used goods worth rejuvenating. You'll know a piece is salvageable if its lines, proportions, and shape hold appeal. Given these characteristics, look past the current finish if it can be stripped, sanded, and repainted.

If the furniture unearthed is appealing in design but appalling in appearance, take heart. Even a beat up wood surface can become trendy when further "distressed" with chains to give it a weathered air.

Zippy paint finishes like sponging or stenciling are other ways to breathe new life into old wood furniture. Check paint stores for proper tools and information about these or other techniques. Be sure to look in the library, too, for do-it-yourself books on refinishing by experts, including those by Jocasta Innes.

For a whitewashed look, apply a coat of paint and wipe it off immediately. Then cover the remaining finish with flat polyurethane for durability.

If dilapidated hardware mars the look of an old piece, replace it with something new. But if you like the detailing, consider having it replated.

How do you know if a "find" isn't worth repairing? Unsafe construction is your first clue. Besides taking that into consideration, base your decision upon whether an item will be costlier to fix than to replace.

Teenage treasure hunters looking for designs with or without a history might consider these recyclables or bargain finds:

✔ **Discontinued or "Seconds" Yardage:** Whether a bolt end or several yards, material in a pleasing pattern can make a good cover-up for secondhand seating. If you can't find what you want in a fabric store, look for sheets on sale—a reasonable alternative because of their dimensions.

✔ **Cast-Off Mirror:** Maybe it once hung above a fireplace or a long gone dresser. Refurbished, it can transform a corner of a teen's world into a special grooming center.

✔ **Tired Trunk or Footlocker:** Collage to the rescue of this storage find, which can be cleverly rejuvenated with snapshots, postcards, ticket stubs, magazine pages, or other paper paraphernalia. To adhere the works and keep them intact, use glue beneath each item and a coat of varethane on top. For a table look, add a piece of acrylic. Top the trunk with a cushion and it turns into seating.

✔ **Secondhand Storage Cubes or File Cabinets:** Repainted and topped with a wide board or door, these common pieces assume the role of work surface.

✔ **Family Easy Chair or Ottoman:** Either of these can fill the bill for extra seating in a bedroom when draped and tied with a makeshift cover, such as an old chenille bedspread or cotton duck remnants. Check sewing stores for clever ideas about tucking and tying slipcovers with ribbon or cord.

✔ **Hand-Me-Down Folding Screen:** Covered in heavy-duty material such as burlap, this assumes a new identity as a place for pinups. It's also ideal to zone off work, play, or sleep area.

A woven kilim rug, a futon covered in fanciful fabric, and a streamlined wood wall unit give this teenage retreat certified adult status.

While sleuthing through family cast-offs, be mindful of old lamps, picture frames, and other accessories. If they're suitable and desirable to the one who will be using them, these items and other accents from a bygone era could add interest once revitalized.

TRUE NEW

If the idea of recycled furnishings meets with resistance, think about more modern options. Consider the following cost-effective new alternatives.

Futons: This fold-up furniture converts to stacked seating when closed. Flipped open, it's oriental-style bedding. Some stores sell combination sleeper/sofa futons with elevated frames. These two-for-one designs offer flexibility while saving space.

Oversized and Accent Pillows: Store them on the bed. Stack them in a comfortable pile on the floor. If you're handy with needle and thread, be creative with your designs. Use different parts of outgrown jeans to make assorted pillows. The legs can be stuffed with Dacron fiber fill, and the ends frayed and tied to form miniature bolsters. Recycle the pocket on the old jeans by attaching it to the new pillow. For punch, add a kerchief. Let your imagination be your guide to other outgrown clothing possibilities. Consider a sports jersey that no longer fits. Stuff it with fiber fill, too, and close up all the ends. Like a jeans pillow, it makes a strong personal statement that can be kept as a keepsake.

Platforms: Turn a corner of the room into a relaxation center with a raised, carpeted platform built from sturdy scrap lumber. If you're not a do-it-yourselfer, go the handyman route and design multilevels for sleeping, exercising, or stretching out. For extra mileage, build in storage doors and drawers.

BUYING BETTER FURNISHINGS

If you have a budget that allows you to invest in quality furnishings, get the most for your money by looking at purchases suitable for a teen as well as a young adult.

Better furnishings have several long-term benefits. For starters, they might help furnish a future college apartment or a first home.

When investing in better merchandise for your child, consider individual pieces that offer flexibility beyond the bedroom. A comfortable overstuffed chair acquired for sleep quarters, for instance, may be ideal elsewhere if reupholstered in another fabric. A small table with a drawer or shelf that originally functions as a nigthtstand and is styled with classic lines, can serve well in other areas of a home. Still other pieces that bridge the teen years and adulthood include a low storage unit that fits right into a living room as a low chest; or a modular bedroom chest and shelving unit that adapts to stereo component and/or TV storage wherever it's placed.

Teen bedroom furnishings with adult appeal that remain at home during college, or later years, serve well when personal quarters convert to guest room status. Taking this into consideration, you might opt for a queen size bed rather than a twin or a double if updating the room translates to buying new bedding.

"Because quality and good design are timeless, investment furnishings have lasting value," stresses California interior designer Rela Gleason. Applying this principle to her projects for young people, she always selects better designs that will not be outgrown. "I shy away from what's trendy or cute; it will be outdated quickly," she reasons.

Quality touches for teen quarters à la Gleason often incorporate a window seat for charm as well as extra seating. Without fail, however, she always suggests a big upholstered chair. "It's essential," she says, "for lounging, studying or just providing a comforting touch."

TEENAGE HANG-UPS

Just as a preschooler enjoys exhibiting personal artistry, a teen takes pride in showing off sports or celebrity posters.

A way to display these and other flat "art" dramatically is to treat one wall as a montage. To protect the wall from tack and tape scars, hang lightweight structural board such as Homasote, a recycled newspaper material. About the thickness of drywall, it's available in 4- by 8-

A comfortable old lounge chair and a recycled family room table turn this well-lit alcove in a student's room into a study haven.

The benefits of having a relaxing private setting to retreat to on a daily basis aren't lost on the family dog. Awash in white with blue accents, this room spotlights furnishings that easily make the transition from childhood to adulthood.

What looks like room for one accommodates two when the bed pictured is rolled out and the separate bed stored underneath it is pressed into duty. "Secret" storage is also behind the sleeping unit in a compartment that hides games and toys.

foot sheets that cut easily for use as a bulletin board. Since it's intended as building material, it looks good for display only when its unfinished appearance can be camouflaged. Do this by stretching material over it. Choose a fabric with give, such as burlap or wool, and create a tackable surface that recovers from the impressions pushpins make.

Besides providing the room with a decorative touch, fabric-covered insulation adds sound absorbency—an ideal feature the rest of the family will appreciate if your teen likes music at a high volume.

Another way to show off large, flat items such as posters is to give them a 3-D effect by backing them with foamboard. A resilient polystyrene material that's strong and rigid but very lightweight, it's available through craft and stationery stores in 4- by 8-foot white, black, and multicolored sheets that cut easily and cleanly to any size. All it takes is spray mount to adhere the poster or other material to the foamboard.

Although small as compared with a wall, the back of a door also accommodates certain hang-ups. To keep the door from becoming damaged, however, get a sheet of thin corkboard and apply it to all or part of the surface.

ALL THAT OTHER STUFF

Sports gear and trophies . . .

Ribbons and trading cards . . .

Music tapes and videos . . .

School photos and pictures of performing artists . . .

And clothes, clothes, and more clothes . . .

Face it. By the time many kids reach high school, they're certified pack rats. Chances are they've accumulated all or most of the preceding items, not to mention all sorts of collections and collectibles.

Finding places besides the middle of the room to store all that stuff is a constant challenge. For starters, a teen should be encouraged regularly to weed through belongings and put what's outgrown in a box for the needy. What's worth keeping can be corralled on floor-to-ceiling shelves, over-the-door hanger valets, and in other catch-alls. Still other places to commandeer for storage include:

- **Under the Bed:** Bulky sports equipment and other big items tuck away easily in large roll-out bins made for this location.

- **By the Bed:** Store books and goods worth seeing in stacked wire baskets. Top it with a shelf and a bedside table is born.

- **On a Free Wall or Door:** Arrange decorative hooks or pegs in a row or in a zigzag pattern to herd hats, ties, belts, etc.

HODGEPODGE, ANYONE?

However interestingly teens assemble their life treasures, to a conservative parent they may look like a crazy quilt of possessions. But try to be tolerant. For someone on the brink of maturity, being allowed to express taste encourages a sense of style and a sense of self. Like getting a driver's license, it's all part of growing up!

CUSHIONING THE JOLT OF A MOVING EXPERIENCE

Whether it's a move across the hall or a move cross-country, relocating at best is a bittersweet experience for a child.

On one hand, it's exciting to imagine a new room that may be bigger or more "grown up" than present quarters. On the other hand, it's unsettling, and maybe even scary, to contemplate giving up familiar surroundings.

Before the normal chaos accompanying any move sets in, think about ways you can ease the transition as it pertains to children. A little preparation goes a long way toward soothing the situation.

"The trauma and confusion of moving can be greatly minimized with smart planning," contends psychologist and relocation consultant Patricia Cooney Nida, author of *Families on the Move*. And some of those plans, she says, should definitely include younger members of the household, too.

"Experts agree that children should be involved as much as possible in a move," Nida explains. Besides letting them decide what to pack, she encourages establishing family traditions that move with you. "Doing things together as a family," she stresses, "makes you feel at home no matter where you live."

GIVING A POSITIVE NUDGE TO BUDGE

If you're faced with uprooting your family, accentuate the move's positive points and deemphasize its negative ones. For instance, if your child is going from solo to shared quarters, downplay the fact that private space will now be at a minimum. Instead, stress the camaraderie that will come from this experience.

One of the best ways to get ready for moving is to consult the experts. Start with a few major moving companies that supply free checklists and brochures. Many have children's kits including special labels, stickers, storybooks, and clever post-move ideas for creating play structures from large cartons.

For other moving advice and strategies, look in the library for books on relocating. First, check the adult section for titles by parents who have survived the experience. Then consult the children's librarian about juvenile literature that talks about moving in ways your child will understand.

If you want current firsthand information about moving, seek newcomers in your old neighborhood. Parents who've recently experienced the adventure probably will be more than willing to share fresh memories of what worked and what didn't with children of different ages.

Long before moving day, seriously evaluate with your child his or her current room. Together, list simple things this room lacks that a new room might provide. More light? A different wall color? Additional storage?

Inspect the new room with an eye for incorporating these features. If an actual visit isn't possible, consult photos or floor plans to make preliminary decisions with your child.

While moving provides adults with motivation to part with old or "tired" possessions, parents shouldn't assume that their children will embrace the opportunity to do likewise.

"It might be wise to keep many of your child's old, familiar possessions, even if they are hopelessly broken or worn-out" advises Lillian G. Katz, Ph.D., an early childhood education specialist. "Such old but well-loved toys," she explains, "may help the child feel a sense of continuity." For that reason, Katz also suggests keeping a few favorite objects handy during the actual move from the old to the new place.

COLOR THE BLUEPRINTS BROWN

In any moving odyssey with young children, common household items are ideal aids. For starters, get a brown paper bag like the kind from the supermarket. Not only is this familiar arts-and-crafts material to a child, but it's also large enough to accommodate a good-size drawing.

Use the brown bag in the same way an architect does a blueprint so it becomes the "Master Plan" you and your child concoct for his or her new room. Before initiating plans, get scissors, tape measure or yardstick, cardboard, and multicolored crayons, including black. Now follow these steps with a junior designer:

- Cut the paper bag wide open. Discard the bottom and turn the side without advertising so that it faces up.

- With tape measure or yardstick in hand, calculate the distance between each corner along one wall of the room. On the drawing, 1 foot will equal 1 inch. Therefore, if the room measures 10 by 12 feet, the drawing will be 10 by 12 inches.

- Using a black crayon, sketch simply on the bag the room's significant details. Mark the location of windows, doors, and electrical outlets.

- Next, measure the width and depth of your child's bedroom furniture so you can make cardboard shapes representing each piece. Using the same scale of 1 foot equals 1 inch, identify pieces as "Diana's chair" or "Nicky's toy box."

Once you inventory all the other basics, such as bed, desk, and dresser, direct questions to your child in plain language he or she will understand. For example, you might ask:

"Where will you sleep—near the window or by the closet door?"

"Where will you do your homework?"

"Where will your stuffed animals live?"

As each question is answered, tape down or paste each cardboard piece of furniture into the position selected. Labels such as "sleep," "study," and "stuffed animals" are all easy references.

If the place your child chooses is unrealistic, spell out the reasons. A bed targeted for the doorway obviously would prevent entry and prohibit visitors. Discussing these things before moving deters tears and builds positive expectations.

Once the basics are decided upon, add playful touches by making sure familiar treasures resurface. Phrase questions so that your child doesn't think there's a right or wrong answer. A few inquiries might be:

Label choices on the drawing in simple jargon.

> ✔ "Where do photos of special friends belong?"
> ✔ "What's a good place to display awards and trophies?"
> ✔ "What wall rates posters and art?"

Be sure to take a break if your child is overwhelmed by too many choices. After a few days, continue this exercise. But don't be surprised if the "Master Planner" wants to reconsider a previous decision. That's fine. This is an ideal time for changes.

Once final selections are made, let color enter the picture. Hand your child a rainbow selection of crayons and his or her paper plan to color as he or she wants. When coloring is done, discuss choices and offer needed suggestions. For example, if the entire room is colored purple, you may want to propose limiting purple to one or two items such as a pillow or throw rug. Realize that your input is as important as your child's, since the room is part of the house.

From the onset, take time to explain that every idea in a Master Plan, including your own, may not work in the new room for one reason or another. It's possible what looks good on paper won't translate to reality. Perhaps old furniture won't fit as you thought. Maybe existing floor covering has to stay temporarily even though it's not the color your child would like it to be.

A SMOOTH MOVE

Undergoing a major upheaval connected with a move is never easy for kids who thrive on familiarity and routine. Involve them in a lighthearted way, however, and create excitement and anticipation about a new environment that no doubt will broaden their perspective about people and places.

Pioneering Positive Moves

A pioneer spirit to forge new paths and settle unfamiliar territory shaped this country.

But pioneering a new homestead today takes more than gumption to entice kids onto the wagon train.

Before forging a new frontier with your brood, consider individual age and development. Both dictate a child's concerns and involvement in a family transplant. To help cushion the experience, give older children stationery and address labels to encourage communicating with old friends. To welcome a child to new surroundings, also consider the gift of a stuffed animal placed on a new bed to discover on arrival.

Here are some other ways to foster positive moves for different ages:

WEE ONES

Packing fuss and commotion confuses infants, tots, and preschoolers. Therefore:

- Reassure young ones that everything, including them, will be transferred to the new site.

- Reduce anxieties on moving day by keeping a familiar blanket and a few favorite toys nearby.

- Dismantle last, if possible, a young child's room in the old house, and arrange it first in the new one.

KINDERGARTENERS THROUGH THIRD GRADERS

Fear of the unknown overwhelms 4- to 8-year-olds. This is why moving may trigger worries about where they'll sleep and what their rooms will look like. Therefore:

- Diminish fears by showing photos or a video of the place where you're going to live.

- Encourage fantasy play about moving, using dollhouse furniture or dolls, suitcases, and a wagon. Act out unpacking, too!

- Sort the toy box together so your child can help pack special playthings and discard others that are damaged. Those outgrown could be given away.

- Bring on the crayons once a child's cartons are full, so the contents can be labeled with his or her name or drawing.

FOURTH GRADERS THROUGH PRETEENS

Eight- to 12-year-olds involved in group activities may resist moving from schoolmates and pals. Therefore:

- Let a child know it's OK to be upset and that you, too, feel the pain of separating from friends.

- Make a collage of keepsakes to display in your child's new room to rekindle memories and maintain faraway relationships.

- Stimulate interest in your new home area by hanging a detailed map indicating nearby landmarks, points of interest, etc. Let your child write the tourist bureau for this information.

TEENS

It's tough for teens to move if they have strong bonds with boyfriends or girlfriends and clubs or teams. Therefore:

- Allow high schoolers, as you would a child of any age, to express their worries. Have a straight talk with your teenager about why you are moving and how he or she can contribute to the venture's success.

- Encourage teens to put a few mementos aside before packing everything. A strange motel room en route to a new home may seem more hospitable with a cherished possession on the dresser.

208

All in all, if a child senses a parent's optimism about a move, positive feelings and reassurances will be transmitted.

PARENTAL GUIDANCE THAT CAMOUFLAGES THE BLAHS

When home is rental property with little leeway for modification, enlivening a kid's room calls for clever tactics, especially if a neutral palette prevails.

Obviously, it's a challenge to carry out decorating maneuvers in a plain setting where major alterations are as welcome to the landlord as skipping the rent.

But there are ways to conquer lease limitations without eviction. Before considering camouflage or other means, however, reread the lease. To clarify restrictions, call the owner.

Maybe the clause prohibiting changes can be eased to sanction strippable wallpaper. Or maybe the provision against interior painting can be amended with an agreement to return what's painted to its original state in the event of a move. Walls will most likely need some refurbishing before the next tenant settles in. With that in mind, perhaps the landlord will negotiate on the color if consulted before the metamorphosis takes place.

After conferring with the owners of her past two addresses, West Coast designer Lynnette Reid got the nod to sponge paint the quarters for her 4- and 6-year-old daughters, Tayler and Colby. By watering down pale paint in both rooms, she gave the walls a cloudy effect. A "soft" look, it was easy to cover with one coat after her family moved. The ploy obviously worked. She was neither chided nor fined for leaving muted walls behind.

Once you're clear about what can and can't be done where you live, take measures as bold as possible. Therein lies the difference between insipid or inspired rental space.

DETAILS, DETAILS

Like a basic black outfit that looks different depending on what adorns it, a bland room destined for child occupancy comes alive with a few embellishments.

If you're stuck, for example, with furnished drab draperies, add contrast. Baste on playful trim that can be removed without damaging the material. Or hang a valance of

An area rug in a bold design and bedroom doors painted red add color and zip to a child's otherwise subdued setting.

whimsical fabric over the window treatment. It, instead of the draperies, will catch the eye. If a covering can fit inside the frame, use a tension rod. It requires no screws to install.

Consider a similar disguise if less than ideal miniblinds furnish the space. Hang a rod in front of them and casually drape it in colorful yardage or a sheet. For more zip, continue the pattern down the wall with matching side panels.

Dashes of detail like these downplay the covering underneath.

Adding drama and color also dresses up a no-nonsense rental setting. In some cases, you need only look at the nearest toy bin to find elements that provide splash.

Regarding other ways to give rental property a lift, do-it-yourselfers take note. You can spiff up one of the major elements of the room if you play the substitution game. Take off the closet door, for instance. Tuck it away. Replace it with a bright curtain. Or hang an inexpensive new door, vividly painted or otherwise detailed. Come moving day, resurrect the original fixture and return it to where it belongs.

However you spruce up the space, enlist the input of the one living there. Fostering fascination with the project may spark interest in the room long after its transformation.

BOTTOMS UP!

If your child is either crawling or sprawling, ground yourself, too. Just because a rental unit has bare floors or mundane coverings doesn't mean you can't revitalize it. Let's say plain carpet is already in place. Cover the part that gets the most traffic with a bright area rug in a snappy design. Instantly, you give the space a focal point and personality. What's more, you provide an extra level of comfort that your child will welcome whether curling up with a book or spreading out with a board game.

A hand-painted canvas floorcloth is another way to conceal all or part of an existing covering. Check stenciling books or a craft store for pattern ideas. After buying the cloth at a paint or crafts store, involve your child in decorating it. One design that often appeals to kids is an oversize checkerboard that invites play.

If there's enough open floor space in a corner of the bedroom, build in a small plywood platform and cover it in a carpet remnant. The raised area provides both stage and seating possibilities plus opportunity for different displays. Once it's time to move, the platform can be easily dismantled for further engagements at another address.

"That little step creates an environment for kids' events to happen and sparks imaginative play," says New York architect Jamie Wollens. Besides providing touches like platforms, he believes, the way to give kids opportunity to unleash their creativity is to enrich visual environment. In the loft bedroom his two children share, he's done just that by securing 14 side-by-side stacked cubes to the wall like a bookcase. Both kids continually change the contents of the boxes. One week it's pictures and cards. The next it's craft projects and toys.

WALL CALL

Because walls command so much space and, therefore, attention, focus on them as a means to provide some visual interest.

If the walls in your rental quarters are in poor condition, conceal imperfections with posters or photo blowups. First spray mount one or more pictures to inexpensive, lightweight foamboard sold at art supply and stationery stores. This adds sturdy backing and cuts down on nails if a collage of pictures is being hung. Other cover-ups that enliven a space include:

Tackable Boards: Once covered in bright burlap, wool or another fabric with "give," a piece of lightweight 4- by 8-foot Homasote structural board becomes a punchy tackable surface for pinups, posters, or artistry. Renters who share a common wall with neighbors will appreciate this board's sound-deadening quality.

Wall Borders: Hang a wallpaper border that's strippable around the room, or self-stick repositionable appliques of animals or characters. For a 3-D border, put up tiles, blocks, or sponge designs with double-sided foam tape.

Shelves: In rental space that lacks architectural features, add staggered shelves to provide some vertical interest. Fill them with stuffed animals or childhood collections. And double the collector's pleasure by hanging mirrors behind them to reflect the treasures. A young child may also relish a very low shelf to use as a tabletop for tea parties, and so forth. On the other hand, an older child into sports may appreciate a shelf on high for prominent display of trophies, ribbons, and other treasures.

Miniature pieces of furniture filled with toys and doll clothes create a three-dimensional effect and vertical play space for a young girl. They also add interest to plain rental quarters.

Vignettes: Look to your child's toys for another three-dimensional decorating idea. Imagine a miniature chair with a little doll sitting in it. Or picture a small hand-painted box with pint-size furniture as decor. Now envision either of them hung in the room at child height. These one-of-a-kind vignettes add charm to a room and promote interaction.

Hanging Tip: Come moving time, fill nail and tack holes with patching compound. Available at a hardware store, it comes in 1-pound packages nominally priced.

SIGNATURE LOOKS

If you move often, it may not be easy for your child to put a personal stamp on his or her private space, especially if the landlord is averse to even minor changes. In that case, channel your decorating energies into your child's furnishings.

Whether something small, such as a colorful wooden toy chest, or something large, such as a headboard in a cloud motif, painted furnishings enliven a youthful setting. Many interesting techniques transform plain pieces into punchy ones. Consider your child's interests and needs as well as what suits the space before taking paintbrush in hand.

If painted furniture doesn't appeal to you, make a bold furnishing statement with a folding screen. Build one from plywood by hinging two or three pieces together, or buy a ready-made version easy to adapt. Covered in bold material that coordinates with the rest of the room, a fabric screen provides much flexibility in a young person's setting. It zones off work, play or sleep areas, or if padded, serves as a large pinup board for whatnots. In addition, screens hide architectural flaws in a room, as well as unsightly pipes or a chimney.

Last but not least, focus on the bed. Choose bright, colorful covers and sheets. This decorative spark will lift the room's look along with your child's spirits.

MORE THAN MEETS THE EYE

Being creative in a rental home where the owners impose restrictions, teaches a lesson in resourcefulness. Beyond that, it underscores the value of making the most of a situation.

ALLERGY-FREE KIDS' ROOMS: NOTHING TO SNEEZE AT

Caution! Children's bedrooms could be hazardous to their health.

As ridiculous as that may sound, the message is no laughing matter to millions of kids with allergies or asthma linked to their indoor environments.

For them, dust, dander, smoke, and other common substances provoke respiratory ailments. Their coughs, sneezes, weezes, and, in some cases, gasps for breath, are not only irritating but at times debilitating, causing more school absence than other illnesses. Some kids with asthma "outgrow" it when their airways reach adult size, but the condition may recur. For most, it's a lifelong ordeal with very individual provocations and symptoms.

While people of any age may suffer from asthma, more than half the cases are found in 2- to 17-year-olds. Of those under 15, the American Lung Association (ALA) reports, asthma alone is the most frequent reason for hospitalization due to chronic disease. Most alarming is this past decade's 48 percent rise in cases. There's no medical explanation for this increase. Yet even ALA speculates in its brochure *Air Pollution in Your Home?* that saving energy by practicing diligent conservation has provoked airtight homes that trap indoor pollutants.

Fortunately for allergy and asthma sufferers, medications stave off flare-ups. But they don't alter the setting aggravating these conditions. That's where constant parental monitoring of a child's surroundings makes a difference. Studies show episodes induced by indoor allergens notably decrease if specific causes are eliminated largely from sleep areas.

It's no surprise bedrooms are a major target. Kids occupy them a third or more of each day and while they are there come in close, long-term contact with bedding, carpeting, and other fibers. While comforting touches to most of us, these furnishings contain most allergy sufferer's biggest enemies: dust mites. Microscopic creatures, they thrive in humid and warm conditions, shedding particles that trigger symptoms even after the insects cease to exist.

But mites aren't so mighty when technology enters the picture. If modern inventions are used to eradicate them, living is much easier for kids sensitive to the Great Indoors. Today, besides removing the fuzzies such as wool blankets and nonwashable stuffed toys, parents can install medical-grade air cleaners, operate dustless vacuums that even NASA uses, and obtain other less costly aids that keep allergies at bay.

STAYING AWAKE TO THE SITUATION

Alleviating the misery dust-sensitive kids suffer starts with setting the goal of a dust-free bedroom. The first hurdle to overcome—the bed. That's because a child sleeps there hours on end and a mattress is the resort capital of the dust mite's world. Pillows and blankets are popular spots, too.

Consequently, kids with dust allergies should rest on mattresses and box springs encased in zippered, dust-proof covers. Although readily available vinyl ones are OK for the box spring, on a mattress they induce sweat which causes eczema. A more comfortable "no sweat" choice sold by allergy supply firms is a cotton-poly cover with a protective backing. Even this should be wiped often and masked with duct tape along the zipper.

Encasing pillows is also important. Otherwise, sleep movement kicks up allergens that are then breathed in. Many doctors give the nod to washable polyester and nix anything feathered, including down comforters. Others qualify their recommendations saying neither fluffy nor nonwashable materials are off-limits if placed in zippered, airtight casings. As with any medical condition requiring treatment, let your own physician guide your actions.

A newer bedding option is a special comforter encasing over which a duvet may be used. This allows kids an opportunity for a standard duvet more colorful than most allergy-resistant linens. But be sure to choose splashy fabric that stands up to frequent laundering.

Washing bed linens in hot water is crucial, too. Water below 120° F prevents scalding, but it must be 135° F to kill dust critters. For hotter water without scalds, get an "instant flow" device, which supplies hot water at a specific point of use, such as for a washer.

Because bunks, canopies, and upholstered headboards attract dust, avoid them. And don't allow a bed on the floor. It fosters dampness, because the bedding can't "breathe," and dampness means moisture—an ideal condition for mite survival.

DON'T OVERLOOK WHAT'S UNDERFOOT

If allergies persist, dustproofing calls for beyond-the-bed tactics. The next place to concentrate on is the floor. Mites claim it as private stomping grounds, too.

Regarding allergens, the research-intensive University of Virginia maintains that carpets are very likely to have as much as 100 times more allergen than a wood floor. Besides hardwood, tile and vinyl are good flooring alternatives. You'll still need to remove traces of dust on them and on woodwork, however, by using water, wax, or oil on an ongoing basis. Even using a damp cloth every day helps.

As for small rugs and throws, they're all right if they're washable and laundered often.

When carpet removal is impossible, there are still ways to reduce dust. Dr. Gerald Klein, author of Keys to *Parenting the Asthmatic Child,* notes low-pile carpet is usually not as troublesome to an allergy sufferer as high shag. Regardless of what carpet you have, he suggests these ways to reduce mite population in it.

1. A vacuum with a high-efficiency particulate air (HEPA) filter. It captures particles without spewing exhaust dust such as a standard vacuum's paper filters do, thereby recirculating escaping allergens. A HEPA filter eliminates 99 percent of dust. Also effective is a central vacuum system that pulls dust into a central motor or cannister usually installed in the basement or garage. By removing dust to an outdoor or out-of-the-way location, this system prevents particles from being recirculated indoors.

2. Chemical carpet products that either reduce or destroy allergens. A moist powder is sold in all states but California. A tannic acid spray is available there.

3. A central or portable air purifier with a HEPA or electrostatic filter to remove irritating particles and some dust mites. Keep in mind it's only effective on what's airborne.

4. A refrigerated air-conditioning system that prevents hot and humid conditions that stimulate mite growth, if ducts are kept professionally cleaned. Central heating ducts demand similar maintenance and synthetic filters to prevent dirt particles from circulating.

The Vista, California, allergist's general recommendations include keeping relative indoor humidity below 50 percent by using a dehumidifier during humid seasons.

THE MITE FIGHT, ACT III

Decreasing dust in a child's bedroom demands other action if symptoms continue. Some professionals advocate stripping the room of all conceiveable allergens, from wall pennants to wicker baskets. But a more conservative approach is fostered by other allergists, including Stanford University assistant professor Steven Machfinger, M.D.

"If you control mites in the carpet and the bed," Machfinger contends, "you've probably done 95 percent of what you need to do to decrease a child's exposure to dust."

For this reason, he downplays extreme measures unless an extreme condition warrants them.

Machfinger's ideas for ridding a room of more possible allergens include:

Books: Keep them in a closed cabinet if necessary.

Clothes: Store them outside the room if your child has serious allergies or asthma. Otherwise, keep them in a closet behind closed doors. When laundering, be sure the dryer vents outside so dust sucked from the fabrics won't go indoors.

Furniture: Avoid upholstered items. Wood, metal, or plastic is preferable.

Pets: Animal dander, saliva, and other irritants, including dust their fur collects, may cause allergic reactions. In particular, do not let a family cat, dog, or pet mammal or bird stay in your kid's room. For a child who must have a pet, get a fish or iguana. If the family can't part with a furry household member, get a bedroom HEPA filter.

Smoke: A respiratory irritant, smoke compounds problems for a child with allergies. If you use cigarettes, do so outside only. If there's a wood stove or fireplace, install a tight-fitting glass cover, but be aware some smoke will escape upon opening.

Toys: If you can, eliminate stuffed toys. If you can't, let one stay but spray it with a mild tannic acid solution. Otherwise, get a washable stuffed toy or playthings made of plastic, wood, rubber, or metal. All are easy to clean.

Wall Hangings: Posters are better than cloth decorations. As for the walls, paint is less likely to attract dust than wallpaper, but consider adding an antimildew agent.

Windows: Choose washable curtains or roller shades over draperies or blinds.

If you wonder how well you're eradicating mites, some labs analyze vacuum dust sent to them. Dust collection kits are available through them or allergy supply companies.

BREATHING EASY

As continuous a task as it may be to keep your child's room—and ideally, the rest of the house—free from irritants, it's worth the effort. It not only adds up to fewer allergy and asthma episodes and less medication, but also provides livable surroundings. The American Lung Association motto says it best: "When you can't breathe, nothing else matters."

The Not-So-Serious Side Of Allergy-Free Settings

A bedroom for a child with allergies or asthma doesn't have to look sterile. Surroundings that must be decoration-shy call for an enlivening use of color.

If your child is sensitive to paint or stain, keep him or her away from home during application and use finishes with low or no VOC (volatile organic compound) ratings. When you're unsure about a product, contact the manufacturer about pigments or possible irritants that might cause reactions.

For a more colorful room, allergy-free design architect Robert Kobet of Butler, Pennsylvania, suggests some of the following ideas:

In a child's room where dust collectors such as carpet, draperies, and stuffed animals contribute to allergies, painting the walls and ceiling with decorative details adds playfulness.

Furniture: If cutting down on dust means cutting back on furniture, pick colorful new hardware for the furniture you'll keep. Try a peppy finish on the drawer fronts. Or consider futons in allergy-free encasings.

Floors: A bare floor can look bleak. Add color with dark stain, bold paint, stenciling or a vinyl pattern. For a soft look, get a washable cotton rug.

Walls: Without toys on shelves or other hang-ups that attract dust, a kid's room can seem lifeless. Fight plain walls with color by tracing and then painting details such as a bird, flower, wall clock, or street sign with your child's name. An overall mural overwhelms a room; a partial one adds interest.

217

Windows: Compensate for lack of traditional fabric by painting the frame either a bold color that contrasts with the walls, or two or more colors. Also consider aluminum blinds with dust-repellent features. Some brands cut down on dust particles by as much as 50 percent or more.

Accessories: If dust collectors such as ribbons or pennants can't be exhibited, display them inside a cabinet with glass doors. Or tuck them under clear acrylic made to fit on top of a desk or dresser. Having a favorite picture laminated works well, too.

If sensitivity prohibits these decorative ideas, shed some light on the subject. But make it colored light to create a playful mood.

Fungus Among Us?

As intriguing as crawl spaces, closets, and Christmas trees can be to kids, they top the list of the things to avoid when allergies mean sensitivity to mold.

Microscopic fungi that thrive in high humidity indoors and out, molds are the most widespread living organisms. Like plants, they come in thousands of different varieties.

Some are produced in the home in areas of high humidity; others come to life outdoors where they're dispersed through the air and consequently enter the home.

A mold-sensitive child should avoid dark, damp, poorly ventilated places at home, school, and elsewhere. In a residential setting, this may include basements, closets, bathrooms, laundries, kitchens, and other areas where water accumulates. Although various products kill fungus, there are other ways to fight it.

In their book *Keys to Parenting the Asthmatic Child*, coauthors Dr. Gerald Klein and Vicki Timerman offer the following suggestions for combatting mold at home:

BATHROOMS
- ✔ Wash or frequently change shower curtains.
- ✔ Remove mold and mildew as soon as possible.
- ✔ Repair leaks immediately.
- ✔ Use a dehumidifier to keep humidity down, if necessary.
- ✔ Avoid aerosol sprays by replacing them with pump sprays, liquids, or roll-ons.

CLOSETS

✔ Keep the doors open to help ventilation.

✔ Keep a low-voltage light on to help prevent mold growth.

✔ Use a dehumidifier to help kill mold.

✔ Avoid moth balls, because chemicals may trigger irritation and asthma symptoms.

LIVING AND FAMILY ROOMS

✔ Be sure carpeting doesn't become wet or damp, since mold can readily develop. If it does get wet, lift and thoroughly dry it.

✔ Keep houseplants to a minimum. The more there are, the higher the mold content. Also remove dried or silk arrangements, which can gather dust and grow mold. If plants are kept, avoid wicker containers; mold grows there as well as in soil. Check and clean other containers, too.

BASEMENTS

✔ Keep children allergic to mold from playing in damp areas.

✔ Use a dehumidifier if an area becomes wet or damp, and remove mold promptly.

KITCHENS AND LAUNDRIES

✔ Check areas under the sink, refrigerator, and washers for leaks and mold.

✔ Do not allow food to become moldy.

✔ Avoid using cleaning products unless the area is well ventilated.

✔ Be cautious of damp paper products.

HOBBY AREAS

✔ Never allow hobbies that entail working with glue, flux, or solder in an area not well ventillated. Supervise the asthmatic child working with paint or glue and discontinue using these products if asthma difficulties arise.

OVERALL

✔ Keep heating and cooking systems cleaned, since they're primary mold sources.

✔ Be mindful of large aquariums, where mold content can be a problem.

✔ Use disinfectants regularly to reduce mold growth.

219

To reduce humidity indoors, Dr. Klein further suggests keeping the home well ventilated and the relative humidity below 50 percent. As a way to reduce humidity, he recommends air-conditioners. They not only filter out large fungal spores, they also lower the indoor mold- and yeast-particle count.

CHAPTER 7

OTHER
IN MY^WORLDS

A doorbell rings, and its singsong sound echoes through the entryway and entices someone young to investigate . . .

A pot of food simmers in the kitchen, and its aromas attract a child there . . .

A light glimmers from the bath and draws a toddler down the hall toward its shine . . .

Everyday home occurrences, these happenings hardly enthrall adults experiencing them day in and day out. But to a child mesmerized by grown-up activities, all sights, sounds, and smells connected to them are like fireworks too colorful to ignore.

Adapting your entire home to accommodate children comes with the territory of raising a family.

And no matter how comfortable or well equipped your kids' private quarters are, they're not likely to captivate them around the clock.

Once crawling begins, so does the thrill of discovery beyond the perimeter of personal space. Rather than squelch exploration in rooms parents occupy, encourage it as much as possible so home is a welcoming environment all over, from the kitchen to the bath to the family room and beyond.

With thoughtful consideration and planning, most rooms can pass the child-friendly test. Whether that means displaying youthful treasures down low or rearranging breakables on high, let safety measures guide the adaptations you make. Then bells or smells or sights that beckon younger members of the household won't sound an inner alert. Instead, they'll signal comforting touches that make home the best place to be.

◄ *Hand carved and painted by the artist/sculptor who lives here with his family, this clever kitchen island is inset with three-dimensional wooden food. Besides adding whimsical decor to the child-friendly setting, it's sturdy enough to resist the sticky fingers of the young twins who inspired it.*

WHERE THE LIVING IS EASY

In the hillside house young Michael, Stephen, and David call home, the family room renovation started like a treasure hunt.

At the top of the search list—a coffee table. But not just any coffee table. This table needed to be interesting in an artsy way so it could serve as a focal point in a sunken setting. Yet it also had to be sturdy and impervious to the everyday energy output of three active boys.

While driven by the desire to find something durable, the designer masterminding the remodel kept clinging to one idea. The piece should be playful as well as practical.

Suddenly, the puzzle became the solution. What Marian Wheeler, *ASID*, devised was a table in a bold design with a metal base and black granite top. It looked and felt indestructible and served likewise. Where the playfulness came in were the drawers. Shaped like eight narrow puzzle parts, they were each stained differently. Those earmarked for the boys reflected their individual color preferences and interests.

Michael chose blue for a drawer that would store favorite CDs.

Stephen picked red and put a miniature chess set inside.

David selected a drawer of bright green and filled it with giant playing cards.

"Like the fun and games the room is designed for, the table plays right into the setting," Wheeler explains with well-deserved pride.

But its winning streak goes beyond playfulness. As the designer readily admits, "The table promotes tidiness in a subtle way. It recognizes that each boy has his own private things that deserve their own private place."

Colorful wood drawers add extra interest in this custom puzzle table, a focal point in the family room. Stained to match the preferences of three active boys, the drawers help keep cards, dominoes, and other individual games separated by owner.

Keeping kids' treasures under wraps is not the only message the owners hoped to convey. Just as important to them as neatness was showcasing the entire family in the room they all used most. To do that, Wheeler let their love of animal life surface in a novel way. Finding a menagerie in papier mâché, she asked each individual to choose one and paint it as delicately or wildly as he or she wished. Their designs would become a special display.

"It turned into a terrific family project," the boys' mother confides. "Each creation is totally different. One has graphics. Another features polka dots. A third is detailed with zigzag patterns."

One-of-a-kind focal points, both the puzzle table and the painted decorations go a long way in advertising the fact that kids reside where these furnishings do.

In keeping with the clever ideas featured in this particular setting, a room meant for any other family's use should cater to all household members using it. If doing that in your home poses some problems, perhaps the solution could be another puzzler!

TIME OUT

Whether contemporary or old-fashioned, a family room should communicate one major message—relaxation. With that in mind, make sure some casual seating welcomes your kids, too.

Used furniture with built-in "character" marks is certainly OK and may be preferable if you'd rather not worry about knicks and scratches that could come with frequent use from lounging around. If your children are very young, however, be sure secondhand goods are sturdy and that hardware is screwed on tight. In fact, if the hardware is old-fashioned and elaborately detailed, it may be wise to replace it with something simple that won't snag clothes or other objects.

In some cases, you can childproof old pieces that are safe yet pose the problem of being damaged by someone young. Take a wood side table, for instance. Its top can be

Papier mâché animals come to life in paints and patterns individual family members chose to express their artistry and sense of humor. Displayed along a high bookshelf in the family room, they add personality and presence to a wide open space.

When a room's furniture and furnishings are inviting, family members enjoy relaxing there together, especially when the setting caters to everyone's interests.

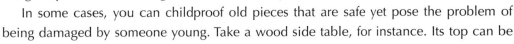

223

A clear acrylic top keeps this Balinese table from becoming knicked and scratched at the hands of kids.

protected with a clear piece of acrylic cut by a fabricator to exacting dimensions. Once children outgrow the stage when you need to worry about sticky fingers, simply remove the plastic top and store it away in case a young child ever comes to visit.

When it's time to consider something new to outfit the family room, think about lightweight pieces that provide flexibility for kids. Beanbag chairs and large floor cushions are two good seating options. So are stadium-style cushions covered in comfortable fabric. Also ideal for young people is a foam futon chair. Some styles are designed as a two-for-one furnishing that flips open for use as a sleep surface.

Since leisure time to a child often translates to playing board games, select a spot where some can be stored. A shelf, a modular cube, and a decorative trunk are all worthwhile candidates. Even more important, however, is arranging the room to allow plenty of open space for playful activity.

Take into consideration the age, interests, and idiosyncrasies of your children before deciding on furniture placement that will please them. Perhaps space for stretching out on the floor should take precedence over space for a game table. Then again, if an activity like table tennis is a family favorite, it may make more sense to keep a Ping-Pong table set up permanently and forgo other space plans.

A small bench, a miniature rocker, or other child-size furniture is appropriate here, too. If there's a piece from your childhood languishing in the attic, reupholster it to fit the decor and your child's taste.

With everyone frequenting a family room, it's also an ideal area for an informal grouping of family photos. To spark your children's interest and contribute to their self-image, involve them in selecting the pictures that should be displayed.

No matter how seldom children are allowed to play in the living room, for instance, it can still reflect their interests. Display one or two of their special treasures, such as an heirloom doll or toy. Or frame a crayon sketch and hang it near the fine art. Even craft projects such as papier-mâché masks rate family or living room status if arranged interestingly.

To incorporate her school-age son's creations into the family area of their home, interior designer Denise Tom-Sera took his artistry into account when remodeling. Two of the four staggered niches inset along one wall were intentionally located so 7-year-old Julian could reach and use them, but they're high enough to foil his baby brother's grasp. Yet the toddler has his own spaces in the room, too. There are large baskets filled with his playthings, including one with his books. When Mom and Dad read, he does, too.

"The whole house is for living," Tom-Sera says of her decision to integrate in subtle ways an area of every room for the boys. Besides display niches and toy containers, this translates to simple low-maintenance features, ranging from a small child-height chalkboard in one end of the house to an art gallery setting at first grader eye level in the kitchen.

"Often children just want your company while they are busy doing their own tasks. If you provide a place for them in every room, they are often able to concentrate longer in the comfort of your presence. Not only does this keep everyone happy," the designer adds,

Papier mâché masks hung next to fine art, and a collection of folk toys displayed on a side table, tell guests that kids call this place home, too.

"it simplifies clean-up by making it easy for children to participate in putting things away." Beyond that, however, the mother of two has learned that accessible spaces throughout a home encourage childhood independence and teach early on a respect for one another's private territory.

A LIVING ROOM THAT'S NOT OFF LIMITS

Since the living room is usually the "best" room in the house, it stands to reason children should be on their best behavior using it.

If your living room is a place reserved for entertaining guests and celebrating special occasions, you may want to restrict it to specific childhood pasttimes, such as reading or playing the piano. In that case, allow only select items to be kept here in something like a big basket that matches or coordinates with the room's color scheme.

If kids are welcome in the living room from time to time, be sensible about the kind of furnishings there. While you don't need to condemn living quarters to dark, dirtproof colors until the kids grow up, you do need to consider mighty materials, sturdy finishes and stain-resistant fabrics that allow even light surfaces to survive childhood. Protective sprays also extend the life of fabrics that aren't pretreated.

As you read about other parts of a home and ways to configure them for child occupancy, remember this. From infancy, a child should look upon home as a safe harbor. Make its many corners a comfort to be in, and create a welcoming environment that a child of any age continually enjoys.

RECIPE FOR A CHILD-FRIENDLY KITCHEN

Hot apple cider and pumpkin pie . . .

Gingerbread cookies and homemade jam . . .

From the time their olfactory senses start identifying tempting aromas that come from the kitchen, kids are drawn there like bees to honey. Long before kitchen territory becomes a favorite hangout, however, take stock of how child-pleasing and childproof this hot spot is in your home.

There's more than food preparation at issue here, and not only from a safety standpoint but from a functional one as well. After all, kitchen counters are intentionally placed at the height of the grown-ups using them. Appliances, too, are often out of children's reach or intentionally off-limits to them. Naturally, altering this setup to accommodate the kids is as preposterous an idea as expecting them, if you actually did, to willingly embrace all the kitchen chores.

But don't let a kitchen's configuration, or its potential risks, stop you from spicing up the decorative fare so it appeals to the young people living there. A growing family should find more than food in the kitchen to welcome their daily presence. With some simple ingredients, you can even concoct a setting that teaches kids a thing or two.

PUTTING ART ON THE MENU

A whimsical wake-me-up is what Paula McChesney, *ASID*, had in mind when re-designing an old kitchen for a California household including 3-, 5- and 8-year-old children.

Positioned on the wall by their breakfast table is a large painting of a royal character eyeing the Four-and-Twenty-Blackbirds pie of the famous nursery rhyme. To stretch a young viewer's imagination and tickle a funnybone or two, the kitchen designer dramatized both the wall and the adjacent stained glass window with images of blackbirds in flight. Talk about pie in the sky!

"In a magical way, these artistic touches suggest anything's possible," McChesney reasons. "It reinforces that message every day when the kids gather for family breakfast."

Whether humorous or instructional or both, kitchen art also can acknowledge the younger generation by showing off their own artistry. This not only reinforces parental appreciation for personal creativity, it indicates a "masterpiece" is valued enough to be displayed in a more public home setting where others can see it.

Ask most parents where they hang their kids' art, and chances are the kitchen ranks high on their list anyway. That's because an invention called the refrigerator has come of age in this century as more than cool storage. Today it's also a message center and/or exhibit space for drawings, photos, notes and other memorabilia.

With birds flying off the canvas at this breakfast table setting, a child's imagination soars right from the start of each day.

But "the fridge" needn't be the sole magnet for children's artistry. There are definitely other showcase areas in the kitchen. Turn the back of a door, or a wall for that matter, into a tackable surface by stretching and stapling material with a little give over a piece of sound deadener board cut to fit. Similar to corkboard, it's usually preferable because it's not only easier to find nowadays, but also less expensive, too.

Side-by-side floor-to-ceiling tackable surfaces, like the kind hung in a Bay Area home designed by Rhonda Luongo, *ASID*, serve both children and parents. Alphabet reference charts and children's school and art works are displayed on lower areas. School calen-

With its alcove for a child-size table and stools and its floor-to-ceiling tackable surfaces to display art, homework assignments, and other materials, this kitchen welcomes the kids who live here.

dars and memos are placed higher up for Mom's and Dad's easy reference. Besides utilizing dead space and providing a display, they minimize clutter for the family of four.

STICK-'EM-UP

Laminating kid stuff to hang in the kitchen also has merit, because it's easy to clean. You can wipe off any food stains from sticky fingers or cooking residue. Depending on size, laminated items also make good table place mats that can be rotated on a seasonal basis.

If easy-to-clean wall hangings sound appealing, try the clear-coated pages of a child's cookbook. *The Bake-a-Cake Book* by Marie Meijer, for instance, has delightful illustrations painted on acetate pages that explain in words and pictures how to make a cake start to finish. Although designed solely as reading material, the book's spiral-bound pages seem ideal for removing and hanging individually or sequentially. They offer an engaging way to teach about measurements, utensils, and ordinary skill that transforms ingredients into special dishes. Still other kitchen showcase ideas include the following:

A Gallery: Prop winning reports and other small treasures on the ledge of a chair rail. This decorative molding, designed to prevent chair backs from rubbing against plaster, hangs below a wall's midway point. If your home doesn't include this feature, it's easy to add such molding not only for exhibit's sake but also for architectural interest.

A Moveable Show: Hang adhesive school emblems or removeable stickers on a sliding glass door. A side benefit of doing this is the signal it provides to those headed indoors or out, that a see-through barrier is in their path.

Communication Station: Secure a roll of paper or a chalkboard on a free door and keep markers or chalk nearby. Besides providing a place for messages, this helps a child keep a grocery list. Depending on your kitchen layout, this station might also work in a recessed area. The right location will be far from cooking areas and capable of accommodating something low enough for a child to use.

Geography Center: If there's space, a kitchen wall is also a candidate for a map. A laminated one encourages marking places of interest or tracking current events.

Photo "Studio": If for nothing else, press the outside of the refrigerator into service as a mini-gallery for photos by using magnetic clear plastic frames hung low where children can enjoy pictures of themselves, the family pet, or whatever else you choose to hang.

THE COOK'S SHADOW

As do grown-ups, kids enjoy the kitchen beyond mealtime for other activities.

Part of the attraction is being near caregivers as they cook, bake, or relax there. It's not just a matter of observation; imitation is part of the allure. For beginner chefs, this translates to cutting out cookies, using pots and pans, and helping with minor tasks.

To foster kitchen activity away from hot ovens or foot traffic, localize it to a safe spot. Store a child's nonbreakable utensils here in a plastic bin if shelf or cabinet space isn't available. Encourage cleanliness by keeping an apron or washable art smock on a low peg inside a closet or under the sink.

For a child helping with mealtime chores, keep some nonbreakable everyday dishes in a low cabinet. As an added safety measure, be sure it's located away from cooking areas. Also, if there's an extra slide-out breadboard, cut a hole in it to anchor the mixing bowl so young, and old, can stir ingredients with less strain.

An out-of-the-way recessed area in the kitchen becomes a gallery for children's artwork once vinyl cable is strung along it clothesline fashion. Colorful vinyl-coated clips keep the art in place without tearing into the construction paper.

DISHING UP A LITTLE LEARNING

Once school begins, the kitchen often becomes an extended classroom with the table as desktop. For a student claiming this room as homework terrain, set aside a bottom drawer for supplies. Or hang a wire storage rack on the door or wall and consign paper, pencils, and other tools of the learning trade to lower shelves more accessible to a child.

More likely than not, in off-study hours the kitchen table may be requisitioned for board games. If that's the case in your home, allocate a cupboard shelf or drawer for a few favorites. By keeping these handy, putting game or puzzle parts away becomes easier.

Other inviting kitchen ideas for kids include a reading nook and a project spot. In the nook, keep a young reader's cookbooks and literature on a low shelf. If there's a window

Zippy paint colors detail the child-size table and chairs tucked along one wall in this kitchen. The original art above it represents the work of a 3-year-old.

seat, designate it as a child's reading retreat during non-mealtime hours. Utilize any built-in storage below for a few kids' belongings such as toys that tend to be used there.

If there's sufficient floor space, establish the project spot by setting up a child-size table with a washable laminate surface—an appreciated feature when arts and crafts are in progress. Because the kitchen is better for messy play than the bedroom, create a corner where this can be done occasionally without disrupting everything else. For the sake of room and convertibility, instead of small chairs for the table, get strong stools that also can be used at the sink to stand on to wash hands.

CUSTOMIZED FOR KIDS

Since kids grow up, customizing a kitchen to their needs is difficult at best, not to mention expensive. If you are remodeling, however, there are many child-friendly design details you should consider from a practical standpoint.

Among them are the following:

- Cabinetry and counters with rounded edges so bumps pose less of a peril.

- Hardware that's smooth and easy to grasp for drawers that children need to access.

- Paint that's washable so smudges can be removed.

- Appliances with controls in the back instead of the front so risks are minimized.

- Surface materials like laminate or Corian so cleanup is easier.

- A low pull-out drawer that can accommodate a kid's "kitsch" and then tuck it away.

- A low pull-out platform—"hidden" in the toe-kick area—to act as a step stool.

For inspiration, consider what artist Rodney A. Greenblat, owner of the Center for Advanced Whimsy, custom designed for his family. It's a Manhattan kitchen where kids can play with food without ruining it or getting themselves messy. Little hands feel around the holes in a giant block of Swiss cheese made of wood. And small fingers scrutinize the seeds in a gargantuan melon slice. When the kids aren't toying with this cornucopia, they climb it to view hot pink cabinets with cartoon drawings on the front and mouth-watering messages like "Yum!"

Sound like the stuff of fairy tales? It is, but only in the sense that fantasy inspired it. The "please touch" fruits, veggies, and other groceries are three-dimensional plywood pieces painted as brilliantly as ripe produce and then inset like a collage on the low face of a kitchen island. They're there to delight young twins Cleo and Kimberly, the daughters of Greenblat and his wife, hat designer Deena Lebow. And as wild as the counters and cabinets may sound to some conservatives, they are practical as well as playful.

Like a children's museum with its "touch me" features, this culinary wonderland has instigated many "hands on" experiences by the girls. Admittedly created for them to enjoy from their perspective, the kitchen's crowning glory is its twin water towers that rest on the cabinetry and actually serve as stereo speaker stands.

WHAT'S COOKING?

Whether you start from scratch to customize a kitchen design or stay with what you've got and try to personalize it, take your entire family's tastes and interests into consideration. After all, with its interesting mix of aromas and activities, a kitchen continually captivates kids as well as grown-ups. Make yours inviting, and what's cooking will always be more than a good meal.

Lending a hand in the kitchen is a piece of cake when design eliminates unnecessary strain. One example of this is a breadboard cut out to support a mixing bowl.

Keeping Kitchens
Safe For Kids

Colorful gadgets that look like toys and clever appliances that sound like noise-makers aren't so whimsical when they cause an accident.

With kid-related kitchen emergencies common, take precautions. Store gadgetry, knives, scissors, and other possible perils out of sight. If you're distracted when using something sharp and must go elsewhere, put the item in a safe place. Minimize other risks as follows:

- Install safety latches or locks on all drawers, cabinets, and, if necessary, appliances. Likewise, put a hook on the wall by the phone so the cord won't pose a danger.

- Never let cords dangle on appliances, either. Those placed safely above the counter and table level should never be near a high chair. When not in use, cover outlets.

- Put pans on rear burners and turn cookware handles to the inside or back of the stove when cooking. To be safe, buy a guard so a child can't touch burners. Also, don't store food above cooking areas where kids could be tempted to climb for it.

- Place a microwave out of reach and make it off-limits until kids are old enough to use it. Even then, teach that microwaved items can cause burns.

- After cooking, keep hot food away from a counter or table edge.

Certain kitchen products are also cause for worry. Consequently, store cleansers, medicine, and unopened pet food in locked cabinets in original containers listing ingredients. That information is crucial if something harmful is accidentally ingested. Items such as plastic wrap in serrated boxes pose threats, too. Keep them out of child reach, and when using plastic, be wary of the risk for suffocation if it's placed over the head.

Do not encourage play on the kitchen floor while anyone is cooking. Hot food may spill if the cook trips. Also keep floors clean and free of anything a child could choke on, and discard trash in a container with a hard-to-open lid or in a compactor.

Last but not least, take fire safety seriously. Install a smoke detector and mount a fire extinguisher near an exit out of child reach and at least 6 feet away from the cooking area.

When it comes to kids and kitchens, the National Safe Kids Campaign emphasizes the need for kids to have certain "no zones" in the kitchen where dangers often lurk. Establish them early on so avoiding common perils is as easy as eating apple pie.

The Muck Stops Here!

Neither flood nor mud causes consternation indoors when home has a special alcove for removing outerwear.

Whether it is a laundry or a mud room, this entry/exit area should contain plenty of room for kids and grown-ups to shed raincoats, boots, parkas, and other weather gear.

Either an open wall with pegs or closed cabinets like lockers solve the problem. High and low shelves also help corral goods destined for this space. Considering the clothing changes that will take place in this location, be sure to provide some kind of seating, even if it's just a stool or a sturdy chair.

Since it's the last place the family stops before leaving and the first place they reach upon arrival, it's also a good idea to provide separate cubbies. Then each family member knows where to find personal mail, messages, and other small items that need to be transported. When very young children are using this area, make storage easy by color coding or labeling it with peel-off lettering available at the stationery store.

If you're creating this area from scratch by remodeling, consider neutral building materials, since the mix of belongings kept here will provide enough color. Design features to consider include a built-in bench to lend an assist when someone is removing boots or shoes.

When you know ahead of time exactly what equipment will be stored in this setting, measure large or odd-size items to make sure they'll fit. If your family is athletic, for instance, and wears all kinds of sports shoes, knowing approximately how many pairs will need to be kept here should influence how much storage will be allocated for them.

About that mud and crud being tracked indoors: To stop it from going into other parts of the house, situate a sink and laundry facilties nearby.

"The biggest advantage of a mud room is cutting down on wear and tear in the rest of the house," says San Francisco interior designer Marian Wheeler, *ASID.* "It keeps all that stuff needed for outside activities in one central place."

Creating a place for outer gear to be kept minimizes the clutter and dirt tracked into the rest of the house. The long, low shelf doubles as a bench.

233

MAKING A SPLASH IN A CHILD'S BATH

Playful and practical design go hand in hand in this kids' bath. Child-friendly features include a window seat change area with built-in hamper and towel storage, easy-to-clean solid surface countertops, easy-to grasp lever-style faucet controls, and scrubbable wallpaper.

Like Alice in Wonderland momentarily dwarfed in a kingdom of giant proportions, a small child must feel tiny upon entering a bathroom built for grown-ups.

Just picture the scene:

Like mountaintops that are too high to scale, the sink, counters, and mirror above loom in the distance . . .

Towel rods, soap dish, and shower nozzle stand guard, unreachable even on tiptoe . . .

The light switch? It's several growth spurts away from being accessible . . .

Only the lower cabinets come face to face with a small kid who more often than not finds them locked and off-limits because of their contents . . .

To understand a child's frustration in this situation, kneel down in a bathroom that hasn't been designed with children in mind. Now you understand what a young boy or girl must confront several times a day.

Although it may seem that the only way to tailor a bath for use by someone small is through major remodeling, there are less extreme options.

First, acquire a sturdy step stool with rubber feet and place it near the sink so someone with very short legs can reach the faucets at washup time. If planning a bathroom remodel or new construction, a slide-out step stool can be located in the toekick area under the sink.

Slip-resistant strips, like the kind most often used in tubs and shower stalls, are advisable for splash areas on the bathroom floor by the sink and the tub. So are rubber-backed bath mats firmly positioned with double-sided tape. With regard to the shower area, add a hand-held unit to aid with a child's shampoo routine.

With many childhood bathroom accidents attributed to slipping, it's wise to invest in a floor with slip-resistant qualities such as vinyl with silica, rubber flooring, or tile specified as slip-resistant. According to industry standards, characteristics of the latter are a finish with abrasive particles, grooves or patterns in the surface, or a glaze designed for "increased coefficient of friction (COF)." A material with a static COF of 0.5 or greater (wet or dry) is usually considered slip-resistant. To be sure, ask a salesperson or check product literature.

MIRROR, MIRROR ON THE WALL

More than any other feature, a mirror can promote positive self-image by allowing a child to check on his or her appearance throughout the day.

Before investing in one, however, be sure the edges are rounded and smooth, since sharp corners could cause an accident. Polished chrome or other metal can be substituted if a glass mirror poses a risk.

In a bathroom lacking sufficient space for full-length reflection, place a small framed mirror low on a wall. Consider your child's eye level when determining location.

If there's room next to a full-length mirror, hang a marker and a measuring tape there, or stack two yardsticks so that a child can chart his or her new height regularly.

THINK LOW

When it comes to other bathroom essentials, think low, too. Take towels and robes, for instance. Those meant for use by very young members of the family should be kept on towel bars and hooks within a child's reach.

Combs, brushes, and other grooming aids for children should be stored down low as well. Perhaps the bottom drawer of a storage cabinet could contain these items. If so, be sure the drawer pull is simple enough for a child to grasp. The stationary

Low towel bars and hooks make robes and other bathroom essentials easier to access when you're a child who can't reach high places.

panel that fronts most sink cabinets can conceal a perfect hideaway for these items when retrofitted with special hinges and a plastic bin. These are available in kit form; check a bath, kitchen supply, or hardware store for a suitable model.

If a cabinet drawer is not available, supply a small basket or plastic basin that can be kept in an out-of-the-way spot on the floor. If there's room for more than essentials, let your child store a couple of favorite waterproof toys. A side benefit to accessible storage is the ease it provides in maintaining tidiness.

When bathroom storage space is at a premium, look for alternate ways to encourage neatness. Velcro strips, for instance, can be pressed into duty for holding combs, brushes and other similar items. Also effective as a shower catch-all for shampoo, soap, and so forth, is a vinyl organizer with pockets that are pierced so water drains from them.

To foster cleanliness and give a special touch, personalize some of the towels with iron-on initials or symbols.

With stick-on names attached to the section of the mirror behind individual sinks, there's no forgetting territorial borders in this bath. "Co-designed" by the boys using it, it features cup holders made of LEGO bricks and a tissue container decorated with child artistry.

WHEN A BATH DOES DOUBLE TIME

More than towels need indiviualizing when two children share a bath, although towels are a good place to start since labeling linens keep them from getting mixed up.

Color coding is also ideal for distinguishing what belongs to whom. If Peggy likes blue and Marie likes green, for example, match their towels to their toothbrushes, plastic cups, and other personal items.

To promote a sense of self and foster imagination, DeAnna Brandt of Minnesota encouraged her 1- and 3-year-old sons to decorate their individual bathroom cups and tissue dispensers with 3-D paints. The boys' personal touch also details the bathroom tiles and wall mirror from time to time when parent and child play together with stick-on shapes and letters. The colorful vinyl designs range from the boys' names applied to the mirror behind their twin sinks to their favorite decor—dinosaurs, fish, trains, and planes.

"We make whole scenarios," enthuses DeAnna, whose graphic design talents surface in another dramatic way on the walls. Using a mix of red, white, orange, and purple 1-inch and 12-inch square tiles, she installed them randomly in zig-zag fashion all over the room. Where one area dips down to only 4 tiles high, another climbs up 20 tiles to touch the ceiling.

Besides vibrant primary colors on the tile-free portion of the walls and the countertop, what also distinguishes Michael and Daniel Brandt's bath are cabinet pulls, towel bars, and a shower curtain rod that looks like free-form squiggles. The whole room is so much fun to look at, it's not surprising both boys love bath time.

A MATTER OF HYGIENE

Without doubt, promoting personal hygiene is what a bathroom is all about whether it serves children only or the whole family. As serious as this subject is, however, it needn't be taught in no-nonsense terms only. As the Brandts' and other clever children's baths demonstrate, whimsy can drive home the same message.

Brushing teeth, for instance, has never been a favorite childhood pastime. But poster art of amusing bath scenes, or a monumental decorative toothbrush hung on the wall, may be just what it takes to encourage this healthful activity.

An amusing shower curtain enlivens a bath, too. For a personalized design, let a child decorate an unadorned canvas curtain with colored fabric markers that are waterproof. Back this curtain with a plastic liner for an extra measure of dryness.

A humorous toilet paper dispenser adds a whimsical element to a child's bath.

A measuring tape or height chart is also appropriate in a bathroom. It permits growth spurts to be tracked and, if decorative, lends a playful look.

Still other lighthearted touches include cheery wallcovering, decorative tile, or synthetic sponges shaped like animals or other designs. Any of these make appropriate bath borders that convey the message that a child lives here.

Other accents that appeal to a child's sense of humor yet promote good habits— whimsical dispensers for paper towels or toilet paper.

Artistic murals add interest, too, and, in older baths especially, can camouflage age marks or other unattractive features. San Francisco designer Victoria Stone had that in mind when she first viewed two long, narrow utilitarian cabinets in the separate baths a client's children used. By commissioning a muralist to cleverly paint the units and add roof facades, Stone transformed the cabinets into delightful storage spaces that became

237

room focal points. One now resembles a large dollhouse front with unusual architectural features; the other looks like a rocket detailed in paint with many planetary objects.

MIXING WATER AND SAFETY

From a child's point of view, taking a bath means playtime! Gather the sponge animals, add a soap that floats, and let him or her comandeer the flotilla.

As much fun as bathing can be for a child, it should also be safe. To guarantee that, examine bathroom details with an eye toward those that could cause problems. Install recessed soap dishes to prevent bruises and provide grab bars around the tub and the shower so small hands can grip something firm when it's time to get in or out of the tub or shower.

To avoid burns, set your household water at a moderate temperature, keeping in mind that 120° F causes scalding. Shop around for temperature-limiting faucets that minimize the risk of being scalded by allowing you to set a maximum temperature. The National Safe Kids Campaign recommends a maximum hot water setting of 105° F, noting that a child's skin is one half to one third the thickness of an adult's, thus making a child far more susceptible to burns.

In the shower, install a pressure-balanced valve. By guaranteeing consistent water temperature, it prevents the sudden surge of hot water often felt when a toilet is flushed.

One further word of caution about water areas. Make sure they're far away from outlets and electrical gadgets such as razors, Waterpiks, curling irons, and hair dryers. And never leave any of these appliances plugged in on the counter after use.

Fortunately, today's building codes require bathroom outlets be protected by a ground-fault circuit interrupter (GFCI). This instantly shuts off any power to a faulty circuit. If your home was built prior to these codes, you may want to have an electrician replace your existing outlets with newer, safer ones. For an extra measure of safety in an older home with outlets straddling the sink, use childproof outlet covers. Also consider installing a remote-mounted GFCI which enables you to protect all the circuitry in the bathroom from one single control. If you aren't a wiring expert, however, consult your electrician or designer about this feature.

Because pills and ointments are usually stored in a bathroom, childproofing should also take the medicine cabinet into consideration. To minimize the chance of accidental poisioning, install magnetic locks on this cupboard or on any drawers where contents might hold potential dangers. In a home with a very young child, buy special latches for the toilet lid, too.

Bathroom door hardware is also important when a very young person is part of the household. Choose something that can be unlocked from both sides so you can get in, if necessary, in the event of an emergency. As for cabinet hardware, look for easy-to-clean designs that are simple for small hands to manipulate.

SHEDDING SOME LIGHT

Just as a child's bedroom should have lighting that's accessible to him or her, so should the bathroom.

If children can't reach the control switch from the floor or from a step stool, get an extension that allows manipulation of a toggle switch from a low vantage point. Costing only a few dollars, they are sold in hardware and children's furniture stores.

Every bathroom also should have a small night-light to assist sleepy eyes headed there. To cut down on energy use, buy a light with a sensor triggered by darkness. Come daybreak, when artificial illumination is no longer needed, these inexpensive lights shut off automatically. In addition, you should consider low-voltage lighting that eliminates the possibility of electrical shock while still providing good illumination.

A BATH OF MY OWN

While the same rules for a family bath apply in a bath that accommodates a child only, there are a few extra features worth considering when someone small will be using this room exclusively.

First, the toilet basin. Choose a design that is as easy for a child to use as possible. If the bath you are building will be for your son, for instance, keep in mind that a boy of any age may find it more hygenic to use an elongated bowl rather than a standard oval shape.

If you are starting from scratch and your budget allows it, investigate the possibility of installing other child-oriented features that capitalize on safety without compromising the aesthetics.

In creating the ideal safety-conscious bath for an exhibit, designer Gary E. White *CID, CBD,* unleased his creativity to prove such design needn't be bland. His innovative ideas revolved around a tub cushioned with a thick layer of urethane foam. To play up the concept of a "safe harbor," the tub was inset in a custom Corian shell shaped like a boat, complete with a wide edge platform that accommodated a seated entrance. Other safety details included boatlike acrylic railings that served as grab bars and were equipped with fiber-optic lighting.

In keeping with the mission of the project, White designed separate stations for changing and washing up that had built-in safety measures with kids in mind. To limit the risk of falling while dressing or undressing, for instance, the change area had a bench made from Corian material rounded at the edge. And the sink area was designed with a single-lever faucet, easier than separate controls for a very young child to manipulate.

To eliminate the chance of accidental injury, several other custom touches were incorporated for the safe bath exhibit. The following are well worth considering whether you're building a new bath from scratch or updating an old one :

It's smooth sailing and sudsing in this cushioned tub that conforms to body contours. Set inside a custom surround shaped like a boat, the tub invites young bathers, who can sit on the side platform equipped with grab bars illuminated with fiber-optic lighting.

✔ Tip-out compartment in front of the sink: Allows for easy access to children's toiletries such as toothbrushes and toothpaste or combs and brushes.

✔ Concealed cabinet lock: Keeps hazardous items such as razors off limits to kids. It opens only with an accompanying magnetic key.

✔ Shower seat: Eliminates awkward positions that cause slips and falls, by providing a place to sit.

✔ Rounded or radius countertop edges: Eliminates any sharp edges that could could cause accidents by giving countertops smooth corners.

✔ Pull-out platform: Provides a step up for small fry who can't otherwise reach a sink or other area. Tucked below existing cabinetry where toe-kicks usually are, this feature allows a child to slide it back in place easily.

Other amenities to contemplate when constructing a child's bath include a laundry chute. It not only advertises the need to wash dirty clothes, but also encourages their quick removal to the laundry after being taken off so they don't pile up on the bathroom floor. Check into impact-resistant safety glass, too. It keeps shower and tub enclosures extra safe.

BATHING BEAUTY

Keeping kids squeeky clean all the time is highly unlikely. But keeping them tuned in to the importance of personal hygiene is well within the realm of possibility, especially if the bath they use has practical features with them in mind. Like other good habits instilled during childhood, those that continually foster clean living should last a lifetime.

TURNING THE CLOSET INTO THE "OTHER" ROOM

Tuck-aways. Cubbyholes. Nooks and crannies.

With a child's imagination, these odd-shaped areas transform into special places every bit as intriguing as outdoor tree houses or forts.

In a young person's world, they also exist anywhere from under the sheets to inside a cardboard box. Neither square footage nor location seems to matter. What really counts is the private refuge they afford.

To a kid, tuck-aways often provide the added advantage of being big enough for only a pint-size person to maneuver in comfortably. Imagine the lure such a cozy haven has for a girl or boy who goes there to entertain pets, playthings, or make-believe pals.

CLOSET HIDEAWAYS

If your child seeks a playful hideaway more permanent than the bedcovers, consider his or her bedroom closet. It may be an ideal alcove to create another room to retreat to once in a while. With little effort or expense, you can convert part of this overlooked space into a reading loft, a naptime nook, or even a mighty fort that allows a lookout point on high.

For either a single or a double closet, start the remodeling project by removing the door or doors and storing them until the day when enclosed storage is more appropriate. In their place, suspend a shower curtain, sheeting, canvas, or other washable material your child selects, using a simple tension rod sold at bath or hardware stores. Entry to this inner sanctum becomes a snap for small hands, which merely push the covering aside.

Now turn your attention inward and upward. If your son or daughter is too short to reach clothes hanging near the top of the closet, move the rod down low so that everything is within easy grasp. Replace the upper rod with a sturdy lowered shelf reinforced along the walls with supports adequate to hold a small child's body weight.

Along the front of the shelf, add a safety bar to prevent accidental falls, and at one end, secure a ladder angled for easy climbing. Cushion the shelf with pillows or a small

241

Taking advantage of the upper area of a standard closet generally inaccesible to a young child, this design utilizes space on high for reading and relaxing. Besides a custom ladder, all it required were added shelf support and safety bars.

foam mattress and provide good light, even if it's only a battery-operated lamp. The result of your efforts will be a comfy penthouse hideaway.

Closet lofts allow children to enjoy countless hours in a special world. Tempting as they may be as nighttime sleep space, however, they should not be considered a full-time replacement for a traditional bed. A better idea is reserving a loft for occasional naps. As a permanent out-of-the-way rest spot, lofts are excellent for stuffed animals, dolls, and other lightweight toys.

A CHILD'S FORTRESS

Whether beasties or ghoulies in a child's room go "bump" in the night or "bump" in the day, there's a sense of security if a young defender has a fortress to man. An irregularly shaped cranny that defies common usefulness could be the perfect place to position young sentries plotting strategy.

If a closet cubicle is too high for a child to reach, create a stairway to it by fastening horizontally some finished two-by-fours at least 3 inches apart, letting them stretch from the floor to the fort. By doing so, you enable someone small to use the beams as ladder rungs, providing ready access to the opening.

At the entry to this outpost, hang a piece of sturdy cloth slit with flaps from which curious faces can peer out to identify callers as friends or foes. Inside, cushion the command post with beanbag chairs or extra large throw pillows.

ROOM FOR GROWTH SPURTS

As a child stretches toward adulthood and requires more vertical storage to handle longer clothing, it's time to reconfigure the loft closet. That upper shelf that once held toys and tykes may now need to be pressed into duty as storage for more grown-up personal effects.

Carving space for special activities in an older child's closet is particularly appealing to the young person inspiring these changes if it caters to his or her special interests. Consider the following options for closets left "doorless":

Grooming Station: Off to one side of a double closet, place a vanity or tabletop unit with enough space for cosmetics, perfumes, grooming supplies, and other paraphernalia. Add a free-standing makeup mirror and a chair or stool to complete the setting. If your budget allows for some additional changes—and there's easy access to plumbing and electrical systems—consider a station that caters to teens. Adding a small sink, a light, and and an outlet really turns a closet into a functional grooming area that relieves the bathroom of extra traffic when it's shared by siblings. Although having a doorless closet grooming area provides an open look, keeping doors in place allows for closing off this area to maintain neatness.

Caged Pet Storage: Open closet shelves in a well-ventilated area of a closet are sometimes a good location for caged pets such as guinea pigs, hamsters, and mice, especially when there's more than one container to accommodate. Depending on the particular space, aquariums might do well here, too. Regardless of the kind of pet, however, consider the need for indirect lighting as well as temperature control before turning this spot into Fuzzy's or Squeaky's permanent home.

Study Station: Fitted with outlets, task lighting, and sufficient work surfaces, an auxiliary closet may house all or most of a student's homework essentials. Adjustable shelves can customize this space to handle books, reference guides, and other material.

Bathroom plumbing nearby cinched the ability to add a vanity with running water to a bedroom closet. Besides alleviating traffic in the bath, it provides a special place for a young girl to spread out her grooming supplies.

With or without doors, closets can accommodate many other childhood interests. For example:

Doll and Toy Collections: To encourage care of dolls, miniatures, awards, and other fine belongings, outfit an auxiliary closet or part of a large main closet with cubicles and/or adjustable shelves. Expensive collections may require encasing shelves in glass or Lucite to deter dust and sticky fingers.

Exercise Center: To promote a positive self-image and mind/body connection and to provide a means of venting frustrations, incorporate an exercise area into a child's

243

room. That way this activity becomes part of the daily routine. A large spare closet could serve as a mini-gym, with space allotted for an exercise mat, a chin-up board, and possibly a punching bag. If the only closet that can house exercise equipment is small, consider installing a slant board for sit-ups. It works in much the same way an ironing board flips down in a utility closet.

UP, UP, AND AWAY

As children grow and expand their wardrobes, utilizing a closet for anything but storage often is out of the question. In certain situations, however, it's still possible to expand a closet's usefulness by taking advantage of hidden space beyond its confines. Such was the case with the already cramped quarters that designer Linda Runion, *ASID*, enlarged for a 10-year-old in suburban Seattle.

Like many Northwestern homes, the bedroom ceiling in Brian's room vaulted to a height of 14 feet. The highest peak was on the closet side. Above the closet was a portion of the home's ample attic. By claiming a small part of it as an annex to the fourth grader's room, an ingenious hideaway was created for him.

To make the retreat cozy, the attic area being claimed was framed in for a finished space of 7 by 7 feet. Once that was done, the space on high was ready to be connected with the area below. A custom ladder, tailored to fit against the back of the reconfigured closet, provided the main access to the hideaway once a hole was cut in the ceiling of the closet. A hinged hatch cover was added as a safety feature.

A lofty lifestyle is an everyday experience for the boy who lives in this setting. To make room for the hideaway, attic space was comandeered above the closet where the ceiling was vaulted. Entry is by means of a ladder—and the secret password!

To give the young boy using the space a lookout to the room below and to the view beyond outside, a 3- by 4-foot opening was made in the bedroom/attic common wall. To be on the safe side, a window grid without glass was installed.

Now large enough for a jumbo 3-foot beanbag that comfortably accommodates two kids or a parent and child, the closet annex also contains adequate toy and game bins, throw pillows, and wall displays. But the best part of the new hideaway, as far as its owner is concerned, is the bookcase tucked into the side of a corner wall. When slid forward on its wheels, this reading center reveals the unfinished portion of the attic and its access portal to the first floor. To 10-year-olds with fertile imaginations, however, this passageway is an official "secret compartment" that leads to intrigue and mystery.

While not all homes have the kind of architecture featuring abundant vertical space, many residences, particularly older ones, have odd-shaped eaves formed by the roofline. When the eaves are located behind a closet, it may be worth getting professional advice about expanding the existing storage area to take advantage of the otherwise dead space beyond. As a child of parents who did just that when I was 11, I know well the thrill of exploring new bedroom territory where grown-ups can't venture easily because of the space's dimensions.

Hideaways don't require much in the way of furnishings. This one functions adequately with a big beanbag chair, a bookcase, and storage containers.

Besides air conditioning vents, only a toy chest and a few dolls would fit in my awkward closet recess. Small matter. The special childhood journeys that began and ended there needed only room in my mind to happen again and again.

IMAGINE THAT

Manning a fort.

Curling up in a corner with special toys.

Pursuing a hobby where you can work uninterupted.

These are a few reasons why children like closet hideaways. Beyond serving as an auxiliary work or play space, they also appeal to the once-in-awhile need for private refuge when it's time to be left alone.

Knock, Knock

Whether in a home's entry or elsewhere, a closet a child shares with the rest of the household should be detailed to some extent to his or her specific needs. Essentially, that means arranging kids' belongings so kids can retrieve them.

A few ways to do that:

- Place hooks at child height for schoolbags, hats, and other hangables.

- Position an adjustable clothes rod low enough for someone small to reach.

- Install cubbyholes or stack open bins so assorted gear tucks away in them. Label them with a child's name so there's no guessing where items belong.

- Hang a small mirror inside the door where a child can check on his or her appearance before and after going out.

- Keep a few shelves at child height so games and other child-friendly items located here are accessible to the one who will be using them.

- Situate a small bench inside the closet—or if that's impossible, just outside of it—so that changing shoes and boots is easier.

If there's a closetless back door area or mud room with storage possibilities, let a locker come to the rescue. One feature could be special cubbyholes for each child to receive messages.

Besides comandeering the locker's insides for outside wear, press the door into duty as a bulletin board. Use it to tack up chore lists, meeting reminders, and personal messages.

A locker is also a good place for a calendar. But hang it low enough so a child can mark dates, too!

THE INSIDE STORY ON PLAY SPACES

Where can children play indoors when it's too cold, dark, or miserable outdoors?

It's a question all parents confront throughout the year, and the issue becomes more complex as children grow up and expand their circle of friends to entertain at home.

Undoubtedly, the ideal solution is a permanent playroom or recreation room. But if the place where you live doesn't permit that luxury, do the next best thing. Improvise an area for play that takes advantage of auxiliary space you do have.

A walk-in closet. An odd-shaped alcove. An enclosed porch. These are a few suitable locations for indoor play. Depending on your particular setup, the attic, basement, or garage may also assume the role of play space even if only part-time.

Although safety and space considerations impose limitations on indoor play, it's still relatively easy to shape a stimulating home environment that will fuel curiosity and creativity.

NOT IN MY ROOM

Besides curing cabin fever when the outdoors are unwelcoming, an indoor recreation area offers someplace besides the bedroom for leisure and social activities. It also provides a designated setting for social interaction when your child's pals come over. As such, it should be a spot where a certain amount of noise can be tolerated and a project can be left "in progress" without parental disapproval.

The benefits of having play space separate from sleep and study space abound. If your

Waves that wash upon the walls, and sea creatures that dance across the carpet, create a serene seaside atmosphere in this playworthy space.

children work off excess energy away from their bedroom, it saves on the wear and tear that room receives.

For those sharing quarters, an auxiliary space for recreation also offers a regular arrangement whereby each roommate has an optional place to retreat for quiet or noisy endeavors.

Finding ideal play elements for the recreation area you choose can be as pleasureable an experience for you as for your child. Join your kids on their level. Participate in activity that tickles their fancy. Watch intently what amuses them.

After observing their playful pursuits, zero in on favored activities. Plot your next move by devising a setting that incorporates them. The objective here isn't to set up an indoor mini-playground or gym for major sports or other rough play. Instead, the aim is to create a small area for limited physical activity and/or quiet play that a child can engage in whenever the mood for either strikes.

With little effort and expense, you can do much to spark imaginative play. Let's say your young one is a born performer. Put a small platform in his or her play area to serve as a stage, or place a wooden closet rod along one wall as a ballet bar.

Imagination is the name of the game in this kind of setting. As renowned educator Maria Montessori demonstrated, rooms can be filled with items that invite activity and aid a child's mental and physical development. Keep it simple, however, so items can be easily changed.

"Play serves an extremely important function in a child's learning about the world," wrote the late child psychologist Lee Salk, Ph.D., in his *A-to-Z Guide to Raising Your Child.*

"Various objects in an environment," Salk explained, "provide needed stimulation to do this—mobiles to look at, music boxes to listen to, stuffed toys to touch and feel. "

SMALL SPACE FOR SMALL FRY

If there isn't a large playroom where you live, don't despair. An expansive area may be just the opposite of what a young child craves. As research at the University of Tennessee, Knoxville, indicates, little ones generally gravitate toward scaled-down environments in proportion to their size. That's why small nooks and crannies may be more appealing than a big open space.

Generally, the more unusual the alcove, the more exciting it will be to a young person. A niche like the one created by a peaked dormer of a window, for instance, is a child's ready-made retreat. Tack up some corkboard, and it becomes a miniature gallery to display camp ribbons, school pennants, snapshots, and treasures. But don't cram too much into a confined space. Showing off one or two interests is probably sufficient. To decide which ones, ask the one claiming this territory.

Another haven for someone small is the stepped dead space under stairs, which is often enclosed as a closet. Remove the door, light the space with a portable battery-operated lantern, and create a special hideaway that can be personalized with paint in your child's favorite color. To make the space more user friendly and visually expansive, secure a safety mirror to the wall. Now the child's reflection will serve as constant company.

If alcoves aren't options in a house or apartment with a small child, scrutinize the kitchen. Is there a low shelf that could accommodate play cooking gear? If so, then junior cooks can stay engaged when Mom or Dad prepares meals.

Even the kitchen table is a candidate for play once a sheet or long cloth is draped over it. For a child who likes being near grown-ups, this temporary refuge is delightful.

A formal dining room also has possibilities as an exclusive play space when its original function is rethought. To do this, adapt the kitchen or living room for meals. If that's impossible, invest in a drop-leaf table. When the leaves are down, it consumes minimal space and tucks aside to open the floor for low-key play.

Pint-size productions find a suitable theater under the stairs in this urban loft, where door and window openings allow for all kinds of theatrics.

PLAYFUL TOUCHES

To encourage playfulness contemplate other designs, too. For example:

Secret Pass-Through: In homes where bedrooms are side by side, closets are often back to back. If a spare bedroom has been relegated as the playroom and it's next to your child's bedroom, cut a child-size door in the mutual closet wall and hinge it to swing open. A mysterious pass through is now ready to use.

Shelf as Toy Garage: To enable a child to move toy vehicles from one shelf to another, architect Elyse Lewin designed a tiered bookcase with ramps. With miniature trucks and cars stored there, the shelves resemble a multilevel toy garage. A similar unit can

249

A common closet wall between the side-by-side bedrooms of two brothers opens the way for a child-size entry when a hole is cut and a small door added. A latch on either side prohibits passage when one of them prefers solitude.

be created with an existing low bookcase by making an opening in the center of upper shelves that measures approximately 3 to 4 inches wide by 8 to 10 inches long. This should enable most miniature vehicles to roll to the next level without getting stuck. The ramp effect is created by cutting individual pieces of $\frac{1}{2}$-inch thick lumber, measuring 3 to 4 inches wide by the length you need to drop to the next shelf.

Wall as Magnet: DeAnna and Peter Brandt of Minnesota proved how delightful sheet metal salvage can be in a child's playroom when it's used as an interactive wall hanging. Using a piece the size of a school blackboard, they applied auto paint to the metal before framing it with wood strips. Their children add the final touches—anything metal that's magnetized.

IMAGINE THAT

If none of these play ideas appeal to you, exercise your own imagination. Some alternatives may already be nearby.

Kids love a corrugated kingdom, for instance. If you don't have a spare large box, check an appliance store for one. Otherwise, buy a large cardboard container from a moving company. Let your child decorate it with crayons, or other media. To facilitate decorating, provide gift wrap for wallpaper and magazine pictures for wall hangings. If the structure can't remain up forever, disassemble the box in folds for easy storage until next time.

Another standby that promotes play is a card table. Besides accommodating tabletop activity, it serves as a hideaway once draped with a large cloth or sheet. If you can permanently spare a covering, cut a porthole in it.

A collapsible tepee is another play idea that works well indoors, whether it's set up for permanent pow-wows or used only occasionally. For do-it-yourself know-how check out fabric store pattern books or craft stores for information. For an authentic touch, follow the lead of Maureen and Mike Lowe's family in Colorado. Using multicolored permanent markers, their 5-, 6-, 9- and 12-year-old children decorated plain beige broadcloth tepee panels with Indian drawings illustrated in *Indian Picture Writing*, a children's book by Robert Hofsinde found in the library.

A WAY TO SOOTHE GROWING PAINS

Just as children outgrow clothes, they outgrow tiny play areas. Once that happens, look elsewhere for indoor playgrounds.

If a walk-in closet can be spared, transform it into a kid's retreat by cushioning the floor with an area rug or carpet remnant and replacing clothes rods with shelves for playthings. Or turn this area into a mini exercise center with padded mats, sit-up and pull-up bars, and a small round trampoline. Before undertaking this conversion, however, furnish sufficient ventilation, and, if possible, soundproofing material.

In winter months, an enclosed porch or solarium devoid of regular furnishings becomes a place to play. Besides warmth and natural light, a bonus here is an outdoor feeling, since trees and sky are within view. No matter how this space is zoned for play, see that window glass is shatterproof so that a tossed toy won't cause an accident. For comfort, install a window covering that keeps the room temperature controlled.

When the ground is too damp or cold, yet it's sunny enough for outdoor exposure, look to a balcony or deck as a makeshift play area. For safety's sake, be sure first that the rails are spaced no more than a few inches apart. If not, prevent a curiosity seeker from climbing through openings by stretching chicken wire in front of the rails.

For practical purposes, allow only toys that weather well in an outdoor setting. Since a deck or balcony is an ideal place to teach gardening, place a small container there exclusively for junior green thumbs to cultivate plantings. Child-size tools nearby make playing gardener easy.

STRETCHING TOWARD ADULTHOOD

As kids get older and spend more time by themselves, they yearn for independent play space. Teens especially prefer entertaining friends away from family activity. By trying to provide such a place, you let them know their buddies are welcome.

Is attic, basement, or garage space available? Convert it into a recreation room. Carve up the area according to general interests, with sections for reading, music, exercise, and so forth. Since computer games also amuse kids, devote an area to this, too, if it's within the realm of possibility.

When Child's Play Works

From peek-a-boo to prancing around in costumes, playtime interests and abilities depend on many developmental factors.

In their *Child* magazine column, Drs. Michael Schwartzman and Lisa Weiss recommend playing with your child so you both learn about each other. "Play offers a fun forum for sharing, relaxing and growing closer," the psychologists write. To understanding child's play, they offer this timetable.

Birth to 1 (A Fun Foundation): View daily tasks as opportunities to stimulate a baby and have fun. For example: Bathtime becomes playtime when you show how the plastic cup fills with water and spills out. To establish security, let the baby know you enjoy being together.

1 to 3 (Giggles and Games): Captivated by physical and cognitive achievements, toddlers repeat accomplishments for motivation, reassurance, and pleasure. Engage in physical play that shows what they're capable of doing.

3 to 6 (The Power of Pretend): Make-believe, dress-up, and pretend play offer great opportunity at this stage to develop imagination. Encourage eagerness to learn by turning everyday activities such as grocery shopping into fun, educative adventures.

6 to 9 (Simple Pleasures): Social life starts to shift to peers, so capitalize on the child's ability to understand rules of play by teaching good sportsmanship and teamwork. Growing command of language supports wordplay, such as crossword puzzles. Games like magic tricks foster creative thinking and self esteem. Be a receptive audience so the child is encouraged to share new skills with others.

9 to 12 (Growing and Sharing): Be sensitive to expanding skills and developing self-esteem by maintaining a constructive, supportive attitude in play. To establish an avenue of togetherness, introduce the child to hobbies you enjoy, too.

252

After the age of 12, Dr. Schwartzman notes, kids tend to play with peers, so it's harder for parents to engage them in play. "All of a sudden," he says, " rooms become very private and off-limits to parents. Respect the need for privacy and don't poke your nose in too deep." If interaction presents itself, take advantge of it. "Always show the pleasure you feel in spending time with your children, " the psychologist adds.

As for rec room furnishings for kids, take the budget route with inexpensive floor cushions, beanbags, futons, and a card table with chairs. Or make large and small platforms from plywood boxes. Stacked, carpeted, and covered with pillows, they make an impromptu stage, lounge seating, or, once sleeping bags are stretched across, adequate bedding for slumber parties. Finishing touches might include posters that the younger generation favors as well as school or sports memorabilia.

If you're taking advantage of attic space, don't overlook important technicalities. These include extra insulation, air-conditioning, heating, and self-ventilating skylights.

Basements and garages, on the other hand, should be not only insulated and heated, but also water-proofed to seal off any dampness.

HOW YOU PLAY THE GAME

Both indoors and out, a good play environment for a child of any age is one that fosters creativity and self-expression. When that environment is located at home, it gives parents the opportunity to encourage youthful imagination and skill in safe and secure surroundings.

A giant plastic initial of a child's first name playfully reminds him what familiar objects also begin with that letter.

Like a favorite game played again and again, a room with playful elements continually intrigues the child in it. If it stimulates both mind and body, going there will always be an enjoyable experience.

Having play space at home also gives children another important message. Relaxation has a definite role in the way we live.

A FINAL NOTE FROM THE AUTHOR...

Like finding photos of long-ago friends, writing this book unearthed faded childhood snapshots, albeit mental ones. The "finds" popped up at every bend.

Interviewing an educator studying the meaning and exhibition of family photos, I recalled the image of my first bedroom's most intriguing detail—a heart-shaped framed picture of the never-known aunt for whom I was named . . .

Reading about home play spaces, I envisioned the little log cabin from Sears in our yard accessorized with folding table and chairs and a braided rug from the family mill . . .

Surveying kids about what they collect, I flashed back on hundreds of vending machine trinkets I amassed and traded during grade school days . . .

If I could place these mental images in a tangible album, its most worn page would show the time when I was 11. That's where *In My World* begins—in *my* world many summers ago.

It was the year my now late parents realized their notion of a custom dream house near Valley Forge, Pennsylvania. Although it looked *all* new from my vantage point, it was actually a combination of past and present construction situated on our existing home's foundation. Vividly, I remember being awfully haughty about the remodel being launched in my room. I viewed this as symbolic that my needs took precedence over older brother Jimmy's.

Some kids might balk at the demolition of private space; I gleefully anticipated the ruins of mine since wreckers were wiping out walls to capture dead space under the eaves for closet storage the setting lacked. In the long run, this renovation meant an end to traipsing through Jimmy's room on *his* terms to get *my* clothes out of *our* closet. In the immediate sense, it equated to "camping" in the dining room with our toy fox terrier, Sparky.

For me, the chaos connected with remodeling was pure bliss. And I got to share it with 14 neighbor kids, all relatives who lived in adjacent houses on all sides.

Eventually, our family of four had to move so work could transpire safely. The relocation, a mere 200 feet away at Grandpop's, allowed an inquisitive kid like me to fill endless days with a stream of "I witness" events: A side patio poured where a play yard once was . . . An indoor "gallery" created where an outdoor wraparound porch once stood . . . Large picture windows installed where small double-hung ones used to be.

Just as swell as observing progress was investigating it after workmen quit for the day. That's when 10-year-old cousin Felice came from her house next door to join me in playing jacks on a sawdust pile, or in building a fortress with all kinds of discards. How we got away with this, I don't recall. Unless we didn't and I've lost that mental picture.

That summer, I saw my first blueprints. And I met my first architect. Actually, our encounters were more an awareness of each other's presence than any formal how-do. In retrospect, this should have alerted me that my ideas might not factor into the project. But I was young and wanted to believe I was part of the monumental undertaking. As the architect paraded samples, I enjoyed thinking I was a crucial part of the decision process.

Yet by the time painters began working upstairs, no one had asked my opinions, although it's hard to imagine I didn't volunteer some. Anyway, as for coloring my private quarters, I was sure everyone in *my* world knew *my* preference—blue in any shade.

Oh, how I dreamed of a new room that matched the sky! What a shock to find nothing bluish in it. In truth, the pink floral wallpaper I'd stared at nearly a dozen years was gone. But the place was still peppermint pink, a shade I knew to be mother's favorite.

Bless her heart and her intentions. One of nine children always sharing a space, Mom created her perfect refuge—a rosy paradise reflected in cafe curtains, figurine lamps, and chenille coverlet. Even the flowers outside my window were you-know-what color.

Happy as I was to be back looking at familiar treetops and hearing distant trains, I felt a bit cheated at not even being asked how *my* furniture should be arranged. Years later when Dad lived with us after Mom passed away, I asked why my ideas were overlooked. *"You were just a kid,"* he replied. *"What did you know about things like that?"*

As I grew up, I kept moving into places that would look better blue, from a dorm room that cried out for peacock fishnet on the walls, to a studio that longed to be navy.

Those true blue experiences took on new meaning once I focused my journalism career on how environment influences children. In the years since, I've gained new perspective about the young by observing, consulting, and writing about their personal spaces.

I hope this book imparts some insight about shaping surroundings for and with the next generation. If so, may its ideas help you bridge the years between us. What a picture-perfect world this would then be.

—Ro Logrippo

A BIBLIOGRAPHY

Research and information in this book stem from scores of interviews with authorities on design and children, as well as myriad books and reading materials by experts in many fields.

Resources consulted by the author include the following, listed here for those who wish additional information. This listing does not constitute endorsement of the material.

Babbitt, Edwin S.
THE PRINCIPLES OF LIGHT & COLOR
(Citadel Press, New York, NY, 1980)

Better Homes and Gardens
**ALL ABOUT YOUR HOUSE:
STRETCHING LIVING SPACE**
(Meredith Books, Des Moines, Iowa, 1983)
NEW DECORATING BOOK
(Meredith Books, Des Moines, Iowa, 1990)

Birren, Faber
**COLOR: A SURVEY IN WORDS AND
PICTURES**
(Citadel Press, Secaucus, NJ, 1963)
COLOR & HUMAN RESPONSE
(Van Nostrand Reinhold, New York, NY, 1978)

Black, Lynette Ranney, and Wisner, Linda
**CREATIVE SERGING FOR THE HOME AND
OTHER QUICK DECORATING IDEAS**
(Craftsman Press, Seattle, WA, 1991)

Bourke, Linda
IT'S YOUR MOVE
(Addison-Wesley, Boston, MA, 1981)

Brazelton, T. Berry, MD
TOUCHPOINTS
(Addison-Wesley, Boston, MA, 1992)
WORKING AND CARING
(Addision-Wesley, Boston, MA, 1987)

Brown, Laurence Krasy, and Brown, Marc
DINOSAURS DIVORCE
(Little Brown and Co., Boston, MA, 1986)

Carnegie Corporation of New York
**STARTING POINTS: MEETING THE
NEEDS OF OUR YOUNGEST
CHILDREN**
(Carnegie Corporation of New York, 1994)

Children's Environments Research Group / Ph.D.
Program in Psychology/ Environmental
**CHILDREN'S ENVIRONMENTS
QUARTERLY**
(The Graduate Center, City University of New
York; Issued quarterly)

Csikszentmihalyi, Mihaly, and Rochberg-Halton,
Eugene
**THE MEANING OF THINGS:
DOMESTIC SYMBOLS AND THE SELF**
(Cambridge University Press, New York, NY, 1992)

Danger, E.P.
THE COLOUR HANDBOOK
Gower Technical Press, Brookfield, VT, 1987)

Ehlert, Lois
PLANTING A RAINBOW
(Harcourt Brace & Co., New York, NY, 1988)

Eiseman, Leatrice
ALIVE WITH COLOR
(Acropolis Books, Washington, DC, 1983)

Gelson, Hilary
CHILDREN ABOUT THE HOUSE
(Martin Cadbury Ltd., Worcester, England, 1976)

Gilliatt, Mary
DESIGNING ROOMS FOR CHILDREN
(Orbis Publishing Ltd., London, England, 1984)

Gillis, Jack, and Fise, Mary Ellen R. (Consumer
Federation of America)
THE CHILDWISE CATALOG
(Harper & Row, New York, NY, 1990)

Harrington, Leslie, ASID, ARIDO, IDC, with
Mackie, Joan
COLOR: A STROKE OF BRILLIANCE
(B & E Publications Inc., Mississauga, Ontario,
Canada, 1993)

Hofsinde, Robert
INDIAN PICTURE WRITING
(William Morrow, New York, NY 1959)

Hope, Augustine, and Walch, Margaret
THE COLOR COMPENDIUM
(Van Nostrand Reinhold, New York, NY, 1990)

Huffman, Eddie, Draper, Steve, and Levy, Stephen
KIDS COMPUTER BOOK
(Compute Books, Greensboro, NC, 1992)

Hurwitz, Johanna
DEDE TAKES CHARGE!
(William Morrow, New York, NY, 1992)

Imber-Black, Evan, and Roberts, Janine
**RITUALS FOR OUR TIMES: CELEBRAT-
ING HEALING AND CHANGING OUR
LIVES AND RELATIONSHIPS**
(HarperCollins, New York, NY 1992)

Innes, Jocasta, and Walton, Stewart
**PAINTED FURNITURE PATTERNS:
34 ELEGANT DESIGNS TO PULL OUT,
PAINT, AND TRACE**
(Viking, New York, NY, 1993)
THE NEW PAINT MAGIC
(Pantheon Books, New York, NY, 1992)

Isaacs, Susan
**HOW TO ORGANIZE YOUR KID'S
ROOM**
(Ballantine Books, New York, NY 1985)

Jeunesse, Gallimard, and de Bourgoing, Pascale
COLORS
(Scholastic, Inc., New York, NY 1991)

Klein, Gerald L., M.D., and Timerman, Vicki
**KEYS TO PARENTING THE ASTHMATIC
CHILD**
(Barron's Educational Series, Hauppauge, NY, 1994)

Krauss, David A., Ph.D., and Fryrear, Jerry L., Ph.D.
PHOTOTHERAPY IN MENTAL HEALTH
(Charles C. Thomas, Springfield, IL, 1983)

Kron, Joan, and Slesin, Suzanne
**HIGH-TECH: THE INDUSTRIAL STYLE
SOURCE BOOK FOR THE HOME**
(Chanticleer Press, New York, NY, 1978)

Lansky, Vicki
**ANOTHER USE FOR 101 COMMON
HOUSEHOLD ITEMS**
(The Book Peddlers, Deephaven, MN, 1991)
CHILD PROOF YOUR HOME
(Safety First, Chestnut Hill, MA, 1991)
DON'T THROW THAT OUT!
(The Book Peddlers, Deephaven, MN, 1994)

Leach, Penelope
CHILDREN FIRST: WHAT OUR SOCIETY MUST DO AND IS NOT DOING FOR OUR CHILDREN TODAY
(Alfred A. Knopf, New York, 1994)

Leibrock, Cynthia, with Behar, Susan
BEAUTIFUL BARRIER-FREE: A VISUAL GUIDE TO ACCESSIBILITY
(Van Nostrand Reinhold, New York, NY, 1993)

Lott, Jane
CHILDREN'S ROOMS
(Prentice Hall Press, New York, NY 1989)

Ludington-Hoe, Dr. Susan, with Golant, Susan K.
HOW TO HAVE A SMARTER BABY
(Bantam Books, New York, NY, 1987)

Marshall Editions Ltd.
COLOUR
(London, 1980)

Marston, Stephanie
THE MAGIC OF ENCOURAGEMENT
(William Morrow, New York, NY, 1990)

McClelland, Nancy
THE YOUNG DECORATORS
(Harper & Brothers, New York, NY, 1928)

McGrath, Molly, and McGrath, Norman
CHILDREN'S SPACES
(William Morrow & Co., New York, NY, 1978)

Meijer, Marie
THE BAKE-A-CAKE BOOK
(Chronicle Books, San Francisco, CA, 1994)

Montessori, Maria.
THE MONTESSORI METHOD
(Schocken Books, New York, NY, 1970)
SPONTANEOUS ACTIVITY IN EDUCATION (Fifth Edition)
(Schocken Books, New York, NY 1969)

Nida, Patricia Cooney, Ph.D.
THE TEENAGERS' SURVIVAL GUIDE TO MOVING
(Atheneum, New York, NY, 1985)
FAMILIES ON THE MOVE: HUMAN FACTORS ON RELOCATION
(Kendall/Hunt Publishing Co., Dubuque, Iowa, 1983)

Nissen, LuAnn, Faulkner, Ray, and Faulkner, Sarah
INSIDE TODAY'S HOME (Sixth Edition)
(Harcourt Brace College Publishers, Orlando, FL, 1994)

O'Neil, Isabel
THE ART OF THE PAINTED FINISH FOR FURNITURE & DECORATION
(Viking, New York, NY, 1971)

O'Neill, Mary
HAILSTONES AND HALIBUT BONES
(Doubleday, New York, NY, 1989)

Ortho Editorial Staff; Dunham, Christine, project editor
HOW TO DESIGN & REMODEL CHILDREN'S ROOMS
(Ortho Books, San Ramon, CA, 1988)

Peckinpah, Sandra Lee
CHESTER . . . THE IMPERFECT ALL-STAR
(Dasan Publishing, Agoura Hills, CA, 1993)
ROSEY . . . THE IMPERFECT ANGEL
(Scholars Press, Woodland Hills, CA, 1991)

Plaut, Thomas F., M.D.
CHILDREN WITH ASTHMA: A MANUAL FOR PARENTS (Second Edition)
(Pedipress, Inc., Amherst, MA, 1988)

Raskin, Robin and Ellison, Carol
PARENTS, KIDS & COMPUTERS: AN ACTIVITY GUIDE FOR FAMILY FUN AND LEARNING
(Random House, New York, NY, 1992)

Salk, Lee, Ph.D.
THE COMPLETE DR. SALK: AN A-TO-Z GUIDE TO RAISING YOUR CHILD
(New American Library, New York, NY, 1985)

Sharpe, Deborah T.
THE PSYCHOLOGY OF COLOR AND DESIGN
(Littlefield, Adams & Co., Lanham, MD, 1981)

Stuart, Spencer
MARBLING: HOW-TO TECHNIQUES
(Harmony Books, New York, NY 1989)

Sunset Books
CHILDREN'S ROOMS & PLAY YARDS
(Lane Publishing Co., Menlo Park, CA, 1991)
HOME OFFICES & WORKSPACES
(Lane Publishing Co., Menlo Park, CA, 1986)
IDEAS FOR GREAT KIDS' ROOMS
(Lane Publishing Co., Menlo Park, CA, 1993)
KITCHEN STORAGE
(Lane Publishing Co., Menlo Park, CA, 1989)
MAKING YOUR HOME CHILD-SAFE
Don Vandervort with the Editors
(Lane Publishing Co., Menlo Park, CA, 1988)
MORE LIVING SPACE
(Lane Publishing Co., Menlo Park, CA, 1986)

Tobias, Tobi
MOVING DAY
(Alfred A. Knopf, New York, NY 1976)

Torrice, Antonio F., and Logrippo, Ro
IN MY ROOM: DESIGNING FOR AND WITH CHILDREN.
(Fawcett/Columbine, New York, NY, 1989)

Trelease, Jim
THE NEW READ ALOUD HANDBOOK
(Penguin Books, New York, NY 1989)

Wallerstein, Judith S., Ph.D., and Blakeslee, Sandra
SECOND CHANCES: MEN, WOMEN & CHILDREN A DECADE AFTER DIVORCE
(Ticknor & Fields, New York, NY, 1989)

Walsh, Ellen Stoll
MOUSE PAINT
(Harcourt Brace & Co., New York, 1989)

Walton, Sally, and Walton, Stewart
STENCIL IT! OVER 100 STEP-BY-STEP PROJECTS
(Sterling Publishing, New York, NY, 1993)

PAMPHLET BIBLIOGRAPHY

Assorted booklets, guides, and manuals were consulted in doing research for this book. Those available to consumers include the following. Some are free; others involve a cost.

Allergy and Asthma Network/ Mothers of Ashmatics
Informational Material.
3554 Chain Bridge Road, # 200 Fairfax, VA 22030

Allied Van Lines
Carton Capers (Booklet about imaginative structures)
Purchasing Dept., 1515 Centre Circle Drive, Downers Grove, IL 60515

American College of Allergy and Immunology
Pamphlets
85 W. Algonquin Road, Suite 550, Arlington Heights, IL 60005

American Lung Association
Allergy-related brochures
1740 Broadway, New York, NY 10019

American Red Cross
Basic Aid Training (Activity book)
Child Care Course, Standard First Aid and CPR (Brochures)
National Headquarters: 431-18th Street, NW, Washington, DC 20006

Asthma and Allergy Foundation of America
Self-help materials
1125 15th Street, NW, Suite 502, Washington, DC 20005

Atlas Van Lines
Buddy the Moving Van Fun Kit (Activity book)
Available from Atlas agents nationwide

Consumer Product Safety Commission
Tips for Your Baby's Safety
Protect Your Child (English and Spanish editions)
Office of Information/Public Affairs, 5401 W. Bard Avenue, Bethesda, MD 20207

Department of Education
Helping Your Child Learn Geography
Dept. 414-Z, Consumer Information Center, Pueblo, CO 81009
Helping Your Child Learn to Read
Dept. 617-Z, Consumer Information Center, Pueblo, CO 81009

Discovery Toys
Gateway to Imagination (Book Club for 2 1/2- to 5-year-olds)
Box 5031, Livermore, CA 94550

Eastman Kodak Co.
Hot Shots (Booklet)
Information Center, Dept. 841 Literature and Mail, Rochester, NY 14650-0811

ETS Policy Information Center
America's Smallest School: The Family (48-page report)
Rosedale Road, Princeton, NJ 08541

Gerber Products Company
The Gerber Guide to Safety (16-page guide)
445 State Street, Fremont, MI 49413

International Reading Association
You Can Encourage Your Child to Read
Your Child's First School
800 Barksdale Road, Newark, DE 19714

Juvenile Product Manufacturers Association
Crib Safety Alert
Safe and Sound for Baby (Brochures)
JPMA, Box 955, Marlton, NJ 08053

Lazar Media Group
Shop by Mail (Biannual guide)
112 E. 36th Street, New York, NY 10016

Mayflower Transit
Child's Moving Kit (Storybook, stickers, change of address cards)
Distributed through local transit agents with moving estimates

MACIntosh Performa
ABCs of Learning on Home Computers (Booklet)
55 Union Street, San Francisco, CA 94111.

National Institutes for Health Communications
Create a Dust-Free Bedroom (One of several guides)
9000 Rockville Pike, Bldg. 31 #7-A50, Bethesda, MD 20892.

National Jewish Center for Immunology and Respiratory Medicine
Booklet materials
1400 Jackson Street, Denver, CO 80206

National Kitchen & Bath Association
31 Rules of Kitchen Planning (Fact sheet)
687 Willow Grove Street, Hackettstown, NJ 07840

National Safe Kids Campaign
Safe Kids Are No Accident
Parents' Guide to Safety
111 Michigan Avenue, NW, Washington, DC 20010-2970

National Safety Council
Crib Safety
Cumulative Trauma (Booklets)
1121 Spring Lake Drive, Itasca, IL 60143-3201

Reading Is Fundamental
Pamphlets for young readers
600 Maryland Avenue, SW, # 600, Washington, DC 10024

Safety 1st
Child Proof Your Home (Manual)
210 Boylston Street, Chestnut Hill, MA 02167

Sartori, Linda
KIDS Express! (Monthly newsletter for children in divorce and separation)
Box 782, Littleton, CO 80160

United Van Lines
Moving With Children (Pamphlet)
Corporate Communications, 1 United Drive, Fenton, MO 63026)

Wamsutta
Surroundings from Wamsutta (51-page book)
Times Square Station, Box 774, New York, NY 10108

WestPoint Pepperell Consumer Affairs
Decorating with Sheets (20-page booklet)
Box 609, West Point, GA 31833

FEATURED DESIGNERS

The design projects illustrated in this book represent the creativity of many gifted professionals throughout the United States. In spotlighting their work, the author acknowledges their tremendous talent and contribution toward elevating the quality of children's design. Immeasurable gratitude is extended to them for sharing a wealth of ideas so that *In My World* readers can also benefit from their successful projects for young people.

Page Number

Jane Antonacci, Allied Member ASID
Jane Antonacci & Associates   *71*
644 Menlo Avenue # 100
Menlo Park, CA 94025
415/323-9178

Laura Ashley Inc.   *44, 46, 124, 128*
800/367-2000

Susan Behar, ASID   *190, 192*
Universal Design
1732 Hickory Gate Drive, North
Dunedin, FL 34698
813/784-0261

DeAnna Brandt   *14, 20, 35 (top), 54 (top),*
7570 Dogwood Road   *78 (bottom), 105, 236*
Excelsior, MN 55331
612/470-4566

Carolyn M. Carnell, Allied Member ASID   *217*
Elegant Interiors
15 El Toro Street
Morgan Hill, CA 95037
408/778-6544

Design Response   *59, 201 (top)*
Showcase '94 Project Committee
Suzanne Ferrari, ASID, and Sharon Daroca,
Katherine Murray, and Helen L. Carreker,
Allied Members ASID
1168-H Aster Avenue
Sunnyvale, CA 94086
408/244-2479

Nancy Doolittle, Allied Member ASID   *247*
1700 Seabiscuit Drive
Navarro, CA 95463
707/895-3650

Barbara Eden, IBD   *195*
Eden Design Associates, Inc.
111 Congressional Boulevard, Suite 120
Carmel, IN 46032
317/843-5790

Page Number

Suzanne Ferrari, ASID   *274*
Interior Planning and Design
944 Corriente Point Drive
Redwood Shores, CA 94065
415/592-4994

Kim Fiori   *96, 99*
Wild Child Designs
2307 Mill Creek Lane
Healdsburg, CA 95448
707/433-7440

Tia Garvey, Allied Member ASID   *247*
Cynthia Garvey Interior Design
370 Village Lane
Los Gatos, CA 95030
408/395-6511

Rela Gleason   *114, 201 (bottom),*
Summer Hill Ltd.   *223 (bottom)*
2682h Middlefield Road
Redwood City, CA 94063
415/363-2600

Anita Goldblatt, Allied Member ASID   *78 (top), 149, 177,*
Designing Interiors   *202*
401 East 80th Street
New York, NY 10021
212/517-5428

Rodney A. Greenblat   *24, 220, 249*
Center for Advanced Whimsy
New York, NY
212/219-0342

Mary Beth Hagey   *113, 188*
Burlingame, CA

Joan Halperin   *178 (top)*
Joan Halperin Interior Design
401 East 80th Street
New York, NY 10021
212/288-8636

	Page Number		Page Number

Betsy G. Hoffman
Primary Designs and Projects
2521 Devon Valley Drive
Nashville, TN 37221
615/646-9548

97

Diane Pizzoli Studio
2257 Steiner Street
San Francisco, CA 94115
415/775-6434

50 (decorative painting), *158 (floorcloth)*, *247 (decorative painting)*

Carol Jacobson-Ziecik
Doodles & Dots
995 Lone Pine Road
Bloomfield Hills, MI 48302
810/644-2818

Cover, 70, 230

Public Service Committee of California Peninsula Chapter of ASID "Safe Harbor"
Team: *Karen Ross, ASID, the late Tony Torrice, ASID, and Tia Garvey, Nancy Doolittle, Diane Pizzoli and Ro Logrippo, Allied Members ASID, and Susan Pizzi*
ASID California Chapter Office
671 Oak Grove Avenue, Suite E
Menlo Park, CA 94025
415/323-6791

247

Bonnie Jaffey
Kaleidoscope Interiors
P.O. Box 1303
Redwood City, CA 94064
415/367-8144

3

Living & Learning Environments
1017 California Drive
Burlingame, CA 94010
415/340-8489
e-mail:
rologrippo__fm@msn.com

26, 33, 42, 53, 55 (top),
60, 68, 74, 80, 108, 109,
116, 117, 121, 137, 138,
140, 145, 155, 159, 160,
162, 163, 166, 172,175,
178 (bottom), 181, 182,
200, 225, 235, 242, 247,
250, 253, 274

Lynnette Reid * Interior Design
444 DeHaro Street, Ste 122
San Francisco, CA 94107
415/570-6409

79, 84, 126, 142, 151,
158, 212

Karen E. Ross, ASID
Martino's Interiors
111 N. Santa Cruz Avenue
Los Gatos, CA 95030
408/354-9111

247

Merrily Ludlow
Merrily Ludlow Designs
606 W. Lake Sammamish Parkway, N.E.
Bellevue, WA 98008
206/746-7597

183

Linda Runion, ASID
Linda Runion Interior Design
709 177th Lane, NE
Bellevue, WA 98008
206/644-8080

ii, 35 (bottom), 38, 55
(bottom), 73, 88, 127, 154,
167, 243, 244, 245

Rhonda Ruth Luongo, ASID, CCIDC
Devlyn Corp. Interior Design
205 Crystal Springs Center, Suite 104
San Mateo, CA 94402
415/579-2594

54 (bottom), 67, 94,
224, 228, 234, 237

Sandy Schiffman, ASID, FIFDA
Interiors aLa Mode
1550 Johnson Street
Key West, FL 33040
305/296-6900

64

Paula McChesney, ASID
Paula McChesney Design
724 Tulane Court
San Mateo, CA 94402
415/343-9610

175, 227, 231

and

4277 Sherman Oaks Avenue
Sherman Oaks, CA 91403
818/501-0129

Diane A. McGinnis, ASID
Two's Company Interiors
19527 Business Center Drive
Northridge, CA 91324
818/349-9044

8

Nancy Snyderman
San Francisco, CA

130

Susan Pizzi
S. Pzazz
121 Warren Road
San Mateo, CA 94401
415/342-1434

50, 247 (decorative painting)

Irene Sohm, ASID
Interiors at the Village
4,000 Bastani Lane
Santa Rosa, CA 95404
707/538-1668

101

Victoria Stone, Allied Member ASID
Victoria Stone Interiors
893 Noe Street
San Francisco, CA 94114
415/826-0904

43, 81, 84

Marian Wheeler, ASID
Marian Wheeler Interiors
444 De Haro Street , Suite 122
San Francisco, CA 94107
415/863-7766

65, 132, 171, 187, 222,
223 (top), *233*

Summer Hill Ltd.
2682h Middlefield Road
Redwood City, CA 94063
415/363-2600

114, 201 (bottom),
223 (bottom)

Gary E. White, CID, CBD
Kitchen & Bath Design
1000 Bristol Street North
Newport Beach, CA 92660
714/955-1232

240

Denise Tom-Sera
455 Ruby Street
Redwood City, CA 94062
415/366-6171

9, 10, 169, 229

Jamie Wollens, Architect
212/598-4532

210

Stella Tuttle, ASID
Tuttle & Associates
4155 El Camino Way, Suite 2
Palo Alto, CA 94306-4010
415/857-1171

198

DESIGN PROFESSIONALS CONSULTED

Along the way to publication, many designers and architects—other than those whose work appears on these pages—graciously gave time and professional opinions to enlighten the author about what constitutes good design for children. Listing their names is meant to serve as appreciation as well as indication of the recognition they deserve.

Nancy Carroll, AIA
11-A Talcott Forest Road
Farmington, CT 06032

Linda De Martini, Allied Member ASID
P.O. Box 117789
Burlingame, CA 94011

Roberta Florena
Tatutina, Inc.
24 N. Main Street
Attleboro, MA 02703

Gera King, ASID
Scottsdale Community College
Interior Design Department
9000 E. Chaparral Road
Scottsdale, AZ 85250

Robert Kobet, AIA
135 Woodcrest Road
Butler, PA 16003

Pat Lowry
Pat Lowry Design
1607 Independence Road
Greensboro, NC 27408

Pamela Morin
Pamela Morin Inc.
P.O. Box 469
Beacon, NY 12508

Pam Morris
Pam Morris Designs Exciting Lighting
14 E. Sir Francis Drake Boulevard
Larkspur, CA 94939

John Nalevanko
John Nalevanko Architect, AIA
1049 Camino Del Mar, Suite E
Del Mar, CA 92014-2652

Patti A. Neer, ASID
Von Naeher Design
1930 Noel Drive
Los Altos, CA 94024

Janet Anderson Robb
349 West Eisenhower Drive
Louisville, CO 80027

Karen Rosen
KMR Design
80 East End Avenue
New York, NY 10028

Van-Martin Rowe Design
195 S. Parkwood Avenue
Pasadena, CA 91107

Marshall Watson
Watson & Matthews Interiors
New York, NY

PHOTOGRAPHY CREDITS

Shooting interiors—unlike photographing news and sports events, which provide any number of photographic opportunities—requires a particular expertise in lighting and design to make settings come alive. The superior images on these pages are proof positive of the skill and craftsmanship the following photographers have mastered. The author appreciates all of their cooperation and assistance, particularly that of Mike Spinelli, whose commitment to the cause is reflected in 77 outstanding photographs. Without Mike and the rest of the shadow catchers, this book would have been a hollow undertaking.

	Page Number		*Page Number*
Dennis E. Anderson 48 Lucky Drive Greenbrae, CA 94904 415/927-3530	*166*	**Dan Forer** **Forer, Inc.** 1970 N.E. 149th Street North Miami, FL 33181 305/949-3131	*190, 192*
Laura Ashley 800/367-2000	*44, 46, 124, 128*	**David Garland Photography** 889 S. Rainbow Boulevard, Suite 645 Las Vegas, NV 89175 702/243-0036	*240*
Pamela Barkentin Blackburn 1218 N. La Cienega Boulevard, D-1 West Hollywood, CA 90069 310/854-1941	*8*	**Paul Alan Gewirtz** Box 38-H Scarsdale, NY 10583	*178 (top)*
© Antoine Bootz 133 West 22nd Street New York, NY 10011 212/366-9041	*1, 24, 130, 220, 249*	**Hopkins Associates** 2000 47th Street Des Moines, IA 50310 515/277-4954	*26, 68*
John Canham **Quadra Focus** 588 Waite Avenue Sunnyvale, CA 94086 408/739-1465	*54 (bottom), 94, 198*	For Better Homes and Gardens ® Special Interest Publications *Bedroom & Bath.* Copyright Meredith Corporation 1991. All rights reserved.	
Christopher Covey Photography 664 N. Madison Avenue Pasadena, CA 91101 818/440-0284	*64*	**Hopkins Associates** 2000 47th Street Des Moines, IA 50310 515/277-4954	*33, 116, 181*
Michal Daniel 3237 Longfellow Avenue South Minneapolis, MN 55407 612/729-4453	*54 (top), 105*	For Better Homes and Gardens ® Special Interest Publications *Bedroom & Bath.* Copyright Meredith Corporation 1992. All rights reserved.	
© The Detroit News **Photograph by Kathryn Trudeau** 615 West Lafayette Boulevard Detroit, MI 48226	*230*	**Reprinted by permission from** **House Beautiful,** **The Hearst Corporation** Copyright May 1992. Kari Haavisto, photographer.	*210*
Paul Elledge 1808 West Grand Avenue Chicago, IL 60622 312/733-8021	*cover, 70*	**© Christopher Irion** 183 Shipley Street San Francisco, CA 94107 415/896-0752	*223 (bottom)*

Page Number

Jim Jensen   101
Jensen Photographics
402 Upton Street
Redwood City, CA 94062
415/363-0962

J. Micheal Kanouff   55 *(top)*, 60
Paia, HI

Randall E. Klein   34
Gerber Products Company
445 State Street
Fremont, MI 49413
616/928-2000

Kohler Co.   195
444 Highland Drive
Kohler, WI 53044
414/457-4441

Fred Lyon   145, 242
237 Clara Street
San Francisco, CA 94107
415/974-5645

Sharon Risedorph Photography   81
761 Clementina Street
San Francisco, CA 94103
415/431-5851

Nora Scarlett   110
Nora Scarlett Studio Inc.
37 W. 20th Street
New York, NY 10011
212/741-2620

Page Number

Mike Spinelli   *ii, 3, 9, 10, 35, 38, 42, 50, 53, 55*
Mike Spinelli Photography   *(bottom), 57, 59, 65, 67, 71, 73,*
1017 California Drive   *74, 79, 80, 84, 88, 96, 97, 99, 109,*
Burlingame, CA 94010   *113, 116, 117, 121, 126, 127, 130,*
415/348-5789   *132, 137, 138, 140, 142, 151, 154,*
                              155, 158, 159, 160, 162, 163, 167,
                              169, 171, 172, 175, 182, 183, 187,
                              188, 200, 201 (top), 212, 217, 222,
                              223 (top), 224, 225, 227, 228, 229,
                              231, 233, 234, 235, 237, 243, 244,
                              245, 247, 250, 253, 274

Summer Hill Ltd.   *114, 201(bottom)*
2682h Middlefield Road
Redwood City, CA 94063
415/363-2600

Keith Talley   *14, 20, 35, 78 (bottom),*
4435 Parklawn Court #309   *236*
Edina, MN 55435
612/832-9803

Tom Virtue   *4*
4151 S. Verbena Street
Denver, CO 80237
303/793-0943

Darrow M. Watt   *108, 178 (bottom)*
Loma Mar, CA

Alan Weintraub   *43*
1832-A Mason Street
San Francisco, CA 94133
415/553-8191

Paul Whicheloe   *78 (top), 149, 177, 202*
104 Musconetcong River Road
Washington, NJ 07882
908/537-2437

SOURCES

The following image-by-image breakdown of designs serves as a product guide. Because many items are available through wholesale sources, it is advisable to contact the project designer for specifics. Source material has been omitted regarding discontinued and one-of-a-kind merchandise as well as products for which information was unavailable.

Page ii **Closet Design:** Linda Runion, *ASID,* 709 177th Lane, NE, Bellevue, WA 98008.
Closet Fabrication: California Closet Co., 1700 Montgomery Street, #249, San Francisco, CA 94111.
Model Spacecraft Fabrication: Brian and Bud Runion.

CHAPTER 1
Page 1 **Sculpture, Artistry:** Rodney A. Greenblat, Center for Advanced Whimsy, New York, NY.
Page 3 **Changing Table (without wheels):** #2523, Nu Line Industries, Jerry Baby Products Co., 1500 E. 128th Avenue, Denver, CO 80241.
Valance, Bookcase, Heart Wall Hanging, "Wheels" for Changing Table: Bonnie Jaffey, Kaleidoscope Interiors, Box 1303, Redwood City, CA 94064.
Page 4 **Infant Stim-Mobile:** Wimmer-Ferguson Child Products, Box 100427, Denver, CO 80250.
Page 8 **Corral, Custom-Built-Ins, Mural:** Two's Company Interiors, 19527 Center Drive, Northridge, CA 91324.
Page 9 **Curved Trim for Pegboard Wall Display:** Corrugated roofing wood closure strips, Home Depot, 2727 Paces Ferry Road., Atlanta, GA 30339.
Page 10 **Wall Grid and Components:** Heller Designs, Inc., 41 Madison Avenue, New York, NY 10010.
Page 14 **Bedding and Wall Quilt:** Designed by DeAnna Brandt, 7570 Dogwood Road, Excelsior, MN 55331.
Bedding Fabric: Hoffman California Fabrics "Fun Zone" and mixture of solid remnants.
Page 20 **Banners, Mats:** Designs by DeAnna Brandt, 7570 Dogwood Road, Excelsior, MN 55331.
Mat Fabrication: A-1 Foam 'N' Fabric, 7608 Lyndale Avenue, South, Richfield, MN 55423.
Floor Tile: Pearl Collection, Colortile Supermart, Box 2475, Fort Worth, TX 76113.
Page 24 **Furniture:** Customized by Rodney Greenblat, Center for Advanced Whimsy, New York, NY.
Page 26 **Table Set:** Button Series, ABI Designs, 1534 College, SE, Grand Rapids, MI 49507.
Wall Tiles: "Designer Accents" and "Ceramic Mosaics," American Olean Tile Co., 1000 Cannon Avenue, Lansdale, PA 19446.
Page 33 **Comforter Fabric:** "Arbor Trellis" #5480-48 by Krupnick at Philippe's, Showplace Square #330, 2 Henry Adams Street, San Francisco, CA 94103.
Comforter Fabrication: Quiltcraft Kids, 1233 Levee Street, Dallas, TX 75207.
Paint: Tan: O-24-6; Orange: O-14-2; Red: R-14-3; Green: G-20-4, Dutch Boy Paints, 101 Prospect Avenue, Cleveland, OH 44115.
Paint Treatment: Classic Painting & Associates, 72 N. Pecos Street, Las Vegas, NV 89112.
Sheets: "Simply Cotton," J.P. Stevens, 1185 Avenue of the Americas, New York, NY 10036.
Trundle Bed: "Simple Pleasures," Stanley Furniture, Box 30, Stanleytown, VA 24168.
Page 34 **Safety Device:** "Break-Thru Window Blind Cord Tassels" #76347, Gerber Products Co., 445 State Street, Fremont, MI 49413-0001.
Page 35 (top) **Drawer Locks:** "Boomerings," Discovery Toys, 2530 Arnold Drive, Martinez, CA 94553.
Drawer Pulls: #548.17.64-6 GKW, HEWI, Inc., 2851 Old Tree Drive, Lancaster, PA 17603.
Page 35 (bot) **Furniture:** Techline, 500 S. Division Street, Waunakee, WI 53597.

CHAPTER 2
Page 38 **Ladder:** Design by Linda Runion, *ASID,* 709 177th Lane, NE, Bellevue, WA 98008.
Page 42 **Butterflies:** Tub Time Sponges, Easy Aces, Inc., 387 Charles Street, Providence, RI 02904.
Fabric and Bedding: Tambourine Floral by Collier Campbell for J.P. Stevens, 1185 Avenue of the Americas, New York, NY 10036.
Frames: "My Frames," Tag Trade Associates, 1730 W. Wrightwood, Chicago, IL 60614.
Paint: Blue Dahlia: Y-29-2; Campanula: V-12-1; Hiddle Isle: R-28-1; Geranium: C-23-2; Kelly-Moore Paint Co., Inc., 987 Commercial Street, San Carlos, CA 94070.
Stackable Drawers: Abee Lifestyles, Staxx Inc., 230 Fifth Avenue, New York, NY 10001.
Page 43 **Bath Design:** Victoria Stone Interiors, 893 Noe Street, San Francisco, CA 94114.
Flooring: Vinyl tile, GMT Floor Tile Inc., 1255-T Oak Point Avenue, Bronx, NY 10474.
Wall and Cabinet Mural: Shelley Masters, 4037 23rd Street, San Francisco, CA 94114.
Page 44 All furnishings by Laura Ashley, Inc., 6 Street James Avenue, Boston, MA 02116.
Bedding and Valance: "Circus Circus"; **Lamp:** Wooden column base with coolie shade.
Page 46 All furnishings by Laura Ashley, Inc., 6 St. James Avenue, Boston, MA 02116.
Pillow Fabric: "Nursery Stripe"; **Table and Window Fabric, Pleated Shade, Frame:** "Hey Diddle Diddle"; **Wallcovering:** "Twinkle" vinyl.
Page 50 **Chair:** Glider rocker, Simmons Co., 1 "T" Concourse Parkway, #600, Atlanta, GA 30328.
Comforter: "Jelly Bean," NoJo, Noel Joanna Inc., 22942 Arroyo Vista, Rancho Street, Margarita, CA 92688.
Custom Stenciling and Wall Treatment: Susan Pizzi and Diane Pizzoli, *Allied Member ASID,* Pzaz, 121 Warren Road, San Mateo, CA 94115.
Posters: Nancy Carlson, Carmel Bay Co., Ocean and Lincoln Avenue, Carmel, CA 93921.
Page 53 **Relief Map:** Kistler, 4000 Dahlia Street, Denver, CO 80216.
Wall Border: Flag Stickers, The Flag Store, 520 Broadway, Sonoma, CA 95476.
Page 54 (top) **Colored Chain:** Boomerings, Discovery Toys, 2530 Arnold Drive, Martinez, CA 94553.
Custom Fabric Board: DeAnna Brandt, 7570 Dogwood Road, Excelsior, MN 55331.
Page 54 (bot) **Cabinet Pulls:** Betco, Cal Crystal Unlimited, 7020 Koll Center Parkway, #130, Pleasanton, CA 94566.
Child's Furniture: Samson-McCann, Inc., 638 Ramona Street, Palo Alto, CA 94301.

Curtain Fabric: "Safari Friends" and "Sprinkles," Westgate, 1000 Fountain Parkway, Box 534038, Grand Prairie, TX 75053-4038.
Custom Cabinetry: Rhonda Luongo, *ASID*, Devlyn Corp., 205 Crystal Springs Center, Suite 104, San Mateo, CA 94402.
Paint: Custom "Pearl," Benjamin Moore, 51 Chestnut Ridge Road, Montvale, NJ 07645.
Walls: Vertical Surfaces/Tek-Wall 1000, Maharam, Box 6900, Hauppauge, NY 11788.

Page 55 (top)   Custom Bed/Chalkboard: Living & Learning Environments, 1017 California Drive, Burlingame, CA 94010.
Page 55 (bot)   Grid and Hooks: Hellermade, Heller Designs Inc, 41 Madison Avenue, New York, NY 10010.
Grid Dry Erase Board: Boone International Inc., 1935 Deere Avenue, Irvine, CA 92714.
Grid Storage Bin: Interdesign, Box 39606, Solon, OH 44139.

Page 57   Glow-in-the-Dark Paint: "Polymark, " Polymerics, Inc., .24 Prime Parkway, Natick, MA 01760.
Page 59   Cardboard Valance: Design Response, 1168-H Aster Avenue, Sunnyvale, CA 94086.
Window Gauze: Norman S. Bernie Co., 1135 N. Amphlett Boulevard, San Mateo, CA 94402.
Page 60   Bed, Bookcases: Muurame, Inc., 80 King Spring Road, Windsor Locks, CT 06095.
Cubes: Unfinished furniture.
Page 64   Child's Table and Chairs: Sonrisa, 7609 Beverly Boulevard, Los Angeles, CA 90036.
Day Bed and Cabinetry: Good Wood Inc., Pomona, CA.
Day Bed Fabric: "Los Pajaros," F. Schumacher & Co., 79 Madison, New York, NY 10016.
Wallcovering: "Pacha Kanaq," F. Schumacher & Co., 79 Madison, New York, NY 10016.
Paint: Dunn-Edwards Corp., 4885 E. 52nd Place, Los Angeles, CA 90040.
Painted Floor Design: Sandy Schiffman, *ASID, FIFDA*, Interiors aLa Mode, 1550 Johnson Street, Key West, FL 33040,
Painting: Scott Alpert and Ron Slack, Calabassas, CA.
Pillow Fabric: Imported from Guatemala
Page 65   Bedding: "Brighton Rock" and "Sultan Stripe"; Laura Ashley, Inc., 6 St. James Avenue, Boston, MA 02116.
Bedding and Drapery Fabrication: Quiltcraft Kids, 1233 Levee Street, Dallas, TX 75207.
Doll Bed Fabrication: Rita's Dressmaking, 1175 Chula Vista, Burlingame, CA 94010.
Dollhouse: Shellie's Miniature Mania, 176 W. 25th Avenue, San Mateo, CA 94403.
Wall "Photo Frameables": Studio Shop, 1103Burlingame Avenue, Burlingame, CA 94010.
Hatbox Border: "Ribbons," Laura Ashley, Inc.
Paint: 1/C-822, Benjamin Moore Paints, 51 Chestnut Ridge Road, Montvale, NJ 07645.
Rug: "Arista," Floor Designs, 25 Rhode Island, San Francisco, CA 94103.
Window Coverings and Tablecloth Fabric: "Stocks," Laura Ashley Inc.,
Page 67   Closet Doors: Designed by Rhonda Luongo, *ASID*, Devlyn Corp., 205 Crystal Springs Center, Suite 104, San Mateo, CA 94402.
Eyelet Curtains: Verosol Pleated Shades, 215 Beecham Drive, Pittsburgh, PA 15205.
Ram Rocker: Horizons International Accents, 904 22nd Street, San Francisco, CA 94107.
Page 68   Carpet: Masland Carpets, 2500 Windy Ridge, # 320, Atlanta, GA 30067.
Storage Bins: Storage Station, 8801 University Avenue, Des Moines, IA 50325.
Wall Tiles: "Designer Accents" and "Ceramic Mosaics," American Olean Co., 1000 Cannon Avenue, Lansdale, PA 19446.
World Shower Curtain: Wings Over the World Corp., 15 W. 27th Street, New York, NY 10001.

CHAPTER 3

Page 70   Bed Covers: Antique quilts.
Bookcase "Tops": Carved planter boxes, unknown origin.
Dollhouse and Ladder: Custom designed and painted by Doodles & Dots, 995 Lone Pine Road, Bloomfield Hills, MI 48302.
Floor Covering: Pier I Imports, 301 Commerce Street, Fort Worth, TX 76102.
Unfinished Bed, Bookcase: Archbold Furniture, 303 E. Mechanic, Archbold, OH 43502.
Page 71   Adult Chair: "St. Moritz," Beverly Interiors, 4859 Gregg Road, Pico Rivera, CA 90660.
Adult Chair Fabric: "Penrose 33893," and Child's Chair Fabric: "Idyllic Bough 73819," Payne Fabrics, 3500 Kettering Boulevard, Box 983, Dayton, OH 45401.
Child's Chair: Booster Seat, Fisher-Price, Inc., 636 Girard Avenue, E. Aurora, NY, 14052.
Page 73   Carpet Swatch and Gold Fabric: Remnants
Dark Denim: #11858, Kravet Fabrics, 225 Central Avenue, S., Bethpage, NY 11714.
Light Denim: "Chambray," Red Pillowcase: "Coastal Red," and Striped Sheet: "Cape Stripe," Ralph Lauren Home Collection, 1185 Avenue of the Americas, New York, NY 10036.
Red Bandana: "Wamcraft," Marks Handkerchief Mfg., Box 2226, Augusta, GA 30913.
Page 74   Custom Furniture: Living & Learning Environments, 1017 California Drive, Burlingame, CA 94010.
Hardware: # 5481396, HEWI Inc., 2851 Old Tree Drive, Lancaster, PA 17603.
Page 78 (top)   Built-In Bed, Storage, and Desk: Custom designed by Anita Goldblatt, *Allied Member ASID,* Designing Interiors, 401 E. 80th Street, New York, NY 10021.
Lamp: Hansen Swing Arm, Hansen Lamps, D&D Building, 979 Third Avenue, New York, NY 10022.
Page 78 (bot)   Bedding Fabrication: Custom designed by DeAnna Brandt, 7570 Dogwood Road, Excelsior, MN 55331.
Fabrics: Crayola "Favorite Color" Collection by Cannon Royal Family, Fieldcrest Cannon Inc., 1271 Avenue of the Americas, New York, NY10020.
Twin Bed with Trundle and Bookcase Headboard: Minnesota Panel Systems, 6421 County Road 36, Finlayson, MN 55735.
Wall-Mount Coat Rack: Lilly's Kids, Lillian Vernon Corp., 543 Main Street, New Rochelle, NY 10801.
Page 79   Armoire: Caesar's Unfinished Furniture, 1717 S. El Camino Real, San Mateo, CA 94402.
Custom Painting and Birch Window "Rod": Lynnette Reid * Interior Design, 444 De Haro Street, #122, San Francisco, CA 94107.
Iron Child's Chair: Antique.
Page 80   Area Rug: Unknown origin.
Carpet: "030 Timeless," Floor Designs, 25 Rhode Island, San Francisco, CA 94103.
Furniture: Muurame, Inc., 80 King Spring Road, Windsor Locks, CT 06095.

Page 81 **Custom Platform:** Victoria Stone Interiors, 893 Noe Street, San Francisco, CA 94114.

Fabric: Kinross plaid in red, Brunschwig & Fils, 75 Virginia Road, North White Plains, NY 10603.

Platform Light: Becca Foster Lighting, 340 Bryant Street, #300, San Francisco, CA 94107.

Page 84 **Art:** Original drawings by Colby and Tayler Reid.

Computer Color Printer: Hewlett Packard DeskJet 320, Hewlett-Packard Co., 3000 Hanover Street, Palo Alto, CA 94304.

Computer Station: LARS Design, 1625 Larimer Street, Suite 2105, Denver, CO 80202.

Wallcovering: Apple Border: YS-8211B; Striped: Yellow AA-4685. York Wallcovering, Box 5166, York, PA 17405.

Page 88 **Chair:** Viking Office Products, 13809 S. Figueroa Street, Los Angeles, CA 90061.

Computer and Keyboard: Apple Macintosh IIsi, Apple Computer, Inc., 1 Infinite Loop, Cupertino, CA 95014.

Furniture and Articulating Tray: Techline, 500 S. Division Street, Waunakee, WI 53597.

Adjustable Desk Lamp: "Lollipop Desk Lamp" 20909, Scan Import, 12130 Bel-Red Road, Bellevue, WA 98005

Page 94 **Adjustable Arts and Crafts Station:** Custom designed by Rhonda Luongo, *ASID*, 205 Crystal Springs Center, Suite 104, San Mateo, CA 94402.

Child's Chair: Samson-McCann, Inc., 638 Ramona Street, Palo Alto, CA 94301.

Page 96 **Table and Chairs:** Wild Child Designs, 2307 Mill Creek Lane, Healdsburg, CA 95448.

Page 97 **Switchplate:** Betsy G. Hoffman, 2521 Devon Valley Drive, Nashville, TN 37221.

Page 99 **Rocker:** Wild Child Designs, 2307 Mill Creek Lane, Healdsburg, CA 95448.

Page 101 **Beds and Bedside Chest:** 1940s vintage.

Bed Refinishing: Spraymate, 2684 Middlefield Road, #D, Redwood City, CA 94063.

Fabric: P-497, Westgate Fabrics Inc., 1000 Fountain Parkway, Grand Prairie, TX 75053.

Fabrication: Toshi's, 4131 Business Center Drive, Fremont, CA

Stenciling: Suzanne Mastrolucca, Impressions in Paint, 1509 Alma Terrace, San Jose, CA 95125.

Toy Chests, Coat Rack: Custom designed by Interiors at the Village, 4,000 Bastani Lane, Santa Rosa, CA 95404.

Page 105 **Construction Game on Table:** Marbleworks, Discovery Toys, 2530 Arnold Drive, Martinez, CA 94553.

Numbered Stacking Blocks, Wall Clock, Texture and Activity Wall Quilt: Custom designed and fabricated by DeAnna Brandt, 7570 Dogwood Road, Excelsior, MN 55331.

Play Table "Conversion": Accent Store Fixtures, 6100 Wayzata Boulevard, Minneapolis, MN 55416.

Wood House Numbers: Ace Hardware house numbers customized by DeAnna Brandt.

Page 109 **Paneling:** Slatwall, Spacewall International, 1976 Williams Street, San Leandro, CA 94577.

CHAPTER 4

Page 110 **Paint:** Martin-Senour Paints, 101 Prospect Avenue, NW, Cleveland, OH 44115.

Page 113 **Bed:** Sleigh Bed, Speigel Co., 3500 Lacey Road, Downers Grove, IL 60515.

Fabric: "Princess," by Jay Yang for Croscill Home Fashions, 261 Fifth Avenue, New York, NY 10016.

Stenciling: Mary Beth Hagey, Burlingame, CA.

Page 114 All furnishings by Summer Hill Ltd., 2682h Middlefield Road, Redwood City, CA 94063.

Balloon Shade and Dust Ruffle: "Anda Lucia"; **Bed and Dresser:** "Brighton"; **Bed Coverlet:** "Erin Cable"; **Checked Pillow on Bed:** "Biarritz" check; **Side Chair and Scalloped Pillow Fabric:** "Frambois"; **Square Pillow on Bed:** "Ceylon".

Page 116 **Area Rugs:** "Isis" and "Skyline," Foreign Accents, 2825-E Broadbent Parkway, NE, Albuquerque, NM 87107.

Bed: "Simple Pleasures" #146-14, Stanley Furniture, Box 30, Stanleytown, VA 24168.

Chest: ABC Chest #2605-09 by The Lane Co., Box 151, Altavista, VA 24517.

Clocks: Environments, Inc., Box 1345, Beaufort Industrial Park, Beaufort, SC 29902.

Drapery, Comforter Fabric: "Arbor Trellis" #5480-48 by Krupnick at Philippe's, Showplace Square, 2 Henry Adams Street, # 330, San Francisco, CA 94103.

Drapery, Comforter Fabrication: Quiltcraft Kids, 1233 Levee Street, Dallas, TX 75207.

Folding Chair: #JRC, The Stakmore Co., Elm Street, Owego, NY 13827.

Marker Board: Davson, 1047 Ardmore Avenue, Itasca, IL 60143.

Paint: Tan: O-24-6; Orange: O-14-2; Red: R-14-3; Green: G-20-4, Dutch Boy Paints, 101 Prospect Avenue, Cleveland, OH 44115.

Paint Treatment: Classic Painting & Associates, 72 N. Pecos Street, Las Vegas, NE 89112.

Window Shades: "Duette Vertiglide", D7-716, Hunter Douglas Window Fashions Division, 1 Duette Way, Broomfield, CO 80020.

Page 121 **Custom Display Shelves:** Living & Learning Environments, 1017 California Drive, Burlingame, CA 94010.

Furniture: Muurame, Inc., 80 King Spring Road, Windsor Locks, CT 06095.

Page 124 All furnisings by Laura Ashley, Inc., 6 St. James Avenue, Boston, MA 02116.

Curtain, Window Seat and Pillow Stripe Fabric: "Studio Stripe";

Roller Blind and Tieback Fabric: "Topsy Toys."

Stuffed Animals: Large and little "Angus" bears and "Boris the Russian" bear.

Wall Coverings: Border: "Bookshelf"; Wallpaper, "Polka Dot."

Page 126 **Cushion Fabric:** "Apple" 259-7805, NY Fabrics, 1948 S. El Camino, San Mateo, CA 94403

Page 127 **Area Rug:** "Aztec" #1356, Foreign Accents, 2825-E Broadbent Parkway, NE, Albuquerque, NM 87107.

Aviation Wall Clocks: TrinTec Industries, Inc., 467 Westney Road S., Unit 3, Ajax, Ontario, Canada, L1S 6V7.

Bed Linens: "Cape Stripe," "Coastal Red," and "Chambray," Ralph Lauren Home Collection, 1185 Avenue of the Americas, New York, NY 10036.

Stagecoach Shade and Square Pillow: #11858, Kravet Fabrics, 225 Central Avenue, S., Bethpage, NY 11714.

Stagecoach Shade Ties: "Wamcraft" red bandana, Marks Handkerchief Mfg. , Box 2226, Augusta, GA 30913.

Framed Earth Poster: "The Living Earth", SpaceShots, Inc., 12255 Foothill Boulevard, Sylmar, CA 91342.

Furniture: Techline, 500 S. Division Street, Waunakee, WI 53597.

"Jeans" Pillow and Stagecoach Shades: Design and fabrication, Linda Runion, *ASID*, 709 177th Lane, NE, Bellevue, WA 98008.

Photo Forms: Fabulous Fotoforms, Inc., 3740 Williston Road, Minnetonka, MN 55345.

Page 128 All furnishings by Laura Ashley, Inc., 6 St. James Avenue, Boston, MA 02116.

Chair Fabric: "Sultan Stripe"; **Draperies and Square Pillow Fabric:** "Cirque"; **Lamp:** Wooden column base; Coolie shade in "Circus Circus";
Storage Unit Stripe Fabric: "Studio Stripe"; **Wall Border, Box, Matching Fabric on Storage:** "Circus Circus."

Page 130   **Bed:** Vermont Tubbs, Inc., Newton Road, Forestdale, VT 05745.
Page 132   **Custom Fabrication:** Quiltcraft Kids, 1233 Levee Street, Dallas, TX 75207.
            Drapery, Table Cloth and Bed Pillow Fabric: "Stocks," Laura Ashley, Inc., 6 St. James Avenue, Boston, MA 02116.
            Lamp: Wooden column base with coolie shade, Laura Ashley, Inc.
            Striped Bed Fabric: "Sultan Stripe," Laura Ashley, Inc.
Page 137   **Children's Books:** From the collection of Stephanie Beard Gale, Half Moon Bay, CA
            Comforter: "Navy Star," Arch Associates, 375 Executive Boulevard, Elmsford, NY 10523.
            Dolls: From the collection of Janice Cary, Lewisburg, TN.
Page 138   **Art:** Original drawings by Courtney Gale, Amanda Just, and Dawn Just.
            Birdhouse and holiday ornaments: CJs, 1904 Pickle Road Lewisburg, TN 37091.

CHAPTER 5

Page 140   **Art Station:** Secondhand find.
            Paint: Tan: O-24-6; Orange: O-14-2; Red: R-14-3; and Green: G -20-4; Dutch Boy Paints, 101 Prospect Avenue, Cleveland, OH 44115.
            Wall Treatment: Classic Painting & Associates, 72 N. Pecos Street, Las Vegas, NV 89112
Page 142   **Shelves:** Unfinished, Michaels Stores Inc., 5931 Campus Circle Drive, Irving, TX 75063.
Page 149   **Chair:** Spaghetti Side Chair #620, ICF, 3213 Las Palmas Street, Houston, TX 77027.
            Cork Wallcovering: Wolf Gordon Inc., 3300 47th Avenue, Long Island City, NY 11101.
            Custom Built-Ins: Anita Goldblatt, *Allied Member ASID,* Designing Interiors, 401 E. 80th Street, New York, NY 10021.
            Wooden Puzzle Case: Child Craft Industries, 20 Kilmer Road, Edison, NJ 08818.
Page 151   **Bed Fabric:** "Apple" 259-7805, NY Fabrics, 1948 S. El Camino, San Mateo, CA 94403; "Rockwell" SW2900F, York Wallcoverings, Box 5166, York, PA 17405.
            Custom Bed Treatment including Added Fabrication and Mural: Lynnette Reid * Interior Design, 444 De Haro Street, San Francisco, CA 94107.
            Unfinished Bed Frame: "Bunkie Bed" 1914-"T,"F Decor Unfinished Furniture, 3677 Stevens Creek Boulevard, Santa Clara, CA 95051.
Page 154   **Custom Bookshelf:** Linda Runion, *ASID,* 709 177th Lane, NE, Bellevue, WA 98008.
            Map: U.S. Collectors Series, Hammond, Inc., 515 Valley Street, Maplewood, NJ 07040.
Page 155   **Assorted Science Items:** The Nature Co., 750 Hearst Avenue, Berkeley, CA 94710.
Page 158   **Bamboo Furniture:** A.W. Pottery, 2908 Adeline Street, Berkeley, CA 94706.
            Custom Floorcloth: Diane Pizzoli Studio, *Allied Member ASID,* 2257 Steiner Street, San Francisco, CA 94115.
            Watermelon Play Equipment: Cardboard design and fabrication, The Froot Group c/o Prof. Cigdem Akkurt, Iowa State University, 581 College of Design, Ames, IA 50014.
Page 159   **Butterflies:** Tub Time Sponges, Easy Aces, Inc., 387 Charles Street, Providence, RI 02904.
            Drapery and Bedding Fabric: "Tambourine Floral" by Collier Campbell for J.P. Stevens, 1185 Avenue of the Americas, New York, NY 10036.
            Paint: Blue Dahlia: Y-29-2; Campanula: V-12-1; Hidden Isle: R-28-1; Geranium: C-23-2 Kelly-Moore Paint Co., Inc., 987 Commercial Street, San Carlos, CA 94070.
            Wicker Headboard: Cost Plus World Market, 201 Clay Street, Oakland, CA 94607.
Page 160   **Comforter Fabric:** "Arbor Trellis," #5480-48 by Krupnick, Philippe's, Showplace Square, 2 Henry Adams Street, #330, San Francisco, CA 94103.
            Custom Initial: TAP Plastics, 3011 Alvarado Street, San Leandro, CA 94577.
            Fabrication: Quiltcraft Kids, 1233 Levee Street, Dallas, TX 75207.
            Furniture: "Simple Pleasures," Stanley Furniture, Box 30, Stanleytown, VA 24168.
            Lighting: Track: Halo Lighting/Cooper Lighting, 400 Busse Road, Elk Grove Village, IL 60007; "Venus" 2106 lamps: Basic Concepts, 1425 Rockwell Avenue, Cleveland, OH 44114.
Page 162   **Fabrics:** Metropolitan Furniture, 1635 Rollins Road, Burlingame, CA 94010.
            Lighting: "Dakota Series" by Bridgeport, Bay Commercial Lighting Supply Inc., 1140 Folsom Street, San Francisco, CA 94103.
Page 163   **Assorted Accessory Items:** Galisteo, 590 10th Street, San Francisco, CA 94103.
Page 166   **Custom Furniture:** Living & Learning Environments, 1017 California Drive, Burlingame, CA 94010.
Page 167   **Assorted Posters:** Cost Plus World Market, 201 Clay Street, Oakland, CA 94607.
            Bed and Roman Shade Fabric: "Chambray," Ralph Lauren Home Collection, 1185 Avenue of the Americas, New York, NY 10036.
            Custom Collectibles Cabinet, Bedding Fabrication: Linda Runion, *ASID,* 709 177th Lane, NE, Bellevue, WA 98008.
            Denim Pillow: #11858, Kravet Fabrics, 225 Central Avenue, S., Bethpage, NY 11714.
            Plaid Pillow: #13237, Kravet Fabrics, 225 Central Avenue, S., Bethpage, NY 11714.
Page 169   **Mini Trampoline:** "Jumpking,",Weslo Inc., Weider Health & Fitness, Box 10, Logan, UT 84321.

CHAPTER 6

Page 172   **Custom Railing:** Harry Grover, 13208 McCulloch Avenue, Saratoga, CA 95070.
            Theater Fabric: Zebra Awning Co., 2901 Mariposa Street, #3, San Francisco, CA 94110.
            Theater Fabrication: Elegant Stitch, 1182 Folsom Street, San Francisco, CA 94103.
            Storage Bins: Interdesign, Inc., Box 39606, Solon, OH 44139.
Page 175   **Antique Quilt:** Collection of Marian Brooks.
            Art: Original watercolors by Courtney Gale; Cow print, Cost Plus World Market, 201 Clay Street, Oakland, CA 94607.
            Dolls: Raggedy Ann and Andy; Custom fabrication by Sue Spinelli.
            Frames: "My Frame," Tag Trade Associates Group, Ltd, 1730 W. Wrightwood, Chicago, IL 60614.
            Rag Rug and Wood Animal Accessories: Cost Plus World Market.
            Wicker Table: 1940s vintage.

Page 177   **Cork Wallcovering:** Wolf Gordon Inc., 3300 47th Avenue, Long Island City, NY 11101.

          Custom Built-Ins and Furniture Handles: Designed by Anita Goldblatt, *Allied Member ASID,* Designing Interiors, 401 E. 80th Street, New York, NY 10021.

          Striped Wallcovering: MPARO39, Sonia's Place, D&D Building., 979 Third Avenue, New York, NY 10022.

Page 178 (top) **Custom Beds and Shelf:** Joan Halperin Interior Design, 401 E. 80th Street, New York, NY 10021.

Page 178 (bot) **Wall Grid:** Hellermade, Heller Designs, Inc., 41 Madison Avenue, New York, NY 10010.

Page 181   **Bed and Drapery Fabric**: "Arbor Trellis" #5480-48, Krupnick, Philippe's, Showplace Square, 2 Henry Adams Street, #330, San Francisco, CA 94103.

          Custom Fabrication: Quiltcraft Kids, 1233 Levee Street, Dallas, TX 75207.

          Folding Table JRT2 and Chairs JRC: Stakmore Co., Inc., Elm Street, Owego, NY 13827.

          Flooring: "Light Wood, Limited Edition," B. Forman, GMT Floor Tile, Inc., 1255 Oak Point Avenue, Bronx, NY 10474.

          Furniture Hutches, Roll-Out Bins and Beds: "Simple Pleasures," #146-14, Stanley Furniture, Box 30, Stanleytown, VA 24168.

          Lighting: Track system, Halo Lighting/Cooper Lighting, 400 Busse Road, Elk Grove Village, IL 60007; "Venus" hanging lamps #2106 by Basic Concepts at Bay Commercial Lighting Supply Inc.,1140 Folsom Street, San Francisco, CA 94103.

          Rugs: "Isis" and "Skyline" collections, Foreign Accents, 2825-E Broadbent Parkway, NE, Albuquerque, NM 87107.

          Sheets: "Simply Cotton", J.P. Stevens, 1185 Avenue of the Americas, N ew York, NY 10036.

          Custom Initials: TAP Plastics, 3011 Alvarado Street, San Leandro, CA 94577.

Page 182   **Beds:** Unfinished furniture.

          Custom Desk and Storage: Living & Learning Environments, 1017 California Drive, Burlingame, CA 94010.

          Wall Art: Original drawings by Gregory and Matthew Nagel.

Page 183   **Bedding:** "Congo" by Burlington House, 1345 Avenue of the Americas, New York, NY 10105.

          Carpet: "Cordavel," Gulistan—The Executive Line, by J.P. Stevens, 1185 Avenue of the Americas, New York, NY 10036.

          Furniture: Techline and custom design, 500 S. Division Street, Waunakee, WI 53597.

          Shoji Panel Design: Merrily Ludlow Designs, 606 W. Lake Sammamish Parkway, NE, Bellevuc, WA 98008.

Page 187   **Bedcovers:** ""Brighton Rock" and "Sultan Stripe," Laura Ashley, Inc., 6 St. James Place, Boston, MA 02116.

          Hatbox Border: "Ribbons" wallcovering border, Laura Ashley, Inc.

          Rug: Floor Designs, 25 Rhode Island, San Francisco, CA 94103.

Page 188   **Assorted Bedcover Fabrics and Miniature Chair:** Laura Ashley, Inc., 6 St. James Avenue, Boston, MA 02116.

Page 190   **Custom Design:** Susan Behar, *ASID,* Universal Design , 1732 Hickory Gate Drive N., Dunedin, FL 34698.

Page 192   **Bathroom Tile:** "Il Bagno" collection, Hastings Tile, 230 Park Avenue, S., New York, NY 10003.

          Carpet: Stonecliff "Woodbine," SCS-System, 200 Lexington Avenue, New York, NY 10016.

          Tile: "Mexican Adobe," Dal-Tile, 1135 Reed Hartman Highway, Cincinnati, OH 45241.

          Cabinetry: Mastercraft Industries, 4 Cleveland Street, Clearwater, FL 34624.

Page 195   **Art Glass Mirror:** Fox Studios Inc. 5901 N. College Avenue, Indianapolis, IN 46220.

          Faucet: "Antique Right-Temp," Kohler Co., 444 Highland Drive, Kohler, WI 53044.

          Floor Tile: "Nuance" by Latco at Architectural Brick and Tile, 8000 Castleway Drive, Indianapolis, IN 46250.

          Lighting: Lightolier track and downlight, Luminatae, Inc., 8515 Keystone Crossing, Indianapolis, IN 46240.

          Marbleized Cabinets and Solid Surfacing Material: Avonite Inc., 1945 Highway 3044, Belen, NM 87002.

          Toilet Fixture and Wall-mount Lavatory: "Highline Water-Guard" with elongated seat, Kohler Co., 444 Highland Drive, Kohler, WI 53044.

          Wallcovering: "Artisan" by Dekortex., 6900 Mooridian Drive, P.O. Box 282, Niagara Falls, NY 14304.

Page 198   **Custom Desk:** Stella Tuttle, *ASID,* 4155 El Camino Way, Suite 2, Palo Alto, CA 94306.

          Furniture: Techline, 500 S. Division Street, Waunakee, WI 53597.

          Lamp: "Tizio," Artemide, 20010 Pregano, Milanese, ITA (MI) Via Brughiera.

          Linens: Ralph Lauren Home Collection, 1185 Avenue of the Americas, New York, NY 10036.

Page 200   **Side Chair:** Ligne Roset, 200 Lexington Avenue, #604, New York, NY 10016.

          Bookcase Unit: Scandinavian Designs, 3830 Cypress Drive, Petaluma, CA 94954.

Page 201 (top) **Chair and Lamp:** 1970s vintage.

          Pillow: "Kingsbridge Cloth," F. Schumacher & Co., 79 Madison Avenue, New York, NY 10016.

          Table: "Joan Crawford," Century Furniture Ind., 401-11th Street, NW, Hickory, NC 28603.

Page 201 (bot) All furnishings by Summer Hill, Ltd., 2682h Middlefield Road, Redwood City, CA 94063.

          Bed: "Clipper"; **Bed Coverlet:** "Avignon" with "Henley Stripe" banding and dust ruffle; **Bed Pillows:** "Kristin" (plaid); "Ahoy" (shamrock); "Bits and Pieces" (periwinkle); **Dog's Neck Fabric:** "Picnic"; **Chair:** "Brighton" chair in "Bits and Pieces"; **Club chair:** "Mystic" in "Buttondown" sky welting; **Side Table, Floor and Table Lamps:** "Brighton"; **Window Coverings:** "Regatta" stripe banded in "Buttondown. "

Page 202   **Custom Built-Ins:** Designed by Anita Goldblatt, *Allied Member ASID,* Designing Interiors, 401 E. 80th Street, New York, NY 10021.

          Carpet: "Tyler" in Plymouth Grey, Einstein Moojy, 150 E. 58th Street, New York, NY 10036.

          Desk Light: Say It In Neon, Long Island City, NY.

          Laminate Bed and Surfaces: B.L.Wayne, 200 Lexington Avenue, New York, NY 10016.

          Mirror Globe: SLD Lighting, 318 W. 47th Street, New York, NY 10036.

          Shade: Duck cloth, Sonia's Place, D&D Blvd., 979 Third Avenue, New York, NY 10022.

Page 212   **Mini Armoire:** Shellie's Miniature Mania, 176 W. 25th Avenue, San Mateo, CA 94403.

Page 217   **Furniture:** P.J. Milligan & Associates, 740 Cacique Street, Santa Barbara, CA 93103.

          Muralist: Joyce Oroz, Wildbrush Murals, Morgan Hill, CA 95037.

          Quilt: Leone-Nii Quilt Gallery, 198 Castro Street, Mountain View, CA 94041.

          Wall Mural: Joyce Oroz, Wildbrush Studios, Morgan Hill, CA 95037

CHAPTER 7

Page 220   **Custom Artistry, Sculpture, and Cabinetry:** Rodney A. Greenblat, Center for Advanced Whimsy, New York, NY 10012.

Page 222   **Custom Table:** Marian Wheeler, *ASID,* 444 De Haro Street, #122, San Francisco, CA 94107.

Page 223 (top) **Accessories:** Marian Wheeler, *ASID*, 444 DeHaro Street, #122, San Francisco, CA 94107.

Page 223 (bot) All furnishings by Summer Hill, Ltd., 2682h Middlefield Road, Redwood City, CA 94063.

Chair (foreground): "Mystic" in "Key Largo"; **Ottoman:** "Ipswich"; **Sofa:** "Chatham" in 'Buttondown "; **Table:** "Darjeeling".

Page 224 **Custom Lamp:** Rhonda Luongo, *ASID*, Devlyn Corp., 205 Crystal Springs Center, Suite 104, San Mateo, CA 94402.

Balinese Animal Table: Michael Carr, Box 1480, Aptos, CA 95001.

Tabletop: TAP Plastics, 6475 Sierra Lane, Dublin, CA 94568.

Page 225 **Folk Art Furniture:** Galisteo, 590 10th Street, San Francisco, CA 94103, and Summer House, 21 Throckmorton Street, Mill Valley, CA 94941.

Bamboo Sculpture: Nance O'Bannion. Allrich Gallery, 251 Post Street, San Francisco, CA 94108.

Masks and Carved Animals: Private collection of Freda Scott.

Window Covering: Verosol Pleated Shades, 215 Beecham Drive, Pittsburgh, PA 15205.

Page 227 **Art:** "King" painting by Cathleen Ristow Lambridis at Paula McChesney Design, 724 Tulane Court, San Mateo, CA 94402.

Farm Table and Chairs: Williams-Sonoma, 100 North Point, San Francisco, CA 94133.

Lighting: Ross Lighting, 1300 El Camino Real, Belmont, CA 94002.

Window Covering: Stained glass custom design by Paula McChesney Design, 724 Tulane Court, San Mateo, CA 94402.

Page 228 **Furniture:** Table and stools, Juvenile Lifestyles, 541 Eighth Street, San Francisco, CA 94103.

Walls: Vertical Surfaces/Tek-Wall 1000, Maharam, Box 6900, Hauppauge, NY 11788.

Page 229 **Art:** Original drawings by Julian Sera.

Wire Cable Clothesline: #15742, Wellington Leisure Products, P.O. Box 244, Madison, GA 30650.

Page 230 **Art:** Original fingerpainting by Lacey Jacobson.

Flooring: Black and white sheet vinyl, Mannington Commercial Carpets, Box 364, Calhoun, GA 30701.

Furniture Detailing: Doodles & Dots, 995 Lone Pine Road, Bloomfield Hills, MI 48302.

Page 231 **Kitchen:** Designed by Paula McChesney , *ASID,* 724 Tulane Court, San Mateo, CA 94402.

Props: Merritt Creations, 3670 Sunset Drive, San Bruno, CA 94066.

Page 233 **Cabinetry:** Marian Wheeler, *ASID,* 444 DeHaro Street, #122, San Francisco, CA 94107.

Children's Rain Slickers and Boots: Mudpie, 1694 Union Street, San Francisco, CA 94123.

Page 234 **Fabric:** "Teachers Pet," F. Schumacher & Co., 79 Madison Avenue, New York, NY 10016.

Hardware Pulls: Betco Pulls, Cal Crystal Unlimited, 7020 Koll Center Parkway, #130, Pleasanton, CA 94566.

Floor Tile: "Crystalline," American Olean Tile, 1000 Canon Avenue, Lansdale, PA 19446.

Step Stool: Crate & Barrel, 725 Landwehr Road, Northbrook, IL 60062.

Wallpaper: Marco de Ors, "Confetti," at Philippe's, Showplace Design Center, 2 Henry Adams Street, #330, San Francisco, CA 94103.

Page 236 **Bath Tissue Holder; Alphabet and Animal Figures:** Custom made and designed by DeAnna Brandt, 7570 Dogwood Road, Excelsior, MN 5331.

Cabinets: "Avia," Merillat Ind., Inc., 5353 W. US 223, Adrian, MI 49221.

Cabinet "Locks": Boomerings, Discovery Toys, 2530 Arnold Drive, Martinez, CA 94533.

Hardware: 548.17.64GKW pulls; HEWI, Inc., 2851 Old Tree Drive, Lancaster, PA 17603.

Plastic Mugs: Interdesign, Box 39606, Solon, OH 44139.

Shower Curtain: Crayola "Favorite Colors," Dawson Home Fashions, 295 Fifth Avenue, New York, NY 10016.

Stool: Rubbermaid, Consolidated Plastics, Co., 8181 Darrow Road, Twinsburg, OH 44087.

Stickers: Animals, alphabet: Sandholm Co., Box 7276, Eugene, OR, 97401; Fish: Stikees, 1165 Joshua Way, Box 9630, Vista, CA 92085.

Tile: Floor: "Natura" #8214, Florida Tile., 1 Sikes Boulevard., Lakeland, FL 33802; Walls: "New White," Florida Tile; "Cherry Red" #101 and "Mandarin" #111, American Olean Tile, 1000 Cannon Avenue, Lansdale, PA 19446.

Page 237 **Toilet Paper Dispenser:** "Cycling Man," Seasons, Box 64545, St. Paul, MN 55164.

Wallpaper: Marco de Ors, "Confetti," at Philippe's, Showplace Design Center, 2 Henry Adams Street, #330, San Francisco, CA 94103.

Page 240 **Faucet:** KWC/Rohl Corp., 1559 Sunland Lane, Costa Mesa, CA 92626.

Grab Bars: Custom acrylic equipped with fiber-optic lighting, CSL Lighting Manufacturing, Inc., 25070 Avenue Tibbetts, Valencia, CA 91355.

Tub "Shell": Du Pont Corian custom design by Gary E. White, *CID, CBD,* Kitchen & Bath Design, 1000 Bristol Street, N., Newport Beach, CA 92660.

Tub: International Cushioned Products, 330 S. Pineapple, Sarasota, FL 34236.

Page 243 **Closet, Vanity and Mirror Frame:** Custom design and fabrication, Linda Runion, *ASID,* 709 177th Lane, NE, Bellevue, WA 98008.

Faucet: Classic Bar # 31.054, Grohe America, 900 Lively Bloulevard, Wood Dale, IL 60191.

Sink: Round Series, Carefree, American China, 3618 E. LaSalle, Phoenix, AZ 85040.

Page 244 **Closet Design:** Linda Runion, *ASID,* 709 177th Lane, NE, Bellevue, WA 98008.

Closet Fabrication: California Closet Co., 1700 Montgomery Street, #249, San Francisco, CA 94111.

Model Spacecraft Fabrication: Brian and Bud Runion.

Page 245 **Loft Design and Fabrication:** Linda Runion, *ASID,* 709 177th Lane, NE, Bellevue, WA 98008.

Page 247 **Carpet:** Masland Carpets, 2500 Windy Ridge, #320, Atlanta, GA 30067.

Tables: Wilsonart laminate fabricated by Closet Dimensions, 140 Industrial Road, San Carlos, CA 94070.

Pillows: "Ginza Fish," Barbara Beckmann Studios, 2 Henry Adams Street, #331, San Francisco, CA 94103.

Shades: Hunter Douglas, Window Fashions, 1 Duette Way, Broomfield, CO 80020.

Wall Mural: Diane Pizzoli, *Allied Member ASID,* and Susan Pizzi.

Page 249 **Custom Playhouse:** Rodney Greenblat, Center for Advanced Whimsy, New York, NY 10012.

Page 250 **Closet Design:** Living & Learning Environments, 1017 California Drive, Burlingame, CA 94010.

Red Carpet: "Shazam," Masland Carpets, 2500 Windy Ridge, #320, Atlanta, GA 30067.

Page 253 **"Crayon":** Ralphco Inc., Box 691, W. Side Station, Worcester, MA 01602-0691.

Custom Initial: TAP Plastics, 3011 Alvarado Street, San Leandro, CA 94577.

Page 274 **Puppet:** Bee T-2044, Puppets on the Pier, Pier 39, Space H-4, San Francisco, CA 94133.

Tepee: Shooting Star Designs, 2320 Valley Drive, Missoula, MT, 59802.

** No product information available for images omitted from source list.

RO LOGRIPPO

Ro Logrippo's deep interest in design stems from a childhood in Pennsylvania where her family's rug mill fostered a fascination with colorful yarns and other manufacturing wonders.

The author and syndicated columnist initially covered the design world in the '70s and '80s for a suburban San Francisco daily. Today more than 200 U.S. and foreign papers carry her *In My Room* column distributed by Universal Press Syndicate since 1990.

A graduate of Marquette University College of Journalism, the award-winning design journalist owns and directs Living & Learning Environments, a communications/consulting firm founded by her late partner, Tony Torrice. A highly recognized designer with a background in child psychology and education, he was widely acclaimed for "co-designing" environments with children—the subject of the book he and Logrippo co-authored. *In My Room: Designing For and With Children* was described by media as "one of the most important books on children's design to be published in the past decade."

In My Room garnered the jacket endorsement of noted psychologist Lee Salk, Ph.D. who credits the work with making "an enormous contribution to the mental health of children and the strengthening of family life." It earned a first place national book award in 1990 from The National Federation of Press Women.

Ro's many writing awards include honors from the International Reading Association, American Society of Interior Designers, and International Furnishings and Design Association. In 1994 IFDA's Education Foundation awarded her a grant to poll youth about their rooms in an effort to discover their interests and values.

The author's views on children's design have led to appearances on several television programs including ABC-TV's *Good Morning America* and *Home* shows. Her ideas have been featured in many publications ranging from *Better Homes & Gardens* and *Child* magazines to the *New York Times* and the *Chicago Tribune*.

Two public issues symposiums were coordinated by her for the American Society of Interior Designers. *Design of the Times: The Homeless* roused professionals to renovate homeless shelters nationwide. *Design of the Times: Day Care* spurred them to establish day care interior design guidelines. As co-chair of the National Task Force on Day Care Interior Design, she wrote its award-winning landmark report.

In educational circles, Ro's name is associated with the first graduate level fellowship for research into the affects of design on children. Established by DuPont Co., the Tony Torrice Educational Environments Research Award at the University of Tennessee, Knoxville, is bestowed annually by an Endowment Committee that is chaired by her.

Ro also manages "KidSpace", The Microsoft Network online computer forum for parents and kids. You can link up with her there, or e-mail her through the internet at: rologrippo_fm@msn.com

INDEX

— A

Acoustics, infant hearing, 5-6
Allergy-free rooms, 213-219
  beds and bedding, 214
  checklist for, 216
  decorations for, 217-218
  floors, 214-215
  molds, 218-219
American Lung Association, 213, 216
Americans with Disabilities Act of
  1933, 189
Antiquing, furnishings, 100
Armoire, dual-purpose furnishings, 79
Art center, creation of, 145-146,
  147-149
Art display. *See also* Display
  doors, 67
  kitchens, 227-229
Art/drafting table, 85
Asthma. *See* Allergy-free rooms

— B

Balans chair, 86
Balcony conversion, 177-178
Balloon shades, window treatments, 114
Basement, molds, 219
Bassinet, 12
Bath curtains, door design, 69
Bath mats, flooring, 63
Bathroom, 234-240
  decoration of, 236-237
  fixtures for, 239-240
  hygiene, 237-238
  mirrors, 235
  molds, 218
  physical challenges, 195-196
  safety and, 234-235, 238-240
Bathroom tile, wall design, 51
Beds and bedding. *See also* Sheets
  allergy-free rooms, 214
  crib, 14
  dual-purpose furnishings, 77-79
  guest furnishings, 81-82
  reading, 162-163
  small rooms, 175, 178
Behar, Susan, 190, 191, 193
Benches, decoration of, 99
Blind children. *See* Visual problems
Blinds, window treatments, 113
Blum, Marian, 30
Bolen, Rosemarie, 184, 185, 187
Bookcases:
  dual-purpose furnishings, 79
  safety, 95
Books, reading learning center,
  160-164

Bookshelves, 14-15
Borders:
  rental units, 211
  wallcoverings, 17-18, 45
  wall design, 50-52
Brain development, of infants, 3
Brandt, DeAnna, 10, 236, 250
Brandt, Peter, 250
Bricks, 106
Brothers, Joyce, 185, 186
Buck, Randy, 98
Bulbs, selection of, lighting, 119
Bulletin bar, 54

— C

Calendars:
  message center, 55
  wall design, 52
Carnell, Carolyn, 43
Carpeting. *See also* Flooring
  allergy-free rooms, 214-215
  dual-purpose furnishings, 80
  flooring, 60, 61-63
Carpet squares, 22, 61-62
Carroll, Nancy, 25, 29
Ceiling:
  design of, 56-59
  murals, 43
  wall design and, 50
Ceiling banners, 22-23, 57-58
Chairs. *See* Furnishings; Seating
Chalkboard, 54
Changing table, 14
Chests:
  decoration of, 98-99
  dual-purpose furnishings, 77-78
Christmas tree, 136-137, 139
Clock, message center, 55
Closets:
  door design, 66, 67-69
  learning centers, 145
  molds, 219
  renovation of, 241-246
  shared rooms, 183
  small rooms, 176
Clutter, prevention of, 179
Collectibles:
  closet renovation, 243
  display of, 120-124
Color, 19-30
  bathroom, 236-237
  furnishings, 96-100
  light and, 24-25, 181-182
  paint, 41
  psychology and, 26-30
  selection of, 19-22

small rooms, 177
  teaching potential of, 22-24
  teenagers, 198
  visual problems and, 144
Color vision, infancy and, 4-5
Comforter, dual-purpose furnishings, 80
Communication:
  doors, 66-67
  photographs and, 133
  technology, impaired children, 92
Communication center:
  design of, 52-56
  kitchens as, 228
Computer desk, 85, 87-92
Cork tiles, flooring, 63
Cornice, window treatments, 115
Cradle, 12
Crib(s), 12-13, 77-78
Crib bedding, 14
Crib mattress, 13
Cubes:
  decoration of, 99
  dual-purpose furnishings, 79
  safety, 95
Culture, learning center, 155-156
Curtains:
  safety, 37
  window treatments, 113-114
Curves, rounded edges, 33

— D

Dado, wall design, 50, 51
Dance center, creation of, 145
Decoration:
  allergy-free rooms and, 217-218
  of bathroom, 236-237
  of furnishings, 96-100
  holidays and, 135-139
  nursery design and, 17-19
  of rental units, 209-210
  teenagers and, 201-202
Decorative sponges, wall design, 52
Desks, 83-92
  accessories for, 86
  art center and, 148
  computer center, 87-92
  decoration of, 99
  seating for, 86
  selection of, 84-85
  types of, 85-86
Dhurries, flooring, 64, 65
DiLorenzo, Kevin, 90
Dimmers, lighting, 119
Disasters, emergency preparedness,
  36-37
Display. *See also* Art display

of collectibles, 120-124
  family room, 224
Divider:
  shared rooms, 182-183
  sheets as, 127
Divorce, 184-188
Doors:
  design of, 66-69
  furnishings, 105
  learning centers, 145-146
  safety, 34-35, 76
  small rooms, 175
Drafting table, 85
Draperies, window treatments, 114
Drawers:
  desks, 85
  hardware, 75
  safety, 76
Drawings, furnishings and, 72
Dressers, 15
  decoration of, 98-99
  used furniture, 103
Dual-purpose furnishings, 77-80,
  176-177

— E

Easel, 54-55, 149
Electricity:
  computer center, 87
  safety, 32, 34
Ellison, Carol, 89, 91
Emergency preparedness, 36-37, 119
Energy conservation, lighting and,
  120
Environmental concerns, paint, 49
Ergonomics, computer center, 89-90

— F

Family history, learning center,
  155-156
Family room:
  design of, 222-225
  molds and, 219
Fire safety, 31-32, 36-37
Fitness center:
  closet renovation, 243-244
  creation of, 168-171
Flags, wall design, 52
Flannel board, 54
Flash cards, 4
Flashlights, 119
Flat board, 54
Floor cushions, 126
Flooring, 59-65
  allergy-free rooms, 214-215, 217
  art center and, 147-148

carpeting, 61-63
rental units, 210-211
sisal, 64-65
vinyl flooring, 60-61
wheelchairs, 192-193
wood, 63-64
Foam stamping, furnishings, 100
Footlockers, used furniture, 103
Footrests, computer center, 90
Frischman, Ralph, 132
Fryrear, Jerry, 130
Fungus, allergy-free rooms, 218-219
Furnishings, 71-109
allergy-free rooms, 217
decoration of, 96-100
desks, 83-92
dual-purpose items, 77-80, 176-177
family room, 222-225
guests, 81-83
hardware and, 74-77, 108-109
living room, 225-226
measurements and, 72-73
rental units, 212
safety and, 33
storage, 93-95
teenagers, 198
unconventional, 104-107
used furnishings, 101-104
decoration of, 98
teenagers, 198-200
Futon, dual-purpose furnishings, 78

— G
Garden bench, decoration of, 99
Garden center, creation of, 156-159
Garden planters, 104
Geography, learning center, 153-156
Geometric shapes, wall design, 52
Glare, lighting, 118
Gleason, Rela, 201
Goldblatt, Anita, 23, 24, 178
Greenblat, Rodney A., 24, 230
Greenery, holiday decorations, 139
Grooming center:
closet renovation, 243
creation of, 145
Guardrails, 33
Guest furnishings, 81-83

— H
Halperin, Joan, 177, 178
Halpern, Madelon, 30
Hardware:
bathroom, 238-239
desks, 85
furnishings and, 74-77, 94,108-109
safety, 37

Hearing, of infants, 5-6
Hearing problems, environment and, 144
Hinges, safety, 33
Hobby center:
creation of, 145
molds and, 219
Hoffman, Betsy, 20, 21
Hofsinde, Robert, 251
Holiday decoration, 135-139
Homasote board, 108, 123, 201-202
Hoogenboom, Irene, 21
Hygiene, bathroom, 237-238

— I
Imagination, of infants, 6-7
Impaired children. See also Physical challenges
design for, 189-196
environment and, 144
technology and, 92
Individuality, learning centers and, 141-142
Infants:
brain development of, 3
hearing of, 5-6
imagination of, 6-7
vision of, 3-5
Innes, Jocasta, 199
Isaacs, Susan, 179

— J
Jacobson-Ziecik, Carol, 122
Jerry, Jane, 19, 20

— K
Katz, Lillian G., 205
Kirlian, Semyon, 27
Kirlian, Valentina, 27
Kitchen, 226-232
art display in, 227-229
as learning center, 229-230
molds, 219
safety and, 230-231, 232
Kitchen table, used furniture, 103
Kitchen tile, wall design, 51
Kites, ceiling design, 58
Klein, Gerald, 215, 219
Kobbe, Anna Mae, 131, 187
Krauss, David, 130, 133
Kron, Joan, 107

— L
Language development, environment and, 143-144
Latex paint, 48-49
Laundry room, molds, 219
Leach, Penelope, 6, 29

Learning, environment and, 143-144
Learning center:
art center, 147-149
closet renovation, 243
creation of, 145-146
garden center, 156-159
individuality and, 141-142
kitchen as, 229-230
maps, 153-156
physical fitness center, 168-171
play center, 150-152
reading, 160-164
sports, 165-168
Lebow, Deena, 24
Leibrock, Cynthia, 64, 193
Lewin, Elyse, 249
Light, color and, 24-25, 181-182
Lighting, 116-120
bathroom, 239
bulb selection, 119
computer center, 87-88
dimmers, 119
energy conservation and, 120
glare, 118
holiday decorations, 139
illumination requirement, 117-118
psychology and, 119-120
reading, 162
safety, 34
types of, 117, 118-119
Lillig, Margo, 21, 22
Living room:
design of, 225-226
molds and, 219
Locks, safety, 35
Loft systems, dual-purpose furnishings, 78
Lowe, Maureen, 250
Lowe, Mike, 250
Lubicz, Basia, 20, 21, 23
Ludington-Hoe, Susan, 4
Lumbar roll, computer center, 90
Luongo, Rhonda, 68, 143, 144, 227

— M
Machfinger, Steven, 215
Magazines, wall design, 52
Magnetic board, 54
Maintenance:
collectibles display, 123
flooring, 60, 62, 64
of sheets, 129
Maps, 153-156, 228
Marbling, furnishings, 100
Marston, Stephanie, 131, 132
Mashburn, Judy, 186
Masters, Lowell, 92

Math center, creation of, 146
Mattress, crib, 13
McChesney, Paula, 227
Measurements, furnishings and, 72-73
Meijer, Marie, 228
Melamine, furnishings, 105
Message center, 52-56. See also Communication
Mirrors:
bathroom, 235
small rooms, 177
Mites, allergy-free rooms, 214-215
Mobiles, 4, 5
Modular furniture:
desks, 85
dual-purpose furnishings, 79
safety, 95
Molds, allergy-free rooms, 218-219
Monitors, 32
Montessori, Maria, 74
Moving, 203-208
age level and, 207-208
planning for, 203-206
Mud room, 233
Mug racks, 103, 106
Murals:
ceilings, 57
wall design, 42-43
Murphy bed, 178

— N
Nature, garden center, 156-159
Newborns. See Infants
Newton, Isaac, 27
Nida, Patricia Cooney, 204
Noren, door design, 69
Nursery design:
basic items for, 12-15
color, 19-30
decoration, 17-19
infant abilities and, 2-7
planning for, 7-11
safety, 31-37

— O
Oil-based paint, 48-49
Ornaments, holiday decorations, 139

— P
Paint:
ceilings, 57
furnishings, 96-100
information on, 48-49
wall design, 39-42
Patterns, infant vision and, 3-4
Pennants, wall design, 52

Pet storage, closet renovation, 243
Photographs:
    decorating with, 130-134
    display of, 122-123
    divorce and, 187
    kitchens and, 229
Physical challenges, 189-196
    barrier removal, 194-196
    design for, 190-191
    safety and, 191-192
    technology and independence, 193-194
    wheelchairs, 64, 192-193
Physical fitness center:
    closet renovation, 243-244
    creation of, 168-171
Planters, 104
Plants, garden center, 156-159
Play center:
    creation of, 150-152
    design of, 247-253
Porter, A. P., 137
Posters, 4, 122-123
Prism, 25
Puppetry, play center, 151-152

— R
Ragging, furnishings, 100
Reading:
    encouragement of, 164
    learning center, 160-163
Recreation room. See Play center
Reid, Lynnette, 10, 209
Rental units, 209-212
    decoration of, 209-210
    floor coverings, 210-211
    furnishings, 212
    walls, 211-212
Robb, Janet Anderson, 8, 9
Rocker, 15, 99
Roller shades, window treatments, 114
Rolling cart, dual-purpose furnishings, 80
Rolltop desk:
    described, 86
    safety, 76
Roman shades, window treatments, 114
Room divider:
    shared rooms, 182-183
    sheets as, 127
Room monitors, 32
Rugs. See also Flooring
    allergy-free rooms, 214-215
    dual-purpose furnishings, 80
    sheets as, 126
Runion, Linda, 88, 244

— S
Safety, 31-37
    bathroom and, 234-235, 238-240
    computer center, 89
    doors, 34-35
    emergency preparedness, 36-37
    fire, 31-32
    hardware, 75-76
    holiday decorations, 139
    kitchen and, 230-231, 232
    lighting, 34
    physical challenges and, 191-192
    physical fitness center, 169, 170
    room design, 32-34
    storage, 95
Safety gates, 32-33
Safety hinges, 33
Salapatek, Phillip, 4
Schiffman, Sandy, 7, 64
Schwartzman, Michael, 253
Science center, creation of, 146
Screen divider:
    shared rooms, 182-183
    sheets as, 127
Seasonal display, 22
Seating:
    computer center, 89-90
    decoration of, 99
    desks and, 86
    dual-purpose furnishings, 80
Shades, window treatments, 114
Shared custody. See Divorce
Shared rooms:
    design of, 180-184
    divorce and, 186
Sheets. See also Beds and bedding
    maintenance of, 129
    uses for, 124-128
Shelves:
    learning centers, 146
    rental units, 211
    safety, 95
Shutters, window treatments, 114
Siblings, shared rooms, 180-184
Sisal, flooring, 64-65
Slesin, Suzanne, 107
Sliding screens, 183
Slipcovers, sheets as, 127
Small rooms, 174-178
Sohm, Irene, 101, 102
Spattering:
    furnishings, 97, 100
    paint, 41, 42
Sponges, wall design, 52
Sponging:
    furnishings, 97, 100, 199
    paint, 41, 42
Sports center, creation of, 165-168

Stagecoach shades, window treatments, 114
Stencils, 17
    furnishings, 100, 199
    paint, 41, 42
    wall design, 51
Step stool:
    decoration of, 99
    used furniture, 103
Stone, Victoria, 21, 237
Stools:
    decoration of, 99
    used furniture, 103
Storage:
    bathroom, 236
    clutter prevention, 179
    computer center, 89
    furnishings, 80, 93-95, 106, 108, 109
    hardware, 76
    small rooms, 175
    teenagers, 202-203
Study area, desks, 83-92

— T
Tables:
    decoration of, 99
    furnishings, 105-106
    used furniture, 103
Tabletop easel, 54-55
Tabletops:
    art center and, 148
    learning centers, 146
Technology:
    computer desk, 85, 87-92
    physical challenges, 92, 193-194
Teenagers, 197-203
    decoration, 201-202
    new furniture, 200-201
    planning for, 197-198
    storage, 202-203
    used furniture, 198-200
Throw rugs, dual-purpose furnishings, 80
Tiles:
    flooring, 63
    wall design, 51
Tom-Sera, Denise, 8, 224
Torrice, Tony, 26, 27, 28, 29
Toy chest:
    dual-purpose furnishings, 80
    safety, 76
Trelease, Jim, 161
Trundle beds, 78, 81
Trunks, used furniture, 103

— U
Unfinished furnishings, 97-98

Used furnishings, 101-104
    decoration of, 98
    teenagers, 198-200

— V
Valence, window treatments, 115
Ventilation:
    computer center, 87
    physical fitness center, 169
Vinyl flooring, 60-61
Vinyl wallcoverings, 44
Vision, of infants, 3-5
Visual problems:
    environment and, 144
    technology and, 92
Voice-activated technology, impaired children, 92
Volatile organic compound (VAC) emissions, paint, 49

— W
Wall art, sheets as, 126
Wallcoverings:
    borders, 17-18
    rental units, 211
    wall design, 43-47
Wall design, 39-49
    borders, 50-52
    murals, 42-43
    paint, 39-42
    wallcoverings, 43-47
Wallerstein, Judith, 185, 186, 188
Walls:
    allergy-free rooms, 217
    learning centers, 145
    rental units, 211-212
    small rooms, 175
Weather center, creation of, 146
Weiss, Lisa, 253
Wheelchairs, 64, 192-193
Wheeler, Marian, 222, 233
Wimmer, Ruth, 3, 4, 5, 29
Windows:
    allergy-free rooms, 218
    holiday decorations for, 138
    learning centers, 146
    reading, 162
    safety, 37
    small rooms, 175, 177
Window treatments, 112-116
    checklist for, 115
    planning for, 113
    sheets for, 128
    types of, 113-115
Wood:
    flooring, 63-64
    furnishings, 97-98

"The world is round, and the place which may seem like the end,
may also be only the beginning."

— *Ivy Baker Priest*